Rethinking International Development Series

Series Editors:
Andy Sumner, Fellow of the Vulnerability and Poverty Research Team, Institute of Development Studies, UK.
Ray Kiely, Professor of International Politics, Queen Mary University of London, UK.

Palgrave Macmillan is delighted to announce a new series dedicated to publishing cutting-edge titles that focus on the broad area of 'development'.

The core aims of the series are to present critical work that:

- is cross disciplinary;
- challenges orthodoxies;
- reconciles theoretical depth with empirical research;
- explores the frontiers of development studies in terms of 'development' in both North and South and global inter-connectedness;
- reflects on claims to knowledge and intervening in other people's lives.

Titles include:

Simon Feeny and Matthew Clarke
THE MILLENNIUM DEVELOPMENT GOALS AND BEYOND
International Assistance to the Asia-Pacific

Niamh Gaynor
TRANSFORMING PARTICIPATION?
The Politics of Development in Malawi and Ireland

Caroline Harper, Nicola Jones, Ronald U. Mendoza, David Stewart and Erika Strand (*editors*)
CHILDREN IN CRISIS
Seeking Child-Sensitive Policy Responses

Xiaoming Huang, Alex C. Tan and Sekhar Bandyopadhyay (*editors*)
CHINA AND INDIA AND THE END OF DEVELOPMENT MODELS

Sue Kenny and Matthew Clarke (*editors*)
CHALLENGING CAPACITY BUILDING
Comparative Perspectives

Erik Lundsgaarde (*editor*)
AFRICA TOWARD 2030
Challenges for Development Policy

Sara C. Motta and Alf Gunvald Nilsen (*editors*)
SOCIAL MOVEMENTS IN THE GLOBAL SOUTH
Dispossession, Development and Resistance

Eric Rugraff, Diego Sánchez-Ancochea and Andy Sumner (*editors*)
TRANSNATIONAL CORPORATIONS AND DEVELOPMENT POLICY
Critical Perspectives

Rachel Sabates-Wheeler and Rayah Feldman (*editors*)
MIGRATION AND SOCIAL PROTECTION
Claiming Social Rights Beyond Borders

Jens Stilhoff Sörensen (*editor*)
CHALLENGING THE AID PARADIGM
Western Currents and Asian Alternatives

Andy Sumner and Meera Tiwari
AFTER 2015: INTERNATIONAL DEVELOPMENT POLICY AT A CROSSROADS

Rethinking International Development Series
Series Standing Order ISBN 978–0–230–53751–4 (hardback)

You can receive future titles in this series as they are published by placing a standing order. Please contact your bookseller or, in case of difficulty, write to us at the address below with your name and address, the title of the series and the ISBN quoted above.

Customer Services Department, Macmillan Distribution Ltd, Houndmills, Basingstoke, Hampshire RG21 6XS, England

---

Children in Crisis

Seeking Child-Sensitive Policy Responses

Edited by

Caroline Harper
Research Fellow and Head, Social Development,
Overseas Development Institute, UK

Nicola Jones
Research Fellow, Social Development,
Overseas Development Institute, UK

Ronald U. Mendoza
Associate Professor of Economics, Asian Institute of Management and
Executive Director, AIM Policy Center, Philippines

David Stewart
Chief of Social Policy and Evaluation, UNICEF Uganda

and

Erika Strand
Chief of Social Policy, UNICEF Mexico

palgrave
macmillan

First published 2012 by
PALGRAVE MACMILLAN

Palgrave Macmillan in the UK is an imprint of Macmillan Publishers Limited, registered in England, company number 785998, of Houndmills, Basingstoke, Hampshire RG21 6XS.

Palgrave Macmillan in the US is a division of St Martin's Press LLC, 175 Fifth Avenue, New York, NY 10010.

Palgrave Macmillan is the global academic imprint of the above companies and has companies and representatives throughout the world.

Palgrave® and Macmillan® are registered trademarks in the United States, the United Kingdom, Europe and other countries.

ISBN: 978–0–230–31397–2

This book is printed on paper suitable for recycling and made from fully managed and sustained forest sources. Logging, pulping and manufacturing processes are expected to conform to the environmental regulations of the country of origin.

A catalogue record for this book is available from the British Library.

A catalog record for this book is available from the Library of Congress.

10 9 8 7 6 5 4 3 2 1
21 20 19 18 17 16 15 14 13 12

Printed and bound in Great Britain by
CPI Antony Rowe, Chippenham and Eastbourne

Contents

Tables

Figures

Acknowledgements

The global food price shocks of 2008 and the subsequent period of volatility and crises led child rights advocates and other stakeholders, including experts from the UN Children's Fund (UNICEF), the Overseas Development Institute and other development agencies, to raise international attention to the risks facing children, women and poor families in crises. This volume represents the culmination of many of those collaborations, reflecting both evidence-based policy research and advocacy efforts to promote more effective and equitable policies to protect such groups from the adverse consequences of the crisis.

The volume was also inspired by 'Adjustment with a Human Face', another similar effort to protect child rights during a time of economic volatility, published in 1987 as part of a broader effort to raise awareness about the social and human cost of crises and difficult structural adjustment policies. We would like to thank the team involved in that endeavour for setting such a high standard, in terms of both their lasting analytical contribution and their success in triggering immediate and practical policy reforms in response to the plight of children.

UNICEF and the Overseas Development Institute, in collaboration with the Asian Institute of Management, the Chronic Poverty Research Centre and other partner institutions, have provided invaluable support to this book's development. In particular, we are grateful for the leadership in UNICEF of Richard Morgan, Isabel Ortíz and Gaspar Fajth, in terms of raising the child rights issues throughout the crisis, and of Yoriko Yasukawa, who saw the emerging risks and encouraged this focus on children and crisis.

Several key policy research events helped feature the emerging evidence, providing a forum to discuss policy responses. In November 2009, UNICEF and the Overseas Development Institute organised a conference on 'The Global Economic Crisis: Including Children in the Policy Response'. This convened development practitioners, policy experts and academic researchers from around the world to examine the ways in which food and fuel price spikes, financial market volatility and the global economic slowdown were affecting children and youth in both developing and developed countries, and also to recommend policy responses.

In February 2010, UNICEF and Fordham University organised a policy forum entitled 'Child-friendly Budgets for 2010 and Beyond: Toward Global Economic Recovery with a Human Face'. This brought together development practitioners, researchers and other experts, including from UNICEF, the UN Development Programme, the UN Educational, Cultural and Scientific Organization, the World Bank and the International Monetary Fund, as well as academia and civil society, to discuss the impact of the crisis, related policy challenges and the role of social budgets. It focused on policy options to help ensure recovery with a human face, looking at emerging evidence on crisis impacts on children from developing countries, including Burkina Faso, Cameroon, Ghana, Mali, East Asia and the Pacific Islands. Participants also discussed social budgeting for children, women and the poor and how to ensure a child rights perspective in poverty and social impact analysis.

Similarly, UNICEF country and regional offices have organised policy workshops and events at various levels, contributing to more transparent, inclusive and evidence-based debate on context-specific challenges as well as on the policy options available in terms of responding to the crisis. The volume also builds on ODI's research over the past three years on the effects of crisis on women and children in multiple countries, regions and sectors. This book would not have been possible without the contributions of the various experts, all of whom participated in its development on a voluntary basis.

Finally, we are indebted to Shreya Mitra for her tireless coordination efforts throughout the book writing process and to Roo Griffiths for her excellent editorial support.

Acronyms

4Ps	Pantawid Pamilyang Pilipino Program (Philippines)
ACPF	African Child Policy Forum
ADB	Asian Development Bank
AIDS	acquired immune deficiency syndrome
AIM	Asian Institute of Management
ART	antiretroviral therapy
ARV	antiretroviral
BaU	Business as Usual
BKKBN	Badan Kependudukan dan Keluarga Berencana Nasional (National Family Planning Agency [Indonesia])
BULOG	Badan Urusan Logistik (Bureau of Logistics [Indonesia])
CBPP	Center on Budget and Policy Priorities (US)
CBMS	Community-based Monitoring System (Philippines)
CCT	conditional cash transfer
CDF	cumulative density function
CEE	Central and Eastern European
CEPR	Centre for Economic Policy Research (US)
CFA	Comprehensive Framework of Action
CGE	computable general equilibrium
CIS	Commonwealth of Independent States
CONAPO	Consejo Nacional de Población (National Population Council [Mexico])
CONEVAL	Consejo Nacional de Evaluación de la Política de Desarrollo Social (National Council for the Evaluation of Social Development Policy [Mexico])
CRIN	Child Rights Information Network
CRS	Catholic Relief Services
CSG	Child Support Grant (South Africa)
CSPS	Centre de Santé et de Promotion Sociale (Health and Social Promotion Centre [Burkina Faso])
DAC	Development Assistance Committee (OECD)
DepEd	Department of Education (Philippines)
DFID	Department for International Development (UK)
DHS	demographic and health survey
DRC	Democratic Republic of Congo

DSWD	Department of Social Welfare and Development (Philippines)
EC	European Commission
ECLAC	Economic Commission for Latin America and the Caribbean (UN)
ECOSOC	Economic and Social Council (UN)
EECA	Eastern Europe and Central Asia
ENIGH	National Survey of Income and Expenditure Survey (Mexico) (La Encuesta Nacional de Ingresos y Gastos de los Hogares)
ESA	East and Southern Africa
ESCAP	Economic and Social Commission for Asia and the Pacific (UN)
EU	European Union
FDI	foreign direct investment
FSP	Food Security Programme (Ethiopia)
G8	Group of Eight Countries
G20	Group of Twenty Countries
GDFI	gross domestic fixed investment
GDP	gross domestic product
GFATM	Global Fund to Fight AIDS, Tuberculosis and Malaria
GHS	General Household Survey (South Africa)
GMM	generalised method of moments
GNI	gross national income
HDI	Human Development Index (UNDP)
HH	household
HIV	human immunodeficiency virus
HVMRTWG	HIV Vaccines and Microbicides Resource Tracking Working Group
IADB	Inter-American Development Bank
ICAAP	International Congress on AIDS in Asia and the Pacific
IDP	internally displaced person
IDS	Institute of Development Studies (UK)
IEO	Independent Evaluation Office (IMF)
IES	Income and Expenditure Survey (South Africa)
IFI	international financial institution
IFPRI	International Food Policy Research Institute (US)
ILO	International Labour Organization (UN)
IMF	International Monetary Fund
IMR	infant mortality rate
INEGI	Instituto Nacional de Estadística y Geografía (National Institute of Statistics and Geography [Mexico])

IRIN	Integrated Regional Information Networks
JLICA	Joint Learning Initiative on Children and HIV/AIDS
JUNIMA	Joint Initiative on Mobility and HIV/AIDS
LDC	least developed country
LEAP	Livelihood Empowerment Against Poverty (Ghana)
MDG	Millennium Development Goal
MENA	Middle East and North Africa
MSF	Médecins Sans Frontières (Doctors without Borders)
NAFTA	North American Free Trade Agreement
NCR	National Capital Region (Philippines)
NFA	National Food Authority (Philippines)
NGO	non-governmental organisation
NIDS	National Income Dynamics Survey (South Africa)
ODA	official development assistance
OECD	Organisation for Economic Co-operation and Development
OFSP	Other Food Security Programme (Ethiopia)
OVC	orphans and vulnerable children
PEP	Poverty and Economic Policy
PEPFAR	President's Emergency Plan for AIDS Relief (US)
PIDS	Philippine Institute for Development Studies
PMTCT	prevention of mother-to-child transmission
PPP	purchasing power parity
PSF	Programa Saude da Familia (Family Health Programme [Brazil])
PSNP	Productive Safety Net Programme (Ethiopia)
SAM	Social Accounting Matrix
SARB	South African Reserve Bank
SEDESOL	Secretariat of Social Development (Mexico)
SNNPR	Southern Nations, Nationalities and Peoples Region (Ethiopia)
SSA	Sub-Saharan Africa
TT	targeted transfer
U5MR	under-five mortality rate
UK	United Kingdom
UN	United Nations
UNAIDS	Joint UN Programme on HIV/AIDS
UNCTAD	UN Conference on Trade and Development
UNDESA	UN Department of Economics and Social Affairs
UNDP	UN Development Programme
UNGIVAS	UN Global Impact and Vulnerability Alert System
UNICEF	United Nations Children's Fund
UNIFEM	UN Development Fund for Women

US	United States
UT	universal transfer
VAT	value-added tax
WCA	West and Central Africa
WHO	World Health Organization

Contributors

Steffie Joi Calubayan is Research Assistant at the Poverty and Economic Policy–Community-based Monitoring System (PEP–CBMS) Research Network, working primarily in data collection and processing. She has a BA in Agricultural Economics from the College of Economics and Management at the University of the Philippines Los Baños.

Margaret Chitiga-Mabugu is Executive Director of the Economic Performance and Development research programme at the Human Sciences Research Council in South Africa. Previously she was Professor of Economics at the University of Pretoria. Her interests lie in economy-wide modelling, welfare and industrial and international trade issues.

John Cockburn is the executive director of the Partnership for Economic Policy (PEP) Research Network and Professor in the Department of Economics at Université Laval. He has a PhD from Nuffield College and the Centre for the Study of African Economies at Oxford University on child labour and schooling in rural Ethiopia and the poverty effects of trade liberalisation in Nepal. His areas of specialisation include child poverty, computable general equilibrium (CGE) microsimulation modelling and trade policy analysis. He has provided training and technical support to researchers throughout the developing world since 1990 and is Associate Editor of the *International Journal of Microsimulation*, for which he recently completed a special issue on CGE microsimulation techniques.

Jerónimo Cortina is Assistant Professor in the Department of Political Science and Research Associate at the Center for Public Policy at the University of Houston. Cortina specialises in Latino politics, survey research, political behaviour, immigration and quantitative methods. His work has been published in scholarly and policy journals such as the *American Politics Research Journal*, *Foreign Affairs in Spanish* and the *Harvard Journal of Hispanic Policy*. His recent books include (with Andrew Gelman, David Park and Boris Shor) *Red State, Blue State, Rich State, Poor State: Why Americans Vote the Way They Do* and (with Andrew Gelman) *A Quantitative Tour of the Social Sciences*. He is currently co-editing (with Enrique Ochoa-Reza) *Managing Migration: Maximizing Development and New Perspectives on International Migration and Development* (with Enrique Ochoa-Reza) as part of the Initiative for Policy Dialogue Series.

Bernard Decaluwé is Full Professor in the Department of Economics at Université Laval, Canada. He is also one of the leaders of the Poverty and Economic Policy (PEP) Research Network. His main fields of interest are development economics, international economics and computable general equilibrium models.

Jeremy de Jesus is a research assistant at the Community-based Monitoring System (CBMS) programme, a research project of Angelo King Institute for Economic and Business Studies at De La Salle University. He has co-authored papers on the impact of crises on poverty and missing dimensions of poverty. He also has extensive experience in survey operations and data analysis. He has an undergraduate degree in Development Studies from the University of the Philippines and is pursuing graduate studies in Statistics from the same university.

Nadia Doytch is Assistant Professor of Economics at the University of New Haven. She has a PhD in Economics from City University of New York. Her research areas are international economics and economic development. She has published papers on the impact of the sectoral distribution of foreign direct investment (FDI) on economic growth (*Journal of International Money and Finance*), the employment effects of mergers and acquisitions (*Applied Economics Letters*) and other topics. Doytch's current research focuses on environmental spill-overs from FDI, impacts of FDI on child labour in developing countries and behaviour of social expenditures over the business cycle. Doytch previously worked as a consultant on the Credit Suisse Intangible Infrastructure Investment Index at Credit Suisse in New York.

Ismaël Fofana is Postdoctoral Research Fellow at the International Food Policy Research Institute (IFPRI), based at its West and Central Africa office in Dakar, Senegal. He worked between 2001 and 2010 as Researcher and Resource Person for the Poverty and Economic Policy (PEP) Research Network at Université Laval. He has a PhD in Economics from Université de Paris 1 and a Master's in Economics from Université Laval. His principal area of interest and expertise is in the impact assessment of macroeconomic policies and shocks. His research work is focused mainly on the development of frameworks to assess the macro–micro links of public policy in such a way that issues of poverty, equity, growth and macro dynamics are better understood.

Maricar Garde is Policy Officer for Economic and Social Development at Save the Children UK. She specialises in children's poverty and health issues, particularly inequalities in child survival and access to health care, and her focus is on countries such as Bangladesh, India and

Nigeria. She has previously worked on several research projects while working as an economist in the Philippines including one on international remittances for the Poverty and Economic Policy (PEP) Research Network. She has a Master's in Development Administration and Planning from University College London and another Master's in Economics from the University of the Philippines.

Caroline Harper is Associate Director of the Chronic Poverty Research Centre and Research Fellow at the Overseas Development Institute (ODI) leading a programme on social development with a focus on gender and generations. She has a PhD in Anthropology, and her research interests are in chronic poverty, gender and exclusion, childhood, life course and intergenerational poverty, donor aid policies and child rights and economic crisis and social impacts. Previously, she was Director of the Childhood Poverty Research and Policy Centre (CHIP), a collaborative venture between Manchester University and Save the Children, and Co-director of Young Lives, a longitudinal study of childhood poverty. She worked for Save the Children in several roles in the UK and overseas and also for the UN and the World Bank in East and Southeast Asia and Africa, focusing on issues of poverty, gender, childhood, empowerment, economic adjustment, research, evaluation and policy processes. She is co-author of *Research for Development: A Practical Guide.*

Bingjie Hu is a PhD candidate in Economics at the University of Maryland. She has previously worked as a consultant at the Social Policy and Economic Analysis Unit of the UN Children's Fund (UNICEF) and also as senior economist in the Research Department of Banco Bilbao Vizcaya Argentaria. Her research interests are in economics of institutional governance and economic development.

Nicola Jones is Research Fellow in the Social Development Programme at the Overseas Development Institute (ODI) and also heads a programme of research on the linkages between knowledge, policy and power. She has a PhD in Political Science and has a particular interest in social and poverty policies and their impact on gender and generational relations. Her commissioned research and policy advisory work at ODI has included work on linkages between trade and other economic shocks and experiences of poverty among women, children and youth; social protection and child-specific social and economic risks; donor aid policies and children's rights; gender and the Millennium Development Goals (MDGs); and participatory governance assessments. Prior to joining ODI, she worked with a range of government, non-government and academic agencies in Africa, Latin America, Asia and the Pacific on issues of gender and governance and intra-household dynamics and poverty. She is the author of *Gender and the Political Opportunities of Democracy* and co-author of *Child Poverty, Evidence and Policy: Mainstreaming Children in International Development.*

Ramos Mabugu heads the Research and Policy Division at the Financial and Fiscal Commission of South Africa. Most of his recent work is on the application of computable general equilibrium models to issues of macroeconomics, fiscal policy and poverty. He has taught economic modelling courses on two occasions in the Ecological and Environmental Economics Programme at the Abdus Salam International Centre for Theoretical Physics, and previously lectured at both the University of Pretoria and the University of Zimbabwe.

Hélène Maisonnave holds a PhD in Economics, specialising in Development Economics and Computable General Equilibrium Models. She has worked with the Poverty and Economic Policy (PEP) Research Network at Université Laval, Canada, since 2007 and became a permanent staff member of the network in May 2011. She had also worked for the Environmental and Climate Unit of the European Commission in Seville. She has developed several CGE models mostly on African countries, dealing with trade reforms, education and labour market issues, and the Millennium Development Goals.

Ronald U. Mendoza is Associate Professor of Economics at the Asian Institute of Management (AIM) and Executive Director of the AIM Policy Center. Prior to his appointment at AIM, he was a senior economist with the UN Children's Fund's (UNICEF) Policy and Practice Group in New York. His research background includes work with the UN Development Programme's (UNDP) Office of Development Studies, the Federal Reserve Bank of Boston, the Economist Intelligence Unit and several non-governmental organisations in Manila. He has published extensively on international development policy. His recent work includes 'Trade-induced Learning and Industrial Catch-up' in *The Economic Journal* and 'Why Do the Poor Pay More? Exploring the Poverty Penalty Concept' in the *Journal of International Development.* Mendoza has a BA in Economics from Ateneo de Manila University, a Master's in Public Administration and International Development from the John F. Kennedy School of Government at Harvard University and a Master's and PhD in Economics from Fordham University.

Paola Pereznieto is Research Fellow in the Overseas Development Institute's (ODI's) Social Development Programme. She is an economist specialising in social policy with eight years of international development experience in a range of developing countries, primarily in East and West Africa, Southeast Europe, Southeast Asia and Latin America. Her research focuses on social protection, financing of social policies and programmes, particularly focusing on child-sensitive budgeting; child poverty reduction policy; child-sensitive social protection; public expenditure management; and gender analysis of policies and programmes. She has worked in Mexico's Ministry of Finance and Public Credit and Ministry of Health. After completing her Master's she worked as policy advisor on the Young Lives Longitudinal Study on Childhood Poverty, and then became a freelance consultant researching child-sensitive social protection, child poverty and social sector expenditure and building the capacity of partners in developing countries through joint work and training sessions. She has worked extensively with the UN Children's Fund (UNICEF), including with regional offices in West and Central Africa and the Middle East and North Africa and with country offices in Uganda, Nepal, Vietnam, Kazakhstan and FYR Macedonia.

Aparna Rao works as Investment Banking Analyst at Goldman Sachs and was formerly an intern with the UN Development Programme's (UNDP's) Office of Development Studies. She has also worked with UNDP Mali on rural energy development projects. Rao holds a Master's in International Affairs from the School of International and Public Affairs at Columbia University and a Bachelor's degree in Economics and Math, also from Columbia University.

Nicholas Rees works in the Policy Advocacy Unit at the UN Children's Fund (UNICEF) headquarters in New York. Rees has worked on economic, social policy and advocacy issues for the UN as well as economic policy think tanks and research institutes. His areas of focus include the impacts of the global economic crisis on children, the economic returns to investing in children, child poverty and disparities, infrastructure investments, rural water delivery services and the impact of migration on public health systems. Rees holds a Master's from the London School of Economics and a BA from the School of Oriental and African Studies at London University.

Celia Reyes is Senior Research Fellow at the Philippine Institute for Development Studies. She leads the global Community-based Monitoring System (CBMS) programme and is co-director of the Poverty and Economic Policy (PEP) Research Network. She completed her BA in Statistics and a Master's in Economics at the University of the Philippines. She obtained her PhD in Economics from the University of Pennsylvania.

Véronique Robichaud is engaged in research at the Centre Interuniversitaire sur le Risque, les Politiques Économiques et l'Emploi (CIRPÉE). She has a BA and a Master's in Economics from Université Laval, Canada. Over the years, she has been involved in the development of analytical tools, such as computable general equilibrium models, for the CIRPÉE, Finance Canada, the Department of Finance of Québec and other research centres. She also lectures at the HEC and has participated in numerous research projects related to regional and international agreements, aboriginal issues, international development and environment.

Debra Shepherd is a researcher in the Social Policy Research Group of the Department of Economics at the University of Stellenbosch. She is currently completing a doctorate in Development Economics at Vrije Universiteit under the VU–National Research Foundation Desmond Tutu Doctoral Programme. Her main research interests lie in education and labour market outcomes, with an emphasis on micro-econometric modelling.

Alellie Sobreviñas is Research Associate at the Community-based Monitoring System (CBMS) programme. Previously she worked as an economic development specialist at the National Economic and Development Authority and as a research analyst at the Philippine Institute for Development Studies. She has gained extensive experience in the conduct of research, particularly in terms of designing data collection instruments, survey operations and data analysis. She has co-authored a number of papers related to poverty and development. She has a BA in Agricultural Economics and a Master's in Statistics from the University of the Philippines. In addition, she has a Master's in Development Evaluation and Management from the University of Antwerp.

David Stewart is UNICEF's Chief of Social Policy in Uganda. Between 2005 and 2010 he was UNICEF's Chief of Policy Advocacy where he authored and contributed to UNICEF's State of the World Children Report on issues ranging from excluded and invisible children, gender equality and child and maternal health. He also founded and edited the Social and Economic Policy working papers and policy briefing series. Previously he spent six years at the Human Development Report Office of UNDP where he researched, wrote and presented Human Development Reports on Human Rights, Democracy, the Millennium Development Goals, New Technologies, Cultural Freedom and Development Assistance. He holds a BA in Economics from the University of Sussex and a Master's in Development Economics from the University of Oxford.

Erika Strand is UNICEF's Chief of Social Policy in Mexico, providing technical support at both federal and state levels on public expenditure for children, multidimensional child poverty and the use of disparity mapping to target social policies. Between 2007 and 2010, she served as a policy analyst at UNICEF, contributing to organisational advocacy on social protection and responses to the global financial crisis. Prior to her work at UNICEF, she worked in Honduras, Egypt and Madagascar for the US Government, UNICEF and the World Bank respectively. She obtained her Master's in Public Administration and International Development (MPA/ID) from the John F. Kennedy School of Government, Harvard University, with a focus on poverty analysis and child rights.

Andy Sumner is Research Fellow in the Vulnerability and Poverty Reduction Team at the Institute of Development Studies, Sussex, and Visiting Fellow at the Center for Global Development. He is a cross-disciplinary economist whose research relates to poverty, inequality and human well-being, with particular reference to poverty concepts and indicators, global trends and Millennium Development Goal (MDG)/post-MDG debates. This has led to recent collaborations with Oslo and Harvard Universities, the UN Children's Fund (UNICEF) and the UN Development Programme (UNDP). He has also conducted work for Google and the World Bank and in 2010 was seconded to the UK Department for International Development (DFID) Policy Division as Senior Advisor. He has published more than 30 peer-reviewed articles and five books and is Series Editor for Palgrave Macmillan's 'Rethinking International Development'. Most recently, his research on the 'new bottom billion' has been covered by *The Economist*, Voice of America, Fox News and *The Guardian* and informed the UK Parliament's International Development Committee's inquiry into aid to India. In 2010, he contributed to UNDP's 'MDG International Assessment' for the MDG Summit and the Commission for Africa report 'Still Our Common Interest'.

Nina Thelen is Policy Analyst with the UN Development Programme's (UNDP) Office of Development Studies. Her research areas include market-based strategies to reach the Millennium Development Goals (MDGs), social policy and measuring societies' progress. Prior to joining UNDP, she worked in the Department of Foreign Trade at the German–Brazilian Chamber of Industry and Commerce in São Paulo, Brazil. Thelen holds a BA in International Economics with a specialisation in Latin America from Tuebingen University, where she worked as a research assistant.

Luca Tiberti has a PhD in Development Economics from the University of Florence. His main research interests are health care financing in developing countries, child poverty and social policy, the socioeconomic impacts of economic crises and income and health inequalities. He worked between 2008 and 2010 as a researcher at the UN Children's Fund's (UNICEF) Innocenti Research Centre. In January 2011, he joined the Poverty and Economic Policy (PEP) Research Network as a postdoctoral researcher at Université Laval.

Servaas van der Berg is Professor of Economics and National Research Chair in the Economics of Social Policy at the University of Stellenbosch. His research interests lie in the application of quantitative methodologies to social policy issues relating to poverty and inequality. He has published extensively on social grants in South Africa. His current research focuses on poverty measurement, labour markets and the economics of education in South Africa and other countries in the region.

Dieter von Fintel is Lecturer in Economics at Stellenbosch University. He is currently undertaking a PhD in Labour Economics. His research interests also include development economics and economic history, and particularly empirical work in these fields.

Jenn Yablonski works for the UN Children's Fund (UNICEF) as Social Protection Specialist, based in New York. Her work on social protection includes technical support on policy development and programme design and cash transfer impact evaluation, particularly in Sub-Saharan Africa. She has worked in international development for 14 years, previously for Save the Children UK and Oxfam America, with a focus on inequality, exclusion and poverty analysis. She has a Master's in Economics from the School of Oriental and African Studies at the University of London.

Yanchun Zhang is Policy Specialist with the UN Development Programme's (UNDP) Office of Development Studies. Her research areas include international macroeconomics, sustainable development and economic vulnerabilities. Her research articles have been published in refereed academic and policy journals. Prior to joining UNDP, she taught at San Francisco State University, Santa Clara University and the University of Virginia. She majored in International Finance and has a BA in Economics from Shanghai Fudan University and a Master's and PhD in Economics from the University of Virginia, specialising in international economics, economic development and econometrics.

1

Introduction: Towards Global Recovery for All

Caroline Harper and Nicola Jones

When economic crisis rocks a global or national economy, the impacts on society of both the initial shock and the sometimes-stringent reform measures put in place are much discussed. It is evident, however, that our understanding of these effects is constrained by a lack of age- and gender-disaggregated data, particularly with respect to real-time impacts, which leaves the consequences for some significant groups as a crisis unfolds unexplored and often unknown. Children, youth and women are frequently badly affected. Recent efforts to uncover the actual impacts reveal increases in child mortality and morbidity; high levels of youth unemployment; exploitation of women and children in labour markets; child protection violations; and increases in domestic violence and mental ill health. These are all coming to light as being linked to economic crisis and therefore as requiring consideration in any policy response.

This volume draws together contributions from experts from the global North and South, analysing the implications of economic crises on children. The volume was written in the immediate aftermath of the three successive shocks that precipitated a global crisis – spanning the international food price shock in 2008, the financial crisis in 2009 and the global slowdown, the latter precipitated in 2010 and beyond. The volume analyses some of the key policy responses governments and international agencies have deployed and advances policy responses designed to prevent the crisis from causing permanent harm to children.

It is too early to tell the extent of the crisis and the forthcoming recovery given the economic and social vulnerability that remains even as this volume is being published, and which is likely to persist for years after the initial shocks have passed. However, the analyses and policy recommendations contained herein draw on the amalgam of already available empirical evidence and are for the much longer term, including the volatility we see today.

The expert contributors additionally provide unique insights into the crisis from a historical perspective, advancing policy recommendations to promote an inclusive recovery. By drawing together analysis from multiple regions – Africa, Asia, Eastern Europe and the Commonwealth of Independent States (CIS) and Latin America, the book provides a distinctive and comprehensive lens for analysing crisis impacts on children. In sum, it provides a strong case for policymakers to structure crisis response and recovery policies in a way that is more inclusive for the vast majority of the vulnerable. It also warns that failure to do so risks leaving behind some children, women and poor families permanently, and in turn weakening their resilience to future crises.

The evidence of impact and recovery

Understanding the conditions on the ground is vital to improving the situation of children during crisis and recovery. Based on experience and policy research on the current as well as previous crises, this book synthesises the evidence on the micro-level impacts of macroeconomic shocks, presents a guide to how crises can affect vulnerable children and other vulnerable groups and puts forward practical approaches describing policy strategies that can help ensure recoveries are inclusive.

The underlying framework traces crisis impacts from the macro to the micro level through meso-level economic and socio-political structures. Thus, as crisis hits and as remittances, financial flows, trade and aid contract, responses include governments tightening public spending, employment opportunities and conditions declining and credit fluctuating. Social norms, under pressure, change to become less protective and beneficial. Policy responses, political economy dynamics and civil society can mediate, to a greater or lesser extent, the full effects on people. Effects that are channelled through household economy and social dynamics can challenge household coping reserves, as households have to manage their assets, labour and consumption differently. Time use changes and norms of nurture, care and community life are affected profoundly. The end points for children are very real changes to their survival, protection, development and participation. The evidence within this volume recounts increases in child mortality and morbidity, failures in protection, declines in educational and other developmental opportunities and for youth, declines in work and participation prospects – all linked to crisis effects.

The volume provides a strong case for policymakers to structure crisis response and recovery policies in a way that is more inclusive. It touches on a variety of policy options, including innovative ones that have not yet been absorbed fully in mainstream policy discussions. In order to break away from one-size-fits-all prescriptions, it argues that policymakers could consider (as examples):

1. pursuing a pro-poor countercyclical strategy that preserves (if not increases) social spending and investments;
2. establishing more robust social protection systems that draw on policy innovations in this area by countries that have used social protection to promote better social inclusion and pro-poor growth;
3. setting up community-based monitoring systems (CBMS) that could serve as platforms for rapid data gathering during crisis situations;
4. developing and applying analytical macro–micro modelling tools that could help policymakers better understand the ramifications of crisis transmission and how to respond most equitably and cost-effectively;
5. and developing policies that are nuanced and tailored to particularly vulnerable population groups, including children and families affected by HIV and AIDS, children of migrant families, children at high risk of dropping out of school and girls who are typically at most risk of trafficking and other forms of exploitation.

Challenging orthodoxies

As such, the book challenges mainstream understanding of crisis impacts and their repercussions by drawing on the latest evidence and putting children and a multidimensional rights-informed conceptualisation of poverty and vulnerability centre stage, including an understanding of intra-household dynamics. By doing so, it challenges a number of orthodoxies, which policymakers now need to revisit.

The volume contests the view that a financial or economic crisis will probably not affect the poorest because they are not well integrated into the economy and financial system. The emerging evidence suggests the transmission channels of the crisis to poor and low-income households could actually be strong. This theme is picked up through the historical focus in Part I and in the impact studies in Part II. Thus, a related and widely held view (a second orthodoxy) that blanket macro-stabilisation policies are enough to promote inclusive recovery is also found to be erroneous. Inclusive recoveries are not automatic and they require nuanced policy responses that address the vulnerabilities of those who are most disadvantaged, notably children, and in particular children and their families from various marginalised social groups (for example, as a result of caste, ethnicity, gender, HIV/AIDS status, disability and so on).

A third orthodoxy that does not stand up to scrutiny is the widespread assumption that policies that target households will automatically solve the poverty and vulnerability of women and children. There is now substantial evidence that such responses often ignore intra-household power dynamics and unequal distribution of resources, assets and decision making, such that women and girls often end up shouldering disproportionate burdens of distress coping strategies, including dangerous work and withdrawal from school, and distress-related effects, such as domestic violence and the repercussions of the mental ill health of family members. This is not to deny real effects on boys and men, and thus the need as mentioned above for far better disaggregation of data to nuance policy responses.

These intra-household and gender-differentiated sets of impacts, alongside disruptions to social cohesion and social relations, explain in part why a fourth orthodoxy can be challenged – that which assumes that economic recoveries will automatically bring countries back to both economic and human development trajectories experienced prior to the crisis.

What we now know is that recoveries may be exclusive in the sense that the impact on children could be permanent (and the detrimental impact on human capital and household assets also could be long-lived). It is also likely that pre-existing vulnerabilities and inequity are exacerbated by policy responses that are not nuanced, for example, job creation that ends up mostly for men and programmes that do not consider the burden on women, who become more time-poor.

Thus, the potential impact of the fifth orthodoxy we challenge – that it is acceptable to scale back (sometimes severely) on human capital investments during a crisis, due to more pressing stabilisation-related challenges – becomes clearer. In fact, the authors suggest that social budgets should increase as part of countries' countercyclical responses (this is discussed in depth in Chapter 4). Part of this could be channelled towards boosting social protection systems as well as key social services in an effort to promote an inclusive recovery – one that is informed by a rights-based approach. The promotion of economic arguments for a more robust stimulus effect would preserve long-term human capital investments and growth and human development trajectories.

The chapters presented here put forth a wealth of empirical evidence drawn from recent as well as past episodes of crisis, indicating that these orthodoxies either are no longer relevant in today's interconnected world or that they should be debunked, given our better understanding of the micro foundations and macro linkages of poverty and inequality. Yet many policies still reflect these orthodoxies. Thus, one of the main messages of this book is that policymakers need to revisit and rethink their crisis response and management strategies based on the evidence at hand. This volume synthesises some of this evidence and attempts to contribute to better and more child-sensitive policymaking.

Using the evidence

Interest in the impacts of and responses to the current crisis has been widespread, as highlighted by a number of high-profile events and publications by key international agencies including the Asian Development Bank (ADB), the International Labour Organization (ILO), the United Nations Children's Fund (UNICEF), the United Nations Development Fund for Women (UNIFEM), the World Bank and a range of national governments. Building on this, this book is designed to be accessible so it can serve as a resource for development professionals and policymakers in the global North and South working on social and economic policy issues, notably related to social budgets, social protection and crisis management. It is also intended to serve as a textbook/resource book for graduate and professional schools in international affairs, development economics, public policy, family studies and child/youth studies programmes.

While other volumes on the economic and social fallout of the global economic crisis have emerged (for example Bauer and Thant, 2010; World Bank and IMF, 2010), these have only paid limited attention to child wellbeing – and largely only in the context of implications for reaching the child health and nutrition goals within the Millennium Development Goal (MDG) framework. In contrast, this collection of chapters provides a comprehensive assessment of crisis impacts on children, including their psychosocial wellbeing and their vulnerability to violence, abuse, neglect and exploitation. Importantly, by aiming to provide a fresh perspective on crises, it also highlights often-marginalised concerns and challenges mainstream orthodoxies. Regarding the former, by considering children as a group but also taking a rights perspective, the all-too-often invisible protection and participation implications become apparent, as these are given weight equal to that of the better-anticipated effects on basic human capital indicators. In terms of orthodoxies, we ask the reader to consider that different or more nuanced approaches to handling crises are possible and they should be considered.

The evidence presented

Having highlighted the challenges of integrating a child-sensitive perspective into crisis analyses and presented the conceptual framework we employ in this volume to help make sense of these complexities, we now provide an overview of how the book is organised. The book is divided into three broad parts: (i) impact of crises from a historical perspective, (ii) emerging evidence on the impact of the global financial crisis of the late 2000s and (iii) policies to promote inclusive recovery. We discuss in turn the methodological and substantive contributions of the chapters that each part comprises, focusing on their relevance to the book's broader thematic concern with challenging development orthodoxies. Collectively, the chapters represent a range of novel analytical tools (from historical analysis to computable general equilibrium [CGE] models to Community-based Monitoring System [CBMS]) for examining crisis impacts, which together we believe can equip policymakers with a richer and more robust evidence base, ultimately increasing the chances of not just more effective but also more equitable policy outcomes.

Part I: Impact of crises from a historical perspective

The first part of the book adopts an historical perspective and seeks to synthesise findings from past crises as to the transmission pathways through which children have been affected. The authors of these chapters emphasise that such an approach is critical, as it enables us to capture the breadth and depth of crisis impacts, which often are not visible in the immediate aftermath of economic recession due to data collection constraints that delay the availability of especially statistical evidence on impact, the time lag between macro-level shocks and poverty impacts or both. Historical analyses are also able to draw on a richer set of quantitative and qualitative data and to identify impacts over time. Although the crisis episodes analysed here diverge from the global financial crisis of the late 2000s in a number of ways, lessons learnt from these episodes on how children are affected by shocks and how policy can respond can nevertheless offer important insights and potential policy implications for the current crisis, and hopefully support efforts to respond in a timely, nuanced and age-sensitive manner.

The first chapter, by Harper et al., sets the stage by examining macroeconomic shocks in the recent past from a number of geographical regions, with the aim of understanding how these impacted children's wellbeing broadly defined. Three crisis episodes are examined: (i) the East Asian financial crisis of 1997–8; (ii) the experience of transition in former Soviet Republics in the early 1990s (especially Kyrgyzstan); and (iii) the currency crises in Mexico (1995) and Argentina (2002). What emerges from this analysis is that crisis effects are multidimensional, affecting not only children's educational, health and nutritional development, but also their right to protection from abuse, neglect and exploitation. The chapter also draws attention to the under-discussed psychosocial effects of crisis, especially impacts on mental wellbeing and the need to address this dimension more proactively as part of a comprehensive social protection package of responses.

The second half of the chapter explores the extent to which distinct policy responses undertaken by various national governments (with equally varying degrees of support and inputs by international actors) succeeded or did not succeed in mitigating adverse effects on children and their caregivers. It highlights the importance of political economy dynamics, including the role of civil society, in shaping these policy responses, and the complex tradeoffs that governments have to consider in addressing the macro-, meso- and micro-level effects of economic shocks. The authors draw on the experiences of East Asia and Latin America to underscore the positive human capital dividends that can be derived from a countercyclical approach to public expenditure in times of crisis, and the contrasting experience of transition economies, which witnessed significant reversals, especially with regard to child wellbeing indicators, as a result of widespread cuts and retrenchment of social policy and social protection programmes in particular.

The second chapter, by Mendoza and Rees, explores in more depth the impact of economic downturn and recovery trajectories on the critical area of infant mortality. Based on a systematic review of the empirical literature, the authors argue that, while there is scope for further improving our understanding of the links between economic trends and infant mortality, there is already strong evidence that children face grave risks if the social impacts of economic downturn remain unmitigated. Moreover, economic crises can also erode pre-existing progress in reducing infant mortality. A review of past crises highlights at least three key policy interventions that are critical to minimise impacts on infant mortality:

(i) providing humanitarian relief, including health and nutrition interventions, to the hardest hit and most vulnerable groups;
(ii) expanding social protection to the poorest and most vulnerable; and
(iii) resuscitating growth in a way that is pro-poor and ensures the recovery of household incomes – notably among the poor and low-income households.

As important, however, is adequate investment in social policies that protect children and women in general, as such infrastructure can cushion infants and their caregivers when crises strike.

The third chapter, by Doytch et al., contributes to the literature in this area by analysing the cyclicality of social spending, using data for approximately 100 industrial and developing countries drawn from various databases spanning the period 1980–2008. The authors examine the empirical link between indicators of the business cycle (that is, the output gap and economic growth) and social spending, with a particular focus on education and health spending, given their particular relevance to children's human capital development. Their findings suggest that public education spending appears acyclical and health spending is procyclical in lower-middle and middle-income developing countries. This pattern is reversed in low-income countries. By contrast, high-income countries appear to adopt acyclical or countercyclical public education and health spending. Given this evidence, the authors argue that the challenge for policymakers is to manage and channel the necessary spending and investments in the social sectors – notably in the supply of key services in education and health – in a much more effective way over the business cycle in order to strengthen the resilience of children, women and poor families.

Part II: Emerging evidence on the impact of the global financial crisis of the late 2000s

The second part of the book presents emerging evidence from Asia, Latin America and Sub-Saharan Africa (SSA) on the impact of the global financial crisis of the late 2000s on children and their families, drawing on a range of quantitative and qualitative methodological approaches. The relative weight of the impacts these chapters explore is likely to be revisited in coming years as new data emerge and as the patterning of the lag effects of the crisis on poverty and vulnerability becomes clearer with the benefit of historical hindsight and forthcoming household surveys. We nevertheless believe that these chapters will remain valuable contributions to the knowledge base on crises and children. They offer analytical models for early analyses of crisis-induced vulnerabilities as well as insights into the crisis transmission and policy response options which can help bridge the information gap for policymakers and strengthen evidence-based advocacy for timely interventions.

The first chapter, by Cockburn et al., assesses the impact of the global crisis and policy responses on different dimensions of child poverty in West and Central Africa (WCA) over the period 2009–11. It focuses on three country studies, Burkina Faso, Cameroon and Ghana, which broadly represent the diversity of economic conditions in the WCA region. The methodological approach is a simulation model which seeks to capture the macroeconomic effects of four key transmission pathways – trade, investment, remittances and aid flows – of the crisis and policy responses, and to assess their effects on children's micro-level poverty experiences. The analysis includes a range of different child poverty indicators: child monetary poverty, caloric poverty, school participation, child labour and access to health services. The simulations suggest that the channels through which child wellbeing are affected differ across the three countries: Ghanaian children are likely to suffer most from the global crisis in terms of monetary poverty and hunger, with more modest impacts in the other two countries. By contrast, some effects are expected on school attendance and involvement in child labour in Burkina Faso, while anticipated effects on schooling in Ghana and Cameroon are negligible. Among the policy responses to counteract the negative effects of the crisis on child wellbeing, a cash transfer targeted to poor children is found to be by far the most effective programme (the examination compares a universal and a targeted approach).

The next chapter, by Mabugu et al., adapts a similar methodological approach, combining a macroeconomic (CGE) model with microeconomic analytical tools to provide insights into the magnitude of macroeconomic shocks associated with the global crisis in South Africa, the country's capacity to withstand or cushion these shocks and the extent of fragility in terms of poverty levels and key indicators of child wellbeing. The authors combine both money-metric and non-money-metric indicators and find that the effects of monetary poverty on children, especially the poorest, are significant. The effects on school enrolment are less obvious, in part because of a potential dampening effect produced by school feeding programmes, and in part because existing data are not able to capture the effect on school attendance, which is likely to have suffered as a result of families' inability to pay for school uniforms and supplies. In addition, a dampening effect may have been caused by the fact that few South African school-age children have realistic options of participating successfully in the labour market or of being engaged in subsistence agriculture, given the small size of this sector. In terms of effects on health, the analysis suggests that the impact has been felt not in terms of access to health care but rather in relation to the ability to access quality services, with a switch by some poor families from private to inferior quality public health care facilities. Perhaps the most compelling finding emerging from the authors' analysis, however, is that the magnitude of the impact of South Africa's Child Support Grant (CSG), a monthly social transfer, outweighs the negative effects of the crisis on child poverty, even under the severe scenario. Thus, this *ex ante* social protection measure against poverty and vulnerability offers a type of income diversification to the poor, which has played a valuable role in mitigating child poverty during the crisis.

The third chapter, by Cortina, looks at one specific crisis transmission channel – that of remittance flows – and the responsiveness of existing social protection schemes in compensating for lost remittance revenue in 'left-behind' households in Mexico. Using Mexico's 2006 and 2008 National Survey of Income and Expenditure Survey (ENIGH), a nationally representative survey of more than 40,000 households, the author analyses the impact of a 23 per cent drop in remittances from the US since 2007 on access to social protection schemes. Applying logit regression models, this chapter finds that after controlling for household characteristics, uninsured remittance-recipient female-headed households with children under 18 years of age are more likely to benefit from targeted social protection schemes a year after the start of the economic crisis in comparison with a year before the crisis began. This provides positive evidence of the role of social protection in maintaining household income and mitigating the impact of economic shocks.

Despite these advances in empirical simulation methods, conclusive data and evidence on crisis impact are still forthcoming. Perhaps more closely geared towards assessing actual impact on the ground, rapid and (almost) real-time surveys are another set of tools in policymakers' arsenals to help bridge the information and evidence gap. The chapter by Reyes et al. describes the results of one type of rapid survey in the Philippines, using a CBMS. While the main objective of the chapter is to provide evidence of crisis impacts on children in the Philippines, an associated goal is to underscore the importance of platforms for collecting both social and economic indicators in a timely manner. Having these systems in place prior to the onset of a crisis can be quite fortuitous. In this case, the CBMS offered policymakers access to credible and timely information and evidence, in turn improving the prospects for more efficient and effective policy choices.

The final chapter in this part, by Jones and Harper, turns to an analysis of the global financial crisis of the late 2000s and its potential effects on one particularly vulnerable group of children – those living with and vulnerable to HIV/AIDS. Children are often relatively invisible in global HIV/AIDS policy debates but, given that globally they make up 6 per cent of the infected population but 14 per cent of total deaths, child-specific vulnerabilities deserve urgent attention. Drawing on secondary-level data, the chapter traces the impact pathways through which macro-level shocks are translated into meso- and micro-level impacts on children living with or vulnerable to HIV/AIDS and their caregivers. The authors' findings highlight that the crisis has generally exacerbated pre-existing challenges in this sector. The main impact pathways identified include current or anticipated budget cutbacks to both treatment and prevention programmes, alongside contraction of specific funds, either planned or because of currency devaluation, and increased drug import costs. Such cuts have been compounded by increased household difficulties in accessing services because of rising poverty, and related decreases in nutritional status and thus drug efficacy. Moreover, social protection responses, HIV-targeted or general, have so far been limited by both donor and government resource restrictions stemming from the food, fuel and financial crisis.

Part III: Policies to promote inclusive recovery

The third part of the book turns to a discussion of policy responses to economic crises, the extent to which these are age- (and gender-) sensitive and ways in which responses could be better-tailored so as to mitigate the worst impacts of crises on children and their caregivers and promote their longer-term wellbeing. The authors focus on ways in which policy repertoires can be approached more innovatively so that they can challenge existing orthodoxies of what is possible in terms of protecting social expenditure and what is necessary to promote inclusive wellbeing outcomes.

The first chapter, by Sumner, examines the impact of the global financial crisis on public budgets and child MDGs in SSA, and the potential role of child-sensitive social protection. The analysis is particularly concerned with links between public budget cuts and implications for reaching the child-focused MDGs in the region. It raises concerns that policy momentum that had been building around social protection, an important vehicle for contributing to MDG achievement, may be compromised by future fiscal constraints in the region and limited domestic political support, especially in the context of difficult policy tradeoffs. Moreover, while the World Bank's Vulnerability Financing Facility appears promising in terms of promoting new global partnerships in this area, the extent to which it will translate into substantial new resources remains uncertain.

Sumner's analysis is complemented by Garde and Yablonski's review of the development and evolution of social protection programmes in Ethiopia and Indonesia during previous crises and the consequent impacts for households and children. The authors selected these cases with the aim of teasing out lessons for the 2008-crisis. They argue that, given the impacts of the 2008-crisis in developing countries are in fact the result of multiple economic phenomena (food and fuel prices, financial system disruptions, global economic recession), the introduction of the National Safety Net programme in Indonesia during the East Asian crisis and the evolution of the Productive Safety Net Programme in Ethiopia as a response to repeated food crises are of particular relevance. The chapter concludes that well-implemented social protection programmes can prevent aggregate shocks from causing long-term consequences for children, but that this potential requires attention to a range of design and implementation issues. These include the specific nature of shocks and longer-term vulnerabilities, coverage and targeting challenges, political economy dynamics and gender power relations.

The final chapter in this part, by Zhang et al., reviews the ways that social protection responses have been integrated into fiscal stimulus packages. Many countries have responded to the financial and economic crisis by implementing expansionary monetary or/and fiscal policies. The extent of the monetary easing varies from country to country, as do the size and composition of the fiscal stimuli. Some countries have included certain measures in their fiscal stimulus plans to protect the most vulnerable members of society, notably children, women and poor families. In this chapter, information is collected on the extent of these social protection measures, in order to better understand how policy responses to the crisis have addressed concerns about poverty, vulnerability and deterioration in human development outcomes.

The book concludes with a discussion drawing together the findings of the historical and empirical case studies presented in the volume, and the ways in which these challenge existing development orthodoxies on the impacts of and responses to economic crises. We end by teasing out forward-looking economic and social policy implications, including how to improve crisis response and management in order to prevent crises from exacerbating inequality and poverty. Policymakers will need to look at the array of evidence and use this to rethink and revisit widespread orthodoxies in policymaking that may no longer be relevant in today's world of complex crises. Part of this rethinking would need to reflect an increased openness to innovative and much more nuanced policy interventions, including those that make up more robust social protection systems and stabilised social spending and investments throughout the business cycle. All of this will need to be underpinned by data and evidence in order to help policymakers bridge critical information gaps, particularly during complex crises.

Overall, it is our hope that this diverse set of methodological approaches and empirical case studies will provide a deeper composite understanding of the complex linkages between macroeconomic crises, children's micro-level experiences of related impacts and varied policy responses. The global financial crisis of the late 2000s will certainly not be the last; what is critical is that, as analysts, development practitioners and policymakers, we move beyond orthodox understandings and approaches to crisis-related economic and social vulnerabilities and prepare more strategically and comprehensively to be able to better safeguard children's wellbeing. To do this, we will need to collectively address the very real limitations of real-time crisis impact data availability (especially age- and gender-disaggregated data) and work towards the development of institutionalised mechanisms that capture immediate, more medium- and longer-term impacts. At the same time, we will need to ensure that this evidence base is innovatively communicated and shared with a broad cross-section of policymakers – not just conventional champions of children's rights but also those with decision-making power over macroeconomic policy levers nationally and globally. It is our hope that this book will contribute to an international dialogue on these issues.

References

Bauer, A. and Thant, M. (eds) (2010) 'Poverty and Sustainable Development in Asia: Impacts and Responses to the Global Economic Crisis.' Manila: ADBI and ADB.

World Bank and IMF (2010) 'The MDGS after the Crisis, Global Monitoring Report 2010.' Washington, DC: World Bank.

Part I

Impact of Crises from a Historical Perspective

2

Learning from Past Financial Crises: How Are Children Affected?

Caroline Harper, Nicola Jones and Paola Pereznieto

Introduction

This chapter is motivated by a concern about the effects of the 2008–10 global crisis on children and their caregivers, who are often especially vulnerable when crises strike (Beegle et al., 2008; Duryea et al., 2007). In particular, the adverse effects of shocks on children can have lifelong and sometimes intergenerational consequences. Inadequate nutrition, inadequate or absent health care, being withdrawn from school to work and/or being denied adequate child care and protection may all have consequences that cannot be reversed later, to say nothing of cases of avoidable infant and child mortality (Frankenberg et al., 1999; Harper et al., 2009).

The approach taken here is to look at recent economic shocks in a number of geographical regions to see how these impacted children and to examine the mediating role of economic and social policy responses. We consider evidence from three such crisis episodes: (i) the East Asian financial crisis of 1997–8; (ii) the experience of transition in former Soviet republics in the early 1990s (especially Kyrgyzstan); and (iii) currency crises in Mexico (1994) and Argentina (2002). None of these episodes is directly comparable with the 2008–10 crisis, but we can still learn a substantial amount from them by identifying impact pathways through which children are affected by shocks, and ways that policy can respond. These lessons in turn can be applied to the 2008–10 crisis and ultimately support efforts to respond to shocks in a timely and nuanced manner.

Conceptual framework

Understanding the links between a crisis that originates at the international level and outcomes that affect children at the local level is complex, as the channels of impact are many and often nonlinear, operating at different levels. Here, we use a generic framework that sets out the various possible channels of transmission, from an international and macro level through to meso and micro levels. A number of the channels in the framework, in particular the macro ones, may not be applicable in all cases, but an important number of commonalities emerge and they are of relevance to contemporary debates.

How households react to a contractionary environment and possible reduced access to government services as a result of crisis is mediated not only by intra-household power and resource dynamics, but also by policy responses. The latter are likely to be shaped by local governance arrangements, relationships between national governments and international financial institutions (IFIs) and the relative importance and effectiveness of domestic civil society. Pre-existing basic service infrastructure and social protection systems are also key factors influencing the ability of households to cope effectively with economic shocks.[1]

Macro-level shocks

The regional cases analysed in this chapter cover a spectrum of both discrete and interrelated economic shocks in a range of social, political and economic contexts which influenced the ways they played out, their impacts and related wellbeing outcomes. In this section, we provide an overview of the main macro-level impacts of the crises across the studied regions.

The preconditions for economic crisis in **Mexico** and **Argentina** differed, but both shocks were triggered by currency devaluation resulting from unsustainable pegged exchange rate regimes and loss of investor confidence. Both took place in a context of relative global economic stability which – along with depreciated currencies and trade openness – allowed them to hedge the impacts by increasing their exports (Pastor and Wise, 2004). These factors, along with governmental policy responses, meant both crises were of relatively short duration. Nevertheless, the poverty impacts were long-lasting. For example, the level of poverty in Mexico returned to pre-crisis 1994 levels only in 2002.

In Mexico, a series of political shocks during 1994 undermined confidence in the economy, resulting in capital outflows and an eventual devaluation of the peso. The crisis that ensued cut the peso's value in half, sent inflation soaring and set off a severe recession (Whitt, 1996). Unemployment doubled between 1993 and 1995, real wages declined as a result of inflation and labour market adjustments and worker layoffs led the informal sector to expand (Maloney et al., 2003). On Mexico's request, the IFIs provided a support package amounting to $40 billion, which contributed to the country's recovery.

In Argentina, three consecutive years of recession deepened in 2001 into an economic and financial crisis, exacerbated by a confidence crisis and run on the banks triggered by the International Monetary Fund's (IMF's) refusal to provide any additional financial support unless the country complied with its targets (including a zero deficit). In December of 2001, the government announced a temporary suspension of debt payments. Gross domestic product (GDP) fell by 10.9 per cent in 2002 alone, and unemployment soared, with dire poverty consequences. By early 2003, the IMF agreed to a $3 billion loan and the World Bank and the Inter-American Development Bank (IADB) contributed to new social programmes to help mitigate the worst effects of the crisis (Grugel and Riggirozzi, 2007). By 2005, the administration had resumed debt payments to the IFIs.

In **East Asia,** abundant liquidity and low real interest rates, combined with financial sector deregulation and few prudent controls, encouraged a debt-financed bubble in asset prices, which eventually collapsed. Common factors included rapid financial liberalisation, explosion of short-term foreign-denominated debt and poor macroeconomic management (Paitoonpong, 2001). However, triggers and dynamics varied. Importantly, given the level of contagion to other countries in the region, demand for exports dried up, causing further economic decline in countries whose growth had been largely export-driven.

Thailand's poorly supervised banking sector and mounting foreign debt contributed to the devaluation of the baht. This translated into a drop in foreign investment and a significant contraction in GDP, with wages falling and inflation accelerating. By August of 1997, the government had to seek support from the IMF to avoid 'total collapse' (Hewison, 1999). Conditionalities on assistance led to cutbacks in social expenditure, a restructuring of the financial system and a deepened role for the private sector. The economy recovered, albeit at a slow pace, with GDP growth reaching the pre-crisis 1996 level in 2003 (IMF, 2009 in Jones and Marsden, 2010).

Indonesia also had a poorly supervised banking sector and mounting foreign debt, resulting in rapid devaluation of the rupiah combined with rising inflation and a sharp decline in investment (Dhanani and Islam, 2002). Added to this, the El Niño drought and limited availability of agricultural inputs drove up food prices, which in turn forced down real wages and incomes. Exports declined, unemployment grew and there was a 30 per cent to 50 per cent drop in real wages in 1998 (Gottschalk, 2004). The country recovered only gradually, with GDP growth improving to mid-single digits by 2000.

The Korean economy, which was strong prior to the crisis, was left vulnerable by the rapid increase in short-term foreign debt racked up between 1993 and 1997. The sudden reversal of these capital flows following the crisis in Thailand triggered the collapse of the won. GDP contracted significantly, extreme currency devaluation contributed to a spike in inflation, particularly food price inflation and unemployment rose. As foreign exchange reserves dropped towards zero, Korea had to turn to the IMF for help. However, as much of the debt had been invested in the productive sector, and as the corporate sector had gained strength preceding the crisis and the government had been far more fiscally prudent than its Southeast Asian counterparts, the economy recovered more quickly. By March of 2002, unemployment had dropped and economic growth was firmly back on track (Hart-Landsberg and Burkett, 2001).

Malaysia was in a much stronger economic position than the other countries. While it faced a drop in economic growth, unemployment remained relatively low, and there was no precipitous collapse in real income (World Bank, 2000). Employers were encouraged to use retrenchment as a last resort; instead, many businesses shortened working hours and reduced employee wages and benefits in a bid to reduce costs.

All transition countries of the **ex-Socialist bloc** experienced major economic shocks – a 'transformational recession' – which were generally longer-lasting and deeper than expected (Cornia, 2009). By 1993, only four of the 27 countries were registering some economic growth. Generally, the richest countries – Poland, the Czech Republic and Slovakia – had a quicker transition and therefore saw their welfare indicators suffer least (ibid., 1995). In Commonwealth of Independent States (CIS) countries and countries experiencing conflict, the recession was substantially longer and deeper. Although all countries experienced growth in 2000–07, by 2006 only 7 out of 17 (excluding new European Union [EU] entrants) had surpassed 1989 GDP levels (UNICEF, 2006).

Additionally, patterns of growth have not always been broad-based. Much of the increase in GDP recorded in Azerbaijan, Georgia, Kazakhstan and Turkmenistan is based on oil revenues (either from oil extraction or from pipeline fees); this is not necessarily translated into poverty reduction and human development (ibid.). In some of the poorer CIS countries, such as Armenia, Kyrgyzstan, Moldova and Tajikistan, remittances from migrant workers, rather than growth based on structural transformation of the economy, have been the main engine of poverty reduction (Cornia, 2009).

Meso- and micro-level poverty effects

Across regions, crisis effects translated into increased poverty levels, with significant and potentially underreported effects on women and children. In some countries, the scale of the impact was huge. In Kyrgyzstan, up to one-third of all children were chronically poor a decade after transition, and only 23 per cent were deemed 'never poor' (Falkingham and Ibragimova, 2005). In Indonesia, the proportion of the population living under the national poverty line increased from 15.7 per cent to 27.1 per cent between 1996 and 1999 (Pradhan et al., 2000). In Thailand, the increase was from 9.8 per cent in 1994 to 13–14 per cent in 1998, with rates of income inequality rising (Kakwani and Pothong, 1999 in Tangcharoensathien et al., 2000). In Mexico, the increase in poverty erased previous poverty reduction achievements; both urban and rural poverty increased, although urban impacts were higher, given the transmission of the crisis through labour market adjustments. In Argentina, children and youth were particularly affected, with 75 per cent of children age 18 and under living under the poverty line in 2003 (Pereznieto, 2010).

Households absorbed these micro-level poverty effects of the crisis in a number of ways. Reduced wages and benefits, price increases, loss of employment and lack of access to credit led households to reduce consumption of nonessentials and durable goods, and of transport, educational materials, clothing, primary health care and donations or transfers, so they could allocate a relatively higher share of their budget to food. In more extreme situations, food consumption was reduced, sometimes by adjusting quality, sometimes quantity. In Mexico, poorer families were unable to continue consuming a balanced diet, which may have had important implications for the nutritional status of children and pregnant or lactating women, and the expenditure on primary health care fell (McKenzie, 2001). In Argentina, poor households with children experienced a larger decline in income, making them more vulnerable (Corbacho et al., 2003). Almost 72 per cent of households reduced consumption of school supplies, and 37 per cent of households with children under 12 took their children for medical checkups less frequently (Fiszbein et al., 2003). Health insurance declined markedly among the poor (by 60 per cent in the lowest income groups).

In East Asia, households' purchasing power across countries declined significantly as a result of increased prices of consumer goods and reduced wages. In Indonesia in 1997 and 1998, for example, real per capita expenditures declined by 24 per cent (Frankenberg et al., 1999). In all cases, the food share of total expenditure rose disproportionately, and this was especially damaging in urban areas. Overall, household spending on health was critically affected, appearing generally worse in rural areas. Investment in education tended to be more protected, but it still was affected (ibid.).

In transition countries, almost two-thirds of people in the bottom quintile and one-third of people in the top quintile reduced food consumption (Lokshin and Yemtsov, 2004). Food expenditure as a proportion of household spending rose to 60 per cent in Kyrgyzstan, from 40 per cent in 1989 (Bauer et al., 1998). Most drastically, some households sought to reduce overall expenditure by reducing the number of mouths to feed, that is, by sending children to relatives or into institutional care (Ablezova et al., 2004).

Many households also experienced changes in intra-household power relations, relating to an altered locus of economic power. The burden of these effects was often unevenly shared, depending on pre-existing gender- and age-based power relations. Some adults who did not work before had to take on paid labour; others needed to work longer hours or take on more risky or degrading forms of work; some were forced to migrate and, in some cases, child labour increased as households struggled to cope (Duryea et al., 2007).

Time pressures had knock-on effects related to reproductive responsibilities and increased family stress, with violence linked to depression and alcohol abuse reported widely. Psychological ill health manifested itself in increased incidence of stress-related mortality and intra-household tensions and, although little discussed, this is likely to have affected the care, nurture and protection of children negatively. These impacts were noted in all regions: increased stress, phobias and suicides in Argentina (World Bank, 2003); psychological stress in Indonesia (Friedman and Thomas, 2007) and increased suicide and divorce in Malaysia (Tangcharoensathien et al., 2000). Mortality rates among men rose in Russia and CIS countries, Thailand and Malaysia (Lotrakul, 2006). In Korea, suicide rates surged in conjunction with the financial crisis, again especially among males (Khang et al., 2005).

Impacts of micro-level poverty effects on children's rights

Overall, the negative impacts on children's right to survival (health, nutrition, water and sanitation) were significant in all regions. A rise in infant mortality in Mexico (from 5 per cent to 7 per cent between 1995 and 1996) reversed a decreasing mortality trend up to 1994 (rates fell again after 1997) (Cutler et al., 2002). Child mortality and severe morbidity rose in the northern provinces of Argentina; morbidity increased in Thailand and Indonesia during the crisis years (Waters et al., 2003) and in Russia nutritional status improvements were observed only after the worst of the crisis episodes and after 1998 (Stillman, 2003).

These impacts are linked to the magnitude of economic shocks, rises in food prices, lower spending on health care, declines in the use of health services, the collapse of health services (Argentina) and a shift from the private to public health sector care (Thailand). Such effects are also linked to pressures on parents, who may buffer effects to a degree but pass on others, such as through anaemia in pregnancy (in Indonesia rates rose from 9 per cent to 12 per cent between 1997 and 1998) (Block et al., 2004). In addition, increased parental workloads and migration led to decreases in time for care and nurture (MacDonald et al., 2005). Lack of time is also linked tentatively to increased infant mortality in Mexico (Cutler et al., 2002) and more broadly to child well-being deficits.

Effects on the right to development (education and psychosocial well-being) were mixed, across and within regions, suggesting an income threshold effect and that the relative strength and quality of pre-existing basic services and social protection also shaped deprivations. Thus, household spending (albeit constrained) and government safety nets (such as crisis-related increases in school feeding programmes in Mexico and Argentina) appear generally to have protected educational attendance. In some cases, fewer work opportunities encouraged greater enrolments (presenting its own problems of youth unemployment), although girls' domestic work increased in some countries, such as Indonesia (Cameron, 2000). However, basic school enrolment declined in CIS countries by 10 per cent to 15 per cent in the early 1990s, and upper secondary school enrolment rates fell substantially in poorer countries, as did those in vocational education, indicating a cohort of older children and young people receiving little public investment (UNICEF, 2007).

Evidence on the right to protection (from abuse, neglect and violence) is more limited, but it seems there were important implications for the quality and quantity of care children received from caregivers, a heightened risk of child abuse and mixed impacts on children's engagement in child labour. The number of children living on the streets increased in Indonesia and Thailand, and these children were at increased risk of sex work, drug use and crime (Knowles et al., 1999). There was also an increase in child abandonment and numbers of children taken into care in Indonesia, Thailand and Korea (see Tangcharoensathien et al., 2000). Time poverty increased among women in general (Elson, 2008), and female migration rose in Indonesia in particular (Silvey, 2001).

In transition contexts, there were notable increases in the commercial sexual exploitation of children and, in parts of the region, trafficking of children for sexual exploitation and begging (Tiurukanova, 2006). Other key child protection challenges included children living and working on the streets, particularly in the poorer CIS countries; and, more generally, hazardous and exploitative child labour in agriculture, mining and more visible activities, such as market trading, urban services (for example car washing) and begging (ILO, 2001). A less-noted impact of economic crisis was the increase in the proportion of young children left without adult supervision while their parents or carers were working (UNICEF, 1997).

Finally, there is little evidence as to how crises impact children's and youths' right to participation in decisions that affect their lives. In East Asia, changes in the political system, especially the growing role of civil society, may have opened up new opportunities to realise children's rights (Jones and Marsden, 2010). In transition countries, opportunities for children's participation appear to have declined, related to the loss of organised children's and youth movements in former Soviet republics (Marcus, 2009).

Policy responses and their effects on child wellbeing

In each of the regions, complex and dynamic factors mediated both how deeply the crisis was felt and how quickly and effectively governments could respond. Economic policy responses shaped the general parameters within which governments could make crisis-related social sector investment and reform decisions. For instance, Malaysia and Korea had a greater resource base and fiscal space than Indonesia and Thailand, allowing them greater freedom to protect (and in Malaysia actually increase) social spending (Vijayaledchumy, 2003). Political economy dynamics also shaped decisions about the scope and type of policy response, such as ruling party ideology, balance of power among government agencies and relative influence of organised civil society actors, including champions for women's and children's wellbeing (Croissant, 2004). For example, civil society in Indonesia, Korea and Thailand played a critical role in persuading the government to take measures to temper the social effects of the IMF's economic adjustment measures (in Malaysia, the government itself famously resisted IFI pressures to introduce stringent reforms) (Nesadurai, 1998). By contrast, in the former Soviet Union, comparatively fledgling civil societies had only limited influence on the policy trajectories chosen by their respective governments and donor agencies.

For women and children in particular, the extent to which policy responses reflected age- and gender-specific vulnerabilities often depended heavily on strong government and/or civil society advocates (see Kim and Voos, 2007). In Mexico, a small group of government advisors in the Ministry of Finance concerned about the negative fallout of the crisis on human capital development seized on the opportunity to develop a new safety net programme, *Progresa/Oportunidades*. This subsequently developed into a flagship cash transfer programme of international renown for mothers and their children (although this originally targeted rural areas and thus did not reach crisis-affected urban households). In other cases, however, policy responses have not been sufficiently gender- or child-sensitive. Analysts point out gender biases in the design of public employment and retraining programmes, and inadequate policy attention to rising problems of intra-household violence; reduced care time for children and the incapacitated and the gendered patterning of crisis-induced mental ill health (see Esquivel, 2006).

East Asia

Indonesia, Thailand and Korea all implemented IMF economic reform packages, with Korea recovering the quickest in terms of GDP growth. Malaysia pursued its own path through various capital control measures, a response that has since been credited with yielding important lessons for tackling macroeconomic shocks. Importantly, the crisis coincided with and/or exacerbated periods of marked political change, which in some cases (particularly Indonesia, but also Korea and Malaysia) opened up space for civil society activism (Knowles et al., 1999). This was often highlighted in the significant tensions that emerged between cutting social expenditure and increasing expenditure on social protection. Indonesia and Thailand had a more limited resource base and greater debts when the crisis struck, and so they made significant cutbacks in basic services (some in crucial areas, such as reproductive health and preventative health care in Thailand) (Hopkins, 2006). Malaysia and Korea had greater freedom to protect spending on health and education, with correspondingly greater success in protecting human development indicators. Malaysia actually increased its social sector spending, allowing the government to build on its already comparatively strong social service structures and programmes (World Bank, 2000). Korea was able largely to maintain social spending, with some slight dips in crisis years, combined with a push towards privatisation of the health system (Goh et al., 2005).

Informal social protection mechanisms through family and community links proved critical in shielding the poor and children from negative crisis impacts, especially in the immediate aftermath of the crisis before formal social protection programmes were brought in or scaled up, and for those without access to these programmes (Atinc and Walton, 1998). However, these programmes also came under threat in some contexts, as social capital and social cohesion were eroded, reflected in rising rates of crime, violence, homelessness and drug abuse and falling community participation (Knowles et al., 1999).

All countries introduced (Indonesia) or expanded (Korea, Malaysia and Thailand) social protection programmes to mitigate the worst effects on the poor, with aid playing an important role. This included a range of targeted programmes, including food subsidies, health fee waivers, educational scholarships and public works schemes, fuelled in part by strong civil society pressures (Sumarto et al., 2005). Box 2.1 highlights major differences between countries with pre-existing social protection infrastructure and those that had to develop a system largely from scratch. However, in all four countries, child protection and gender-based violence appear to have been a major gap in the policy responses.

Mexico and Argentina

Mexico was much more aligned with IMF prescriptions; by contrast, the IFI criticised Argentina's crisis response heavily. In both countries, social sector cuts were lower than those in overall spending, although the remaining budget was still inadequate to cope with the expanding vulnerable population. For instance, in Argentina, although social spending fell proportionally less (by 31.7 per cent between 2001 and 2002 compared with overall cuts of 37.8 per cent) (Corbacho et al., 2003), the large increase in the number of poor people meant that real spending per poor person actually declined by 16 per cent (World Bank, 2003).

Box 2.1 Creating versus expanding social protection infrastructure

In pre-crisis Indonesia, social spending was focused mostly on social service provision, such as health and education: informal family and community networks provided the majority of 'social insurance' (Sumarto et al., 2005). In response to the crisis, the government introduced a range of entirely new, more formal social protection programmes. However, given the urgency of addressing immediate vulnerabilities, implementation of these was rushed and not sufficiently systematic. Overall, social safety net programmes were criticised widely for being ineffective and poorly designed and implemented (Paitoonpong, 2001). The bureaucracy lacked the capacity and experience to manage and design them, and this was further complicated by political turbulence in 1998. Another problem related to the need to include effective targeting mechanisms when designing programmes: a large number of the poor were simply not covered. Many of the programmes suffered from substantial leakage to higher quintiles, allowing non-poor beneficiaries to reap benefits. Nevertheless, household participation was generally found to improve consumption, with important protective benefits for children's nutritional wellbeing (Sumarto et al., 2005).

Malaysia, on the other hand, had relatively good initial conditions in terms of service delivery and safety nets. At the onset of the crisis, the government allocated more money to existing safety nets through a fiscal stimulus package that to a large extent protected social budgets (Jones and Marsden, 2009). The existing network of free health and basic education remained virtually intact and provided a solid base to help cushion vulnerable groups (World Bank, 2000). The government focused on opening up income-generating opportunities rather than on cash transfers (ibid.) and tried to avoid creating dependency.

Assistance played a significant role in funding household expenditure and stemming deteriorations in living standards (Islam et al., 2007), particularly of low-income households (Paitoonpong, 2001). Still, safety nets in Malaysia were not sufficiently flexible to adapt effectively to the new poverty landscape that emerged through the crisis, especially the rapid increase in urban poverty (Jones and Marsden, 2009). Existing programmes did not reach significant numbers of newly urban poor, and they were targeted mainly towards rural areas as they had been prior to the crisis (World Bank, 2000).

The crises also highlighted the importance of strengthening existing social safety nets through a sequenced package of reforms and, as in East Asia, provided important opportunities for reform-oriented forces (Barnes, 2005). In Mexico, a key pillar of this package was the major conditional cash transfer programme, *Progresa/Oportunidades*, launched in 1997 under the creative leadership of a small group of policymakers supported by prominent domestic and international researchers. This has been shown to reduce poverty as well as to promote school attendance, along with a range of other health and nutritional improvements (Skoufias, 2005).

In Argentina, too, the crisis at least provided some space for progressive social forces to call for the introduction of new measures to mitigate the worst effects on the poor and vulnerable. The government redesigned an existing small-scale cash-for-work programme for unemployed household heads to reduce aggregate unemployment. This partially compensated many losers from the crisis and reduced extreme poverty. However, it also had key shortcomings, such as the fixed nature of the benefit independent of the number of children in the household and thus the low levels of per capita transfers which were insufficient to allow beneficiaries to move out of poverty (Barbeito and Goldberg, 2003), although they contributed to a better standard of living. The programme also paid limited attention to the gendered nature of poverty and vulnerability: although women increased their participation in the labour force and made up 71 per cent of beneficiaries, they were employed in very low wage and temporary jobs with no child care mechanisms.

Transition CIS countries

CIS countries faced a complex situation, given the systemic-level changes playing out in transitioning from state-controlled planned economies to market capitalist economies (Cornia, 2009). Donor advice and financial support shaped policy choices significantly in many countries, although national political agendas and differing initial institutional and social conditions meant specific policy responses varied from country to country. Overall donor priorities shifted from a very strong emphasis on economic (and governance) reforms in the early 1990s to include greater attention to the social sectors (Anderson, 1998). Civil society sought to mitigate some of the social effects of reforms by providing support services to affected groups.

Economic policy responses were largely neoliberal in nature, with efforts to 'modernise' social services a part of this reform package. Under the Soviet Union, this support had been provided not only through state public services but also by trade unions and state-owned enterprises, which ran social services such as kindergartens. In the early 1990s, social services budgets fell substantially, and such functions were removed altogether (Humphrey, 1995). In theory, these were to be transferred to local authorities; in practice, underfinanced local governments could not afford to run them, and infrastructures such as kindergartens and leisure facilities were sold off or closed. As such, the scaling back of social services was probably the single most significant (and deleterious) consequence of transition for children (Marcus, 2009).

Social assistance was already part of the policy infrastructure pre-transition, but only in the richest Central and Eastern European (CEE) countries such as Hungary, the Czech Republic and Slovakia, was the existing family allowance system used to increase the proportion of resources allocated to crisis-affected families. Most countries shifted from a universal to a targeted (means-tested) system of family allowances or child-oriented income support, which often had significant errors of inclusion and exclusion (ibid.). Indeed, in the poorer countries, the transition-induced recession not only increased the number of people seeking assistance but also simultaneously eroded the resources available. For example, by the late 1990s, the real value of child allowances in Armenia and Moldova had fallen to less than 20 per cent of 1991 levels, and this was reflected in stagnating or declining child welfare indicators (Andrews and Ringold, 1999).

Conclusions

Overall, our findings from past financial crisis episodes point to four key policy implications for children and their families.

Institutionalising crisis-monitoring initiatives

Evidence on past crises not only emerged with a considerable time lag, but also remains fragmented and incomplete in many cases. There is therefore an urgent need to invest in more timely and systematic age- and gender-disaggregated data collection and crisis monitoring, to better inform policy debates on how best to tackle the vulnerabilities children, youth and caregivers face – particularly among rural populations, households dependent on the informal sector and the newly poor. In addition, there is a need to pay attention not just to conventional education, health and nutrition indicators, but also to other areas of social vulnerability, including intra-household tensions, gender-based violence, trafficking, social capital, social cohesion and mental wellbeing. Discussions on child wellbeing often deal only with survival and development deprivations and fail to include issues of protection and care. Accordingly, we need more systematic assessments of experiences of poverty and vulnerability in crisis contexts to be able to take appropriate policy and programming action.

Creating space for countercyclical policy to invest in quality basic services

An important cross-regional lesson is that countries need to be able to react to the downturn without having to cut their social sector public expenditure, at least where fiscal institutions are strong. This is particularly in areas of spending that benefit children directly – education, health, protection – and where deficits for children have lifelong consequences. In East Asia, the crisis did not affect child mortality and long-term malnutrition rates significantly, due in large part to stable investments in basic health services (Korea and Malaysia) and targeted social assistance and social health insurance initiatives (Indonesia and Thailand). Care also needs to be taken to ensure investments are made in supply-side measures, such as maintaining quality accessible health care, so demand-side support fostered by social protection mechanisms can have a meaningful effect on wellbeing outcomes.

Investing in social protection

Both pre-existing social protection systems and tailored crisis-specific responses were decisive in tackling crisis-induced household- and childhood-specific poverty and vulnerability. Even so, developing effective targeting mechanisms in the design of social protection interventions remains important. Given the important role of informal mechanisms in enabling families to cope during crisis episodes, especially in the short term, it is important to foster synergies between formal approaches and existing informal mechanisms, which often come under strain during crisis. Finally, given the importance of international aid in supporting social protection responses during crises, it is critical to monitor aid flows and the extent to which they are prioritising child-sensitive social protection initiatives, especially given how much the aid landscape has changed in the recent past.

Promoting care and protection concerns on the policy agenda

The extent to which policy responses addressed issues of protection and care appears to have been very limited. Despite rising intra-household tensions and violence, there was little increased investment in related social services, and there was a marked absence of response to rising rates of mental ill health and drug and substance abuse in East Asia and transition countries. Similarly, although the gendered effects of under- and unemployment and household poverty were often stark, measures to address women's time poverty and support their greater responsibility for care work and domestic responsibilities do not appear to have been factored into design. Crisis responses must focus not only on threats to wealth and human capital accumulation but also on the ability of communities and households to ensure the adequate care and protection of children.

In sum, this chapter has underscored the complexity involved in the regional patterning of crisis impacts and the importance of adopting context-specific responses. It has also highlighted the need to take into account local political economy dynamics, and especially the relative influence of different institutions and organised civil society in shaping policy dialogues on response initiatives. Nevertheless, a number of common themes emerge with regard to policy approaches to mitigating child-specific vulnerabilities to survival, development, protection and care deprivations. Given that each crisis occurs in unique circumstances, it is not straightforward to anticipate which effects will be most prevalent in which countries in other crises. Some similar patterns in the 2008–10 crisis regarding remittance flows, access to credit and employment conditions and opportunities imply the existence of many of the same effects, depending on the base conditions within particular countries, especially among the most vulnerable.

Note

1. Here we draw on work undertaken by Harper et al. (2009).

References

Ablezova, M., Botoeva, G., Jukusheva, T., Marcus, R. and Satybaldieva, E. (2004) 'A Generation at Risk? Childhood Poverty in Kyrgyzstan.' Report 15. London: CHIP.

Anderson, J. (1998) *Kyrgyzstan: Central Asia's Island of Democracy?* London: Routledge.

Andrews, E. and Ringold D. (1999) 'Safety Nets in Transition Economies: Toward a Reform Strategy.' Social Protection Discussion Paper 9914. Washington, DC: World Bank.

Atinc, T.M. and Walton, M. (1998) *Social Consequences of the East Asian Financial Crisis. Responding to the Global Financial Crisis.* Washington, DC: World Bank.

Barbeito, A. and Goldberg, L. (2003) 'Social Policy and Economic Regime in Argentina: Crisis and Retrenchment of Social Protection.' Geneva: UNRISD.

Barnes, H. (2005) 'Conflict, Inequality and Dialogue for Conflict Resolution in Latin America: The Cases of Argentina, Bolivia and Venezuela.' Occasional Paper. Geneva: HDR Office, UNDP.

Bauer, A., Boschmann, N., Green, D. and Kuehnast, K. (1998) *A Generation at Risk. Children in the Central Asian Republics of Kazakhstan and Kyrgyzstan.* Manila: ADB.

Beegle, K., Dehejia, R.H., Gatti, R. and Krutikova, S. (2008) 'The Consequences of Child Labor: Evidence from Longitudinal Data in Rural Tanzania.' Policy Research Working Paper 4677. Washington, DC: World Bank.

Block, S.A., Kiess, L., Webb, P., Kosen, S., Moench-Pfanner, R., Bloem, M.W. and Timmer, C.P. (2004) 'Macro Shocks and Micro Outcomes: Child Nutrition during Indonesia's Crisis.' *Economics and Human Biology* 2(1): 21–44.

Cameron, L.A. (2000) 'The Impact of the Indonesian Financial Crisis on Children: An Analysis Using 100 Village Data.' Working Paper 81. Florence: UNICEF Innocenti Research Centre.

Corbacho, A., Garcia-Escribano, M. and Inchauste, G. (2003) 'Argentina: Macroeconomic Crisis and Household Vulnerability.' Working Paper 03/89. Washington, DC: IMF.

Cornia G.A. (1995) 'Ugly Facts and Fancy Theories: Children and Youth during the Transition.' Occasional Paper 47. Florence: UNICEF Innocenti Research Centre.

Cornia, G.A. (2009) 'Transition, Structural Divergence, and Performance: EE-FSU over 2000–2007.' UNU-WIDER Conference on Reflections on Transition: Twenty Years after the Fall of the Berlin Wall. Helsinki, 18–19 September.

Croissant, A. (2004) 'Changing Welfare Regimes in East and Southeast Asia: Crisis, Change and Challenge.' *Social Policy and Administration* 38(5): 501–24.

Cutler, D., Knaul, F., Lozano, R., Mendez, O. and Zurita, B. (2002) 'Financial Crisis, Health Outcomes and Ageing: Mexico in the 1980s and 1990s.' *Journal of Public Economics* 84: 279–303.

Dhanani, S. and Islam, I. (2002) 'Poverty, Vulnerability and Social Protection in a Period of Crisis: The Case of Indonesia.' *World Development* 30(7): 1211–31.

Duryea, S., Lam, D. and Levison, D. (2007) 'Effects of Economic Shocks on Children's Employment and Schooling in Brazil.' *Journal of Development Economics* 84: 188–214.

Elson, D. (2008) 'Gender Equality and the Economic Crisis.' IDRC/SID-OG Meeting. Ottawa, 27 November.

Esquivel, V. (2006) 'What Else Do We Have to Cope with? Gender, Paid and Unpaid Work during Argentina's Last Crisis.' GEM-IWG Working Paper 6-6. Salt Lake City: International Working Group on Gender, Macroeconomics and International Economics.

Falkingham, J. and Ibragimova, S. (2005) 'The Dynamics of Child Poverty in the Kyrgyz Republic.' Report 11. London: CHIP.

Fiszbein, A., Giovagnoli, P. and Adúriz, I. (2003) 'The Argentine Crisis and Its Impact on Household Welfare.' *CEPAL Review* 79: 151–68.

Frankenberg, E., Thomas, D. and Beegle, K. (1999) 'The Real Costs of Indonesia's Economic Crisis: Preliminary Findings from the Indonesia Family Life Surveys.' Labour and Population Program Working Paper 99-04. Santa Monica, CA: RAND.

Friedman, J. and Thomas, D. (2007) 'Psychological Health Before, During, and After an Economic Crisis: Results from Indonesia, 1993–2000.' Policy Research Working Paper 4386. Washington, DC: World Bank.

Goh, C., Kang, S.J. and Sawada, Y. (2005) 'How Did Korean Households Cope with Negative Shocks from the Financial Crisis?' *Journal of Asian Economics* 16(2): 239–54.

Gottschalk, R. (2004) *How Financial Crises Affect the Poor.* London: DFID.

Grugel, J. and Riggirozzi, M.P. (2007) 'The Return of the State in Argentina.' World Economy and Finance Research Working Paper 0018. London: Birkbeck.
Harper, C., Jones, N., McKay A. and Espey, J. (2009) 'Children in Times of Economic Crisis: Past Lessons, Future Policies.' Background Note, London: ODI.
Hart-Landsberg, M. and Burkett, P. (2001) 'Economic Crisis and Restructuring in South Korea. Beyond the Free Market-Statist Debate.' *Critical Asian Studies* 33(3): 403–43.
Hewison, K. (1999) 'Thailand's Capitalism: The Impact of the Economic Crisis.' Asia Paper 1. Armidale: UNEAC.
Hopkins, S. (2006) 'Economic Stability and Health Status: Evidence from East Asia before and after the 1990s Economic Crisis.' *Health Policy* 75(3): 347–57.
Humphrey, C. (1995) 'Mythmaking, Narratives and the Dispossessed in Russia.' *Cambridge Anthropology* 19(2): 70–92.
ILO (2001) *In-depth Analysis of the Situation of Working Street Children in the Leningrad Region 2001*. St. Petersburg: ILO.
Islam, M.M., Siwar, C. and Karim, M.A. (2007) 'The Impact of the Financial Crisis on the Living Standard: An Empirical Investigation.' *UNITAR E-Journal* 3(1): 52–75.
Jones, N. and Marsden, H. (2009) 'Assessing the Impacts of and Responses to the 1997–98 Asian Financial Crisis through a Child Rights Lens.' London: ODI.
Jones, N. and Marsden, H. (2010) 'Assessing the Impacts of and Responses to the 1997–98 Asian Financial Crisis through a Child Rights Lens: Including Children in Policy Responses to Previous Economic Crises.' Social and Economic Policy Working Paper. New York: UNICEF.
Khang, Y.H., Lynch, J.W. and Kaplan, J.A. (2005) 'Impact of Economic Crisis on Cause-Specific Mortality South Korea.' *International Journal of Epidemiology* 34(6): 1291–301.
Kim, H. and Voos, P.B. (2007) 'The Korean Economic Crisis and Working Women.' *Journal of Contemporary Asia* 37(2): 190–208.
Knowles, J.C, Ernesto, M.P. and Racelis, M. (1999) 'Social Consequences of the Financial Crisis in Asia.' Economic Staff Paper 60. Manila: ADB.
Lokshin, M. and Yemtsov, R. (2004) 'Household Strategies of Coping with Shocks in Post-crisis Russia.' *Review of Development Economics* 8(1): 15–32.
Lotrakul, M. (2006) 'Suicide in Thailand during the Period 1998–2003.' *Psychiatry and Clinical Neurosciences* 60(1): 90–5.
MacDonald, M., Phipps, S. and Lethbridge, L. (2005) 'Taking Its Toll: The Influence of Paid and Unpaid Work on Women's Well-Being.' *Feminist Economics* 11(1): 63–94.
Maloney, W., Cunningham W. and Bosch, M. (2003) 'Who Suffers Income Falls During Crises? An Application of Quantile Analysis to Mexico 1992–95.' Washington, DC: World Bank.
Marcus, R. (2009) 'Transition to a Market Economy and Children's Rights: Kyrgyzstan in Regional Perspective.' Background Paper. London: ODI.
McKenzie, D. (2001) 'The Household Response to the Mexican Peso Crisis.' Working Paper 01017. Stanford, CA: Department of Economics, Stanford University.
Nesadurai, H.E.S. (1998) 'Accommodating Global Markets: Malaysia's Response to Economic Crisis.' Coventry: CSGR.

Paitoonpong, S. (2001) 'Social Impacts of the Asian Economic Crisis in Thailand, Indonesia, Malaysia and the Philippines: Synthesis Report.' *Thailand Development Research Institute Quarterly Review* 161: 3–14.

Pastor, M. and Wise, C. (2004) 'Picking up the Pieces: Comparing the Social Impact of Financial Crisis in Mexico and Argentina.' Los Angeles, CA: Center for International Studies.

Pereznieto, P. (2010) 'The Case of Mexico's 1995 Peso Crisis and Argentina's 2002 Convertibility Crisis: Including Children in Policy Responses to Previous Economic Crises.' Social and Economic Policy Working Paper. New York: UNICEF.

Pradhan, M., Suryahadi, S., Sumarto, S. and Printchett, L. (2000) 'Measurements of Poverty in Indonesia: 1996, 1999, and Beyond.' Working Paper. Jakarta: SMERU.

Silvey, R.M. (2001) 'Migration under Crisis: Household Safety Nets in Indonesia's Economic Collapse.' *Geoforum* 32(1): 33–45.

Skoufias, E. (2005) 'PROGRESA and Its Impacts on the Welfare of Rural Households in Mexico.' Research Report 139. Washington, DC: IFPRI.

Stillman, S. (2003) 'Health and Nutrition in Eastern Europe and the Former Soviet Union during the Decade of Transition: A Review of the Literature.' CESifo Conference on Health and Economic Policy. Munich, 27–28 June.

Sumarto, S., Suryahadi, A. and Widyanti, W. (2005) 'Assessing the Impact of Indonesian Social Safety Net Programmes on Household Welfare and Poverty Dynamics.' *European Journal of Development Research* 17(1): 155–77.

Tangcharoensathien, V., Harnvoravongchai, P., Pityarangsarit, S. and Kasemsup, V. (2000) 'Health Impacts of Rapid Economic Changes in Thailand.' *Social Science and Medicine* 51(6): 789–807.

Tiurukanova, T. (2006) *Human Trafficking in the Russian Federation: Inventory and Analysis of the Current Situation and Responses*. Moscow: UNICEF/ILO/CIDA.

UNICEF (1997) 'Children at Risk in Central and Eastern Europe: Perils and Promises.' Regional Monitoring Report 4. Florence: UNICEF Innocenti Research Centre.

UNICEF (2006) *Innocenti Social Monitor 2006: Understanding Child Poverty in South-Eastern Europe and the CIS*. Florence: UNICEF Innocenti Research Centre.

UNICEF (2007) 'Education for Some More than Others?' Geneva: UNICEF Regional Office for CEE and the CIS.

Vijayaledchumy, V. (2003) 'Fiscal Policy in Malaysia.' Paper 2. Basel: BIS.

Waters, H., Saadah, F. and Pradhan, M. (2003) 'The Impact of the 1997–98 East Asian Economic Crisis on Health and Health Care in Indonesia.' *Health Policy and Planning* 18(2): 172–81.

World Bank (2000) 'Malaysia Public Expenditures. Managing the Crisis; Challenging the Future.' Report 20371-MA. Washington, DC: World Bank.

World Bank (2003) Argentina, Crisis and Poverty 2003: A Poverty Assessment. Washington, DC: World Bank.

3

Infant Mortality during Economic Downturns and Recovery

Ronald U. Mendoza and Nicholas S. Rees

Introduction

Despite important gains in recent years, the challenge involved in saving the lives and improving the wellbeing of children is still quite considerable. Almost 8.1 million children die before they reach the age of 5 and an estimated 5.7 million before the age of 1. Furthermore, approximately 99 per cent of child deaths and 98 per cent of infant deaths occur in developing countries.[1] Mothers too experience considerable risk. Globally, the lifetime risk of maternal death (that is, the probability a woman will die from complications of pregnancy or childbirth) is 1 in 140; in least-developed countries (LDCs) it is 1 in 37. More than 99 per cent of maternal deaths occur in low- and middle-income countries (UNICEF, 2008). Furthermore, for every woman who dies in pregnancy or childbirth, an estimated 20 others suffer pregnancy-related illness or other severe consequences (ibid.). All these deaths are linked to poverty, particularly where there is poor access to health and maternity services, nutritious food, micronutrients and breastfeeding and clean water and sanitation.

This chapter reviews the empirical literature on the impact of previous crises on children to shed light on the potential risks and main channels of crisis impacts on infants, mothers and young children. It then reviews some of the main policy responses to help mitigate these risks, notably those focused on reducing infant mortality.

A brief review of the empirical literature on economic downturns and infant mortality

Infant mortality[2] is most often associated with preterm birth, asphyxia, severe infections, diarrhoea and other complications (including from endemic diseases). Preterm birth can explain up to 27 per cent of neonatal deaths (deaths within the first 28 days of birth); sepsis/pneumonia and asphyxia up to 26 per cent and 23 per cent, respectively. Tetanus, congenital malfunctions and diarrhoea help account for the remaining 24 per cent (Lawn et al., 2005). Low birth weight – in turn associated with poor maternal health, inadequate antenatal care and more generally, poverty – also contributes, and it is a co-factor in 60 per cent to 80 per cent of neonatal deaths (UNICEF, 2008). Among other outcomes detrimental to health, poor public goods provision, leading to inadequate access to clean water and health care as well as lack of information on weaning and other good infant health practices, can exacerbate the direct causes of infant mortality.[3]

Some of these factors are exacerbated during crisis situations. Aggregate shocks – like those that precipitated the food, fuel and financial crisis that began to unfold globally in 2008 – can cause severe harm to children and other vulnerable groups, through at least two main channels.[4] First, they typically lead to dramatically lower household purchasing power, as a result of job losses, asset depletion and tighter credit conditions, which in turn lead to lower spending on and investment in the health and wellbeing of children and pregnant women. Even where public services are free, there are other costs to seeking health care which might become much more acute during severe economic stress. For example, the opportunity cost of time spent accessing these services could be very high as household incomes decline.

Second, these shocks could lead to more limited access to public services due to tighter government budgets, diminished social spending and inadequate public goods provision. Combined, these factors could contribute to lower birth weight, inadequate antenatal care, lower chances of skilled medical attendance and a poor hygienic environment during delivery. It follows that there is a risk of rising infant mortality.

Nevertheless, the empirical evidence on the countercyclicality of infant mortality is mixed (Ferreira and Schady, 2008). First, a recession could also create an income effect – lower household incomes – which is an inward shift in the entire demand curve, implying less schooling and less health-promoting behaviour and consumption (at any given child and adult wage). Formal credit and insurance markets are missing or imperfect in much of the developing world, thus preventing poor households from smoothing consumption through these shocks.[5]

Second, a recession could create a substitution effect by pushing households along the demand curve for human capital investments, implying more schooling and health-promoting behaviour as a result of falling child and adult wages. For example, mothers who previously worked but who are now unemployed may begin to engage more in time-intensive activities that promote health, such as travelling to health facilities to secure medicine and vaccines, receive antenatal medicines (for pregnant women) and get checkups for children; or collecting cleaner water, breastfeeding and cooking healthy meals. These effects seem to exist predominantly for middle- and upper-income countries. Essentially, the further away from subsistence, the more possible it is this will occur.

However, particularly if families are desperately poor, a recession could result in a negative income shock and a further increase in the time poverty of mothers and families. This would leave even less time to care for children, even if the substitution effect does prevail. Mothers (and other family members) often have to hold down more than one job, travel further to find work (which may be scarcer during crises) and undertake more household chores to save costs (such as switching from gas and oil to wood gathered from outside). Meanwhile, when public health and education services are cut or reduced, the burden often shifts onto households and communities, and the unpaid care burden of household members intensifies. Women usually bear the brunt of child care in the home (UNDESA, 2008).

Hence, the net impact will depend on which effect dominates – the income effect, which tends to reduce human capital investments, or the substitution effect, which tends to increase it. The final implication for schooling and health outcomes is therefore an empirical matter.[6]

Studies show that child education, health and wellbeing indicators could exhibit either countercyclical or procyclical patterns depending on the interplay between substitution and income effects on households' behaviour. Countercyclical patterns tend to show up in middle-income country settings where households may still have some space to adjust to income shocks. Adverse education and health outcomes tend to be more procyclical in poorer countries: aggregate shocks are followed by increases in infant mortality and declines in school enrolment and nutrition. In middle-income countries in Latin America, the results are more nuanced: health outcomes are generally procyclical and education outcomes countercyclical. This is unsurprising because in poorer countries governments tend to be more cash-strapped, and many more households live closer to subsistence and have less means to cope. Thus, in some of the poorest countries, any negative shock on income could translate more easily into lower social and household spending and investment, leading to worse child welfare outcomes.[7]

The large range of estimated impacts of crises (and income shocks) on infant mortality signals that there is still scope to sharpen estimates in this area. For instance, Cutler et al. (2002) used mortality data and population estimates derived from national statistics to examine trends in mortality at the national level for 1980–96 and at the state level for 1982–96. Their analysis thus covered major economic crises in 1982–8, 1986–7 and 1994–5. They found that child and elderly mortality rates in Mexico increased substantially after 1994 compared with the years prior to the crisis. Using a difference-in-differences methodology, they found evidence that children ages 0–4 were especially vulnerable during crises: the increase in their mortality rate during crises was between 6.9 per cent and 10.3 per cent, which was the highest among potentially affected groups. Further, these estimates translated to about 7,000 additional deaths among children age 0–4 in 1990 alone.[8] They also found evidence that a reduction in income and an increase in the burden on the medical sector could play a very important role in determining the level of child mortality. Out-of-pocket health expenditures declined from 3.9 per cent to 3.1 per cent of GDP between 1994 and 1995. Using regressions to examine the factors behind age-specific mortality rates, the authors also found that the inverse association between the number of public sector physicians and mortality rates among children and childbearing women was statistically significant: a reduction of 1 per cent in public sector physicians led to a 0.4 per cent increase in mortality rates for childbearing women and a 0.25 per cent increase in mortality rates for children age 0–4.

Similarly, using demographic and health surveys (DHS) conducted in Peru, Paxson and Schady (2005) constructed a time series on the IMR before, during and after the late 1980s economic crisis, in order to examine impacts on its evolution. This particular crisis was characterised by a sharp economic contraction (a 30 per cent decline in GDP) and a precipitous fall in real wages (by more than 80 per cent in Lima). Public sector spending on health fell by 58 per cent between 1985 and 1990, and from 4.3 per cent to 3.0 per cent of the government budget during that period. The authors estimated linear regressions of infant mortality expressed as a function of maternal characteristics and other controls for each year of birth for 1978–99. To explore possible selection issues (that is, more at-risk women giving birth), they used the parameter estimates to decompose changes in the mortality rate between years, enabling them to analyse changes in the characteristics of mothers giving birth. They found that the IMR increased by 2.5 percentage points during the crisis period – translating into roughly 17,000 more infant deaths. Further examining how different subgroups of women fared, they found that infant mortality was highest among uneducated, younger (and older) and poorer rural women. It also increased across all groups of mothers, suggesting that selection alone was not behind the increase.

Bhalotra (2010) investigated the impact of macroeconomic shocks on infant mortality in India by constructing a rich dataset on infant mortality and other indicators for about 150,000 children born between 1970 and 1997, drawing on India's National Family Health Survey. She attempted to address a number of weaknesses of past studies by including state-specific trends (minimising problems of omitting trends that vary by state) and examining possible forms of heterogeneity in the income effect, such as those linked to rural–urban differences, as well as differing age and education, among other characteristics, of mothers. She also developed a novel identification strategy by examining linked siblings, that is, children born to the same mother but under different economic conditions, allowing her to address selection issues among mothers giving birth. She found that a recession involving a one standard deviation change in the log of income raised infant mortality risk by 1.2 percentage points. Based on this estimate, and using the UN estimate of 26.3 million live births in India in 1990, she estimated that an additional 320,000 infant deaths occurred as a result of macroeconomic shocks. The results also suggested that most of these deaths were of children of mothers in rural areas who tend to be younger and less educated, further confirming the results of earlier studies in other crisis contexts (for example Paxson and Schady, 2005).

On the other hand, studies examining micro-level data in other countries have found very little evidence or mixed results that crises are associated with worsening child health indicators and higher infant mortality.[9] Some even find a positive and procyclical relationship. Miller and Urdinola (2007), for example, use the 1993 Colombian population census and a special household survey to evaluate the Familias en Acción conditional cash transfer (CCT) programme, in order to examine how coffee price shocks affect child mortality. To improve on the identification strategy of past studies, they constructed a novel measure of coffee shocks in Colombia during the period 1970–2000 by reflecting both internal coffee price changes and the economic importance of coffee in the child's county of birth. In a first step, they empirically examined how birth cohort size (in each county in the country) was affected by the coffee shock measure.[10] They then examined how various labour market outcome indicators (for example work the week prior to the survey, hours of work in the past month, log of wages) were associated with the shock. Their empirical findings suggested time was more important than current income in child health production in Colombia during the period examined: child mortality increased as coffee prices rose and decreased as they fell. The largest price increases during the period 1970–2000 (that is, approximately 40 per cent of the long-run mean) were accompanied by a 15 per cent decrease in child survival to age 5.[11]

More recently, a study by Schady and Smitz (2010) found that infant mortality tends to increase only when economic shocks are very deep. Using DHS and focusing on a set of 17 middle-income countries, the authors found that infant mortality tends to be procyclical or acyclical. Only three countries out of the sample had experienced countercyclical trends between GDP and infant mortality. Those three countries, however, were among the top four with the largest year-on-year contractions in GDP. The authors concluded that, in middle-income countries, only when shocks to GDP are 15 per cent or larger are they regularly associated with higher mortality.

While the above literature helps to illustrate the impact of economic and income shocks on infant mortality in specific countries, it does not allow for generalisable inferences across countries: cross-country empirical analyses are required for this. A number of multi-country studies also provide evidence that poorer economic performance is typically associated with higher infant mortality. For instance, Pritchett and Summers (1996) examined bi-decennial child mortality statistics for 58 developing countries during the period 1960–85. They examined the log of infant mortality as a function of the log of GDP per capita (variable of interest), other conditioning variables (for example schooling) and country- and time-specific effects (for example time-specific intercept allows overall mortality to change due to diffusion of or improvements in health technology). Instrumental variables were used to address potential reverse causality issues. Drawing insights from the growth literature, the authors used instruments that could help explain growth but they would not necessarily be linked to health outcomes, that is, the terms of trade shock, investment to GDP ratio, black market premium and deviation of official exchange rate from purchasing power parity level.[12] Their findings suggested that the long-run income elasticity of infant and child mortality in developing countries lies between –0.2 and –0.4.[13] Using these estimates, the authors calculated that about 450,000 infant deaths and over a million child deaths in the developing world in 1990 alone could have been averted had developing countries been able to maintain the same rate of growth in the 1980s as in the period 1960–80.

More recently, and using a dataset covering 136 countries across 10 quinquennia (1960–2005), Cornia et al. (2008) turned to a panel fixed effects model to examine possible factors behind life expectancy at birth, IMR and U5MR. The explanatory variables they used included dummies for each regional grouping (that is, helps account for region-specific effects); female literacy (that is, expected to have positive effects on child health); inequality (that is, signals skewed access to resources for investing in health); immunisation (that is, a measure of health care access); output volatility (that is, reflecting economic and income instability) and log of GDP per capita, the main variable of interest. They found evidence that a 1 per cent increase in GDP per capita is associated with a decline in IMR and U5MR, respectively, by about 14 points and 22 points. Their empirical analysis also suggests that a reduction in average female illiteracy by 10 percentage points is linked to a reduction in IMR and U5MR, respectively, by about 5 and 8 points.[14]

To try to confirm the sensitivity of these, Doytch et al. (2010) built on this dataset to analyse the impact of public spending, indicators of governance and GDP per capita on infant mortality. Their initial results differ slightly but they are broadly consistent with a wider review of estimates of the income elasticity of infant mortality. A similar study of U5MR by Rajkumar and Swaroop (2008) arrives at similar results, using annual data (1990, 1997 and 2003) for 91 countries to study the role of public spending, governance and income per capita in determining health outcomes. The authors found that a 1 percentage point increase in per capita GDP at the margin was associated with a 0.42 per cent reduction in child mortality.

Nevertheless, cross-country studies generally face a number of limitations, including constraints inherent to the data on infant mortality and other child wellbeing indicators. The IMR is typically reported in a bi-decennial manner, with missing information filled in using extrapolation or intrapolation methods. The impact of shocks is also likely to be smoothed out when examining data sets of this nature, precisely because of the methods of collecting and reporting (usually averaged) figures. This makes a study using these figures less informative for examining crisis impact, and perhaps more useful for analysing long-term structural relationships between income and child health outcomes.

Baird et al. (2007) found a way around this by setting up a cross-country empirical analysis at the same time as using data on the IMR with higher (at least annual) frequency. The authors used data from 123 DHS conducted over the period 1986–2004 covering 59 developing countries[15] and 1.7 million births to examine the effects of aggregate income shocks on infant mortality in the developing world. Based on the results from various model specifications, they concluded that a 1 per cent increase in per capita GDP was associated with a decrease in infant mortality within the range of approximately 0.18 to 0.44 deaths per 1,000 children born. Revisiting the issue, Baird et al. (2009) found similar results – a 1 per cent increase in per capita GDP is associated with a decrease in infant mortality by between 0.24 and 0.40 deaths per 1,000 children born.

To complement these main results, the authors also empirically examined unit data in order to control for mother- or child- specific covariates, as well as country-specific deterministic trends, and to inspect possible heterogeneity in the relationship between GDP and infant survival. They found that changes in the composition of mothers giving birth did not change the results. As part of a battery of checks, the authors also examined possible omitted variables bias, such as those resulting from conflict (including civil war) and weather shocks (for example droughts and floods). The specification checks suggested these also had little effect on their results. Nevertheless, given the wide array of factors that could influence infant mortality, it is unlikely that this problem is really eliminated, which is well recognised in the literature.[16] Finally, the authors also explored possible heterogeneity in the relationship between crises and infant mortality, focusing on differences by gender of the child, education and age of the mother, place of residence and birth parity. They found that a one log-unit change in per capita GDP changed the mortality of boys by approximately 28 per cent and that of girls by approximately 77 per cent, suggesting girls are more adversely affected by crises.

In a related paper, Friedman and Schady (2009) restricted the data set in Baird et al. (2007) to cover only the Sub-Saharan African (SSA) countries and found further evidence of adverse effects of aggregate shocks on girls. Using a variety of specifications, a 1 per cent negative deviation in per capita GDP is associated with an increase in infant mortality of 0.34 and 0.62 per 1,000 children born. With an infant mortality rate of 106.7 across the sample of countries, the elasticity of mortality with respect to GDP would be between –0.32 and –0.58. The results are significantly more sensitive for girls than for boys – one set of estimates suggests a 1 per cent negative deviation in GDP is associated with an increase in infant mortality of 0.25 per 1,000 boy births and 0.90 per

1,000 girl births. For very large negative deviations in GDP (1.5 standard deviations), every percentage point decrease in GDP is associated with an increase in 0.046 deaths per 1,000 boy births and 2.14 deaths per 1,000 girl births. Put differently, a negative shock lowering GDP per capita by 10 percentage points is associated with 22 more deaths per 1,000 girls born but has almost no impact on boy mortality. Drawing on this, Friedman and Schady (2009) estimated 30,000–50,000 excess deaths in Africa in 2009, with girls accounting for most of them.

Empirical evidence on the disproportionately larger adverse impact of household income shocks on the health of girls can be found in some parts of the developing world. Bengtsson (2010) used Tanzanian rural household data to examine the response of children's body weight to transitory changes in household income, using weather variation (rainfall) as an instrument for income. He found that female children experienced a 0.4 kg decline in bodyweight for every 10 per cent decrease in household income. A similar income shock results in only a 0.2 kg decline for boys. In rural India, there is empirical evidence that favourable rainfall patterns increase the likelihood of girls' survival more than boys' (Rose, 1999). Bairagi (1986) found evidence of sex-based distribution of food during droughts and crises in northern Somalia and rural Bangladesh, and that food crises in rural Bangladesh resulted in disproportionately worse health outcomes for female children belonging to poorer families.

Figure 3.1 presents the main range of estimates for the income elasticity of infant mortality. The estimates are sensitive to the underlying data used as well as the model specifications. In addition, most studies do not cover much of the developing world, due to a lack of data. Nevertheless, the available studies provide an overall snapshot of the current state of empirical evidence on this topic, and the evidence suggests that, within a certain (negative) range, there is some convergence in the estimated elasticity.

Policy responses to mitigate the risk of infant mortality

An important challenge for national authorities and the international community lies in breaking from past, largely inadequate policy responses by prioritising policy interventions designed specifically to help vulnerable families. Four main sets of responses are summarised briefly here: (1) health and nutrition interventions, including humanitarian relief, for the hardest-hit and most vulnerable; (2) expanding and enhancing social protection systems; (3) ensuring pro-poor growth,

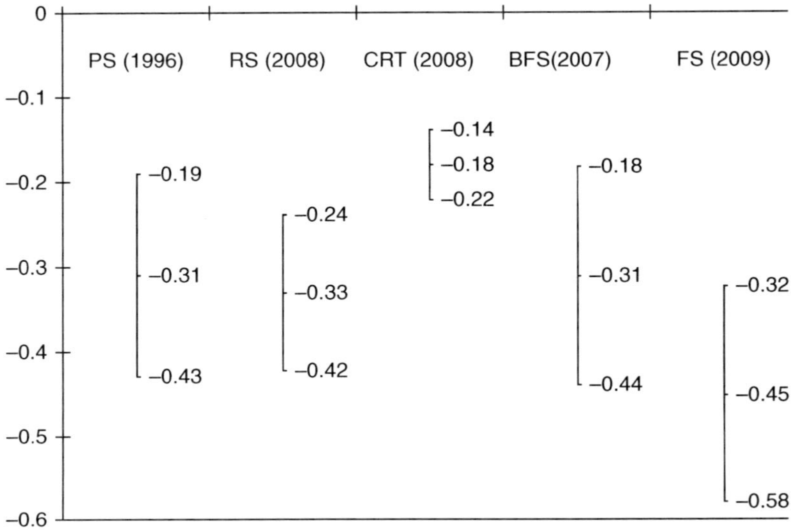

Figure 3.1 Estimates of the income elasticity of infant mortality from selected studies

Notes: All refer to income elasticity of infant mortality except for Rajkumar and Swaroop (2008), who use the U5MR. We note here that the U5MR is correlated with the IMR. In addition, we assume the average IMR is 100 in order to arrive at the estimated elasticities for Cornia et al. (2008).

Sources: Baird et al. (2007); Cornia et al. (2008); Friedman and Schady (2009); Pritchett and Summers (1996) and Rajkumar and Swaroop (2008).

employment and recovery; and (4) rapid real-time monitoring systems that collect accurate information on the most vulnerable in a timely manner and help inform other crisis response strategies.

Health and nutrition interventions

Health and nutrition security is crucial among desperately poor families in any crisis, especially as they face the compounding effects of lower employment and decreased government spending. Interventions are particularly essential for younger children, given that the most nutritionally vulnerable period of a child's life is the first 18 months (Shrimpton et al., 2001). Lack of nutritional investments in children (and also in antenatal care and nutrition for mothers) could have dramatic adverse consequences, not just on the child's health status but also on her/his cognitive and broader capabilities later on in life.

In many cases, health and nutrition interventions provided to a large part of the population can have the greatest effect on mitigating the negative effects of crises, particularly in countries where capacity to implement social protection programmes is very low. Other health-related interventions focusing on the prevention, treatment and control of major causes of infant mortality (including pneumonia, diarrhoea, malaria and deaths during the neonatal period) should also be emphasised to prevent increases in infant and child mortality.

Social protection

One set of policy interventions for which strong empirical evidence of success is available has to do with expanding social protection to poor and vulnerable families, with a focus on investments in the health, education and wellbeing of children. A growing number of countries have incorporated resource transfers specifically targeted at women that are conditional on their children's school enrolment and their participation in health care monitoring and food supplementation programmes. Expanding and strengthening social protection systems could help lower the risk that the global slowdown will harm children and women.

In terms of infant mortality, an empirical study of Mexico's *Progresa/Oportunidades* programme provides empirical evidence that this has helped decrease infant mortality (Barham, 2006). This used a non-experimental method and exploited the phase-in of the programme, which was first introduced in 2,578 localities in 7 of 32 Mexican states in 1997. Using 1991–2001 vital statistics data, including data on mortality and on live births (excluding the state of Oaxaca in 2000), the author used the percentage of rural households in a municipality receiving *Progresa* benefits as a measure of the intensity of programme treatment. The model specification included the IMR in each municipality for each year as the dependent variable, and the *Progresa* intensity measure, year and municipality fixed effects and time-varying municipality characteristics as independent variables. The study found that the average treatment effect obtained from the programme was a 5 per cent reduction in the rural IMR. (At the municipal level, programme coverage reached about half of rural households.) This impact could reach over 10 per cent if the programme were better targeted at poor households.[17] Clearly, impacts of such programmes will depend on a variety of factors, including the country and time context and the exact features of the programme itself.

Cash transfer programmes are not the only form of social protection intervention that could be appropriate across different country contexts. For instance, community-based primary care programmes such as Brazil's Family Health Programme (PSF) – could also help mitigate infant mortality. A decentralised approach to providing core primary care, PSF involves, among other features, first-contact access for new health needs, health care over the life course, coordination of care between different providers and types of health services and family- and community-oriented health promotion initiatives. The programme's roots trace back to the community health agents' programme initiated in Ceara state in the early 1990s. By 2007, it had grown considerably, with 26,730 community-based teams providing primary care to over 85 million people, making it one of the largest community-based primary care systems in the world.

As for evidence on the impact of PSF on infant mortality, a recent study by Macinko and others (2007) used panel data covering all 557 Brazilian micro regions over a six-year period (1999–2004) to examine the impact of PSF coverage on infant mortality, neonatal mortality and post-neonatal mortality. The study also controlled for other factors that could affect infant and child health, for example measures of physicians and hospital beds, Hepatitis vaccine coverage, share of women without antenatal care and with no formal education, low birth weights, population size and poverty rates. It found evidence that a 10 per cent increase in PSF coverage was associated with a 0.45 per cent decrease in the IMR, a 0.6 per cent decline in post-neonatal mortality and a 1 per cent decline in diarrhoea-related mortality.

Clearly, social protection programmes differ in their design as well as their context, which shows there is no single best approach.[18] *Progresa/Oportunidades* costs about 0.4 per cent of Mexico's GDP and covers about 5 million households, or about 23 per cent of the total population (Grosh et al., 2008). Programme coverage in other countries could be much lower than this. For example, Peru's *Juntos* programme, which costs about 0.1 per cent of GDP, covers slightly over 330,000 households, representing 5.3 per cent of the population (ibid.) (Note that over 50 per cent of Peru's population falls under the national poverty line [UNDP, 2007].) Similarly, Jamaica's Programme of Advancement through Health and Education costs about 0.16 per cent of GDP and covers about 8 per cent of the population (Grosh et al., 2008) (about 19 per cent of Jamaicans fall under the national poverty line (UNDP, 2007). Both programme coverage and benefits are among the areas in which social protection could be further enhanced (Lustig, 2000; Mendoza, 2009a).

Implementing some elements of social protection programmes – notably cash transfers – may be difficult to do quickly during an economic downturn or a crisis situation. This is particularly the case in LDCs. The poorest families may be unable to meet the conditionality required for participation in the programme, so it will be necessary to ensure that they are not excluded. These types of programmes require planning and time in order to establish targeting and monitoring mechanisms (Soares, 2009). This underscores the need to build robust social protection systems in anticipation of future crises and as part of inclusive growth and poverty reduction strategies more broadly.

Pro-poor countercyclical policy

Clearly, mitigating the downturn itself and ensuring economic recovery is pro-poor, are critical components of the overall policy response. Empirical evidence reviewed earlier suggests that boosting households' purchasing power and income-earning capacity could be key factors to preventing harmful coping strategies as well as stimulating health-promoting behaviour and consumption that could improve child and maternal health. Thus, stimulus packages designed to hasten economic recovery could also help alleviate the situation for poor and low-income families. However, the nature of this recovery – whether it is pro-poor and benefits low-income and poor families harmed by the slowdown – will be critical. Just as crises tend to have distributional consequences, possibly creating most harm to those least equipped to cope, so too will economic recovery, tending to benefit those with stronger capacity and means to take advantage of economic opportunities. Both ways, poor and low-income people may be at a relative disadvantage, facing great harm during the downturn and benefiting very little during the upturn.

The impact of economic growth on poverty alleviation and human development depends not just on the size and persistence of economic growth episodes, but also on their nature and notably their composition, that is, which sectors benefit most. Empirical evidence suggests that poverty reduction is most successful when the unskilled and labour-intensive sectors (agriculture, construction and manufacturing) are driving growth (Loayza and Raddatz, forthcoming). Studies also show that economic growth is slow to bring about improvements in child wellbeing such as reductions in child malnutrition. For example, one recent study of over 160 spells of change in chronic malnutrition found that an average country with 30 per cent children stunting prevalence and income growth per capita of 10 per cent faced a very marginal reduction in stunting prevalence: from 30 to 29.4 per cent (Heltberg, 2009).[19] Past empirical studies confirm that the elasticity of economic growth and child indicators like malnutrition is small – and typically much smaller than that of growth and poverty reduction (ibid.; Haddad et al., 2003). Some have used this evidence to help justify a more targeted approach to alleviating child malnutrition, among other deprivations, given that growth alone is unlikely to deliver rapid and sustained gains.

Similarly, benefits from an economic recovery process are not necessarily going to trickle down automatically to the poor (Mendoza, 2009b; Ravallion, 2008). A variety of measures exist to help ensure they do, however, and all are germane to the design of the government's policy intervention – notably the countercyclical responses (or lack thereof). Meanwhile, the social and economic impacts of stabilisation programmes themselves are chequered.[20] In past crises, the social sectors were typically among those that remained stagnant or that were retrenched at precisely the time more people were falling into poverty and already existing poor were falling deeper into destitution. A strong case could be made for breaking from these past policies, and instead trying to emphasise pro-poor stabilisation policies or, put differently, 'countercyclical safety nets' (Alderman and Haque, 2006).

The pro-poor countercyclical response could take the form of a surge in social sector spending at precisely the time of the slowdown, when the sector's needs are most acute. China's recent decision to expand its spending in education and health is an important step in this direction. Another example is Brazil's recent decision to expand its *Bolsa Família* social protection programme to an additional 1.3 million poor families in response to global slowdown. Indeed, the government identified this as a key aspect in its policy response, noting how cash transfer programmes not only rescue millions of people from extreme poverty but also turn them into consumers, helping to stimulate local and regional economies (ILO, 2009). Some – though not all – countries have taken decisive steps to try and boost social sectors and bolster social protection, reflecting efforts to scale up existing systems or undertake more ambitious reforms.

Finally, stimulus programmes could also be designed in ways that have broader and more immediate benefits in terms of reaching the poor and low-income people. Investments in infrastructure, for example, could prioritise rural areas and form part of the country's overall strategy to boost productivity in agriculture and improve the country's resilience to climate and other types of shocks. The quality of the recovery, the preservation and strengthening of the country's human capital (and thus the minimisation of social and economic costs) and the resulting resilience (or continued vulnerability) of the country to future shocks will hinge on these investment strategies.

Rapid real-time monitoring

This chapter has illustrated that there is a wide range of estimates of the impact of economic crises on infant mortality, and so the exact impact of the current crisis on children is unlikely to be known fully until after the crisis has come and gone. The importance of real-time monitoring cannot be understated during crises – natural or manmade. Policy responses to protect children during crises will require accurate information that is provided on a timely basis in order to ensure that they are appropriate and address the needs of children.

Conclusion

This chapter has reviewed the empirical literature on the impact of crises on infant mortality, in order to shed light on the risks facing infants, mothers and young children during crises. As evidenced by past economic crises, the downturn may be very 'inclusive' (that is, poor and low-income people will be affected, often disproportionately more than richer people), whereas the recovery is not necessarily so. Policy responses to expand social protection and resuscitate pro-poor growth can mitigate most if not all of the increase in infant mortality. This chapter emphasises four key areas for policymakers to consider:

(i) Providing health and nutrition interventions, including humanitarian relief, to the most severely affected countries and population groups;
(ii) Expanding social protection to the poorest and most vulnerable to mitigate the worst implications of the global slowdown on children and women, blunting their protracted ill-effects;
(iii) Resuscitating growth in a way that is pro-poor and ensuring that the recovery of household incomes – notably among poor and low-income households – is robust and sustained;
(iv) Monitoring impacts in real-time to gain an accurate and rapid understanding of the situation of children.

In addition to these options, policymakers should not lose sight of policies and social sector investments that address the broader challenges of poverty reduction and human development and help lower many of the pre-existing vulnerabilities of children and women. Policy responses in this area include promoting protective household practices for infants, young children and mothers, including care; breastfeeding; diarrhoea prevention; good weaning and complementary feeding practices and hand washing – all of which are not greatly economy-dependent.[21] Furthermore, a gendered perspective and support for mothers, particularly where they become increasingly time-poor as a result of crisis and need to undertake a variety of tasks to keep the family alive, are also a crucial part of policy responses. Escaping poverty and many of the deprivations that characterise this condition often means being much more resilient to crises and income shocks. Thus, the main message of this chapter is that, based on empirical evidence from past crises, the possible impact of crises on infant mortality is nothing that cannot be mitigated by policies that protect children and women and ensure sufficient social sector investments in the first place.

Notes

1. www.childinfo.org.
2. Infant mortality is typically reported in the form of the infant mortality rate (IMR), that is, the number of children who die before the age of 1 per 1,000 births. IMR is highly correlated with the under-five mortality rate (U5MR). In practice, data on U5MR are often used to estimate the IMR when national data sources are not available. For further information on methodologies for compiling IMR and U5MR, see Hill and Amouzou (2006).
3. See Alderman and Behrman (2004); Bhutta et al. (2008); Chopra et al. (2009); Lawn et al. (2005); UNICEF (2008).
4. Aggregate shocks include those that affect: (1) aggregate or macroeconomic variables (for example gross domestic product [GDP], current account, exchange rate); and (2) a large group of people within a country. In most cases, the two parts of this definition overlap, but it is framed in this way to cover aggregate shocks more broadly understood. These shocks vary in their nature, severity, distributional impact, length and other aspects. Clearly, the channels through which these shocks will affect countries and, within them, poor households will vary. No claim is made here that these are the only ones worth considering. For further elaboration, see Mendoza (2009b), for example.
5. Formal credit and insurance markets also typically do not produce financial services that cater to the poor's needs. While the poor may turn to informal credit markets and other risk management methods, these are likely to face their natural limits in the presence of an aggregate shock which affects the entire risk pool. The interested reader may wish to turn to Armendariz de Aghion and Morduch (2005) and Mendoza (forthcoming).
6. Other factors also come into play, including fertility decisions, as discussed later.
7. For a broader review of the literature, see Ferreira and Schady (2008) and Mendoza (2009b).

8. A potential caveat in this study is that it used infants and the elderly as the potentially affected groups and males age 30–44 as the potentially unaffected group. It is not clear to what extent such an approach provides an appropriate control, considering that crises could also affect males directly through job losses and coping through other behavioural changes. (For example, less income and food in the households could spur adult males to eat less or work more, with some possible impact on their health status.)
9. For example, on Indonesia, see Block et al. (2004); Frankenberg et al. (1999); and Rukumnuaykit (2003).
10. Their birth cohort size approach is useful to the extent that it avoids problems of underreporting and other data quality issues in Colombia's household data, it captures foetal deaths, it is complete and it captures the entire population and cumulative mortality.
11. Studies examining infant mortality in the US find a similar procyclical effect. Infant mortality declines during recessions, due to factors such as changes in fertility decisions, maternal behaviour changes (possibly including more child health-promoting behaviour) and reductions in pollution (see, for example, Dehejia and Lleras-Muney, 2004).
12. Robustness tests revealed that all but the black market premium indicator were acceptable instrumental variables.
13. These estimates are very similar to those of Rajkumar and Swaroop (2008), who used annual data (1990, 1997 and 2003) for 91 countries in order to study the role of public spending, governance and income per capita in determining health outcomes. They found that a one percentage point increase in per capita GDP at the margin is associated with a 0.42 per cent reduction in child mortality.
14. A recent UN (2008) study of 30 countries in Asia tracking their progress towards the Millennium Development Goals (MDGs) also found evidence that appears consistent with the abovementioned studies. This study calculated the 'MDG elasticity', or the percentage change on different MDG indicators, for each 1 per cent increase in growth. It found that an increase of 1 per cent of GDP is associated with: (1) a 0.3 per cent fall in maternal mortality; (2) a 0.43 per cent fall in under-five mortality; and (3) a 0.46 per cent fall in infant mortality.
15. The data set is drawn from countries in Africa (33 countries, 68 surveys), Latin America (12 countries, 31 surveys) and Asia (14 countries, 27 surveys).
16. Public health expenditures and foreign aid are among other factors that may also figure into health outcomes during a crisis period. It is possible these will be highly correlated with the crisis event itself, however.
17. Two caveats in Barham (2006) are the non-measurement of possible spill-over effects from programme treatment (that is, programme impact could be overestimated due to inability to exclude non-eligibles from benefiting from the improved health service supply or other programme spill-over effects) and possible underreporting of births and deaths (that is, programme impact could be overestimated if reporting of births is affected by the availability of the programme).
18. As noted earlier, infant mortality itself is owed to a number of factors, each linked to different stages of vulnerability within the first year of an infant's

life. Programme components that include antenatal care and adequate nutrition are crucial even before birth. On the other hand, health worker attendance and hospital care if needed could be critical at the time of birth. Furthermore, adequate postnatal care, good hygiene and sanitation and education on good infant care practices are likely to be important from the time of birth onwards.

19. A spell is the change between any two years for which a given country has observations on both malnutrition and income per capita, drawing on the World Bank's World Development Indicators database. Of this total, Heltberg (2009) covers 45 positive (meaning increasing malnutrition), 118 negative and three zero spells.
20. For a detailed discussion, see, for example, Vreeland (2006) and evaluations produced by the Independent Evaluation Office (IEO) of the International Monetary Fund (IMF) (www.ieo-imf.org/).
21. Empirical studies that suggest the importance of these and other factors in reducing infant mortality include Agha (2000); Aguilera and Marrufo (2007); Chopra et al. (2009); Jalan and Ravallion (2003) and WHO (2000).

References

Agha, S. (2000) 'The Determinants of Infant Mortality in Pakistan.' *Social Science and Medicine* 51: 199–208.

Aguilera, N. and Marrufo, G. (2007) 'Can Better Infrastructure and Quality Reduce Hospital Infant Mortality Rates in Mexico?' *Health Policy* 80(2): 239–52.

Alderman, H. and Behrman, J. (2004) 'Estimated Economic Benefits of Reducing Low Birth Weight in Low Income Countries.' Health Nutrition and Population Working Paper. Washington, DC: World Bank.

Alderman, H. and Haque, T. (2006) 'Countercyclical Safety Nets for the Poor and Vulnerable.' *Food Policy* 31(4): 372–83.

Armendariz de Aghion, B. and Morduch, J. (2005) *The Economics of Microfinance.* Cambridge, MA: MIT Press.

Bairagi, R. (1986) 'Food Crisis, Nutrition, and Female Children in Rural Bangladesh.' *Population and Development Review* 12(2): 307–15.

Baird, S., Friedman, J. and Schady, N. (2007) 'Aggregate Income Shocks and Infant Mortality in the Developing World.' Policy Research Working Paper 4346. Washington, DC: World Bank.

Baird, S., Friedman, J. and Schady, N. (2009) 'Aggregate Income Shocks and Infant Mortality in the Developing World.' Mimeo.

Barham, T. (2006) 'Providing a Healthier Start to Life: The Impact of Conditional Cash Transfers on Neo-natal and Infant Mortality.' Boulder, CO: Department of Economics and Institute of Behavioral Science, University of Colorado.

Bengtsson, N. (2010) 'How Responsive is Body Weight to Transitory Income Changes? Evidence from Rural Tanzania.' *Journal of Development Economics* 92(1): 53–61.

Bhalotra, S. (2010) 'Fatal Fluctuations: Cyclicality in Infant Mortality in India.' *Journal of Development Economics* 93(1): 7–19.

Bhutta, Z. et al. (2008) 'What Works: Interventions for Maternal and Child Undernutrition and Survival.' *The Lancet* 371(9610): 417–40.

Block, S.A., Keiss, L., Keller, H., Kosen, S., Moench-Pfanner, R., Bloem, M. and Timmer, C.P. (2004) 'Macro Shocks and Micro (Scopic) Outcomes: Child Nutrition during Indonesia's Crisis.' *Economics and Human Biology* 2(1): 21–44.

Chopra, M., Daviaud, E., Pattison, R., Fonn, S. and Lawn, J. (2009) 'Saving the Lives of South Africa's Mothers, Babies, and Children: Can the Health System Deliver?' *The Lancet* 374(9692): 835–46.

Cornia, G.A., Rosignoli, S. and Tiberti, L. (2008) 'Globalization and Health.' Research Paper 2008-74. Helsinki: UNU-WIDER.

Cutler, D., Knaul, F., Lozano, F., Méndez, O. and Zurita, B. (2002) 'Financial Crisis, Health Outcomes and Ageing: Mexico in the 1980s and 1990s.' *Journal of Public Economics* 84(2): 279–303.

Dehejia, R. and Lleras-Muney, A. (2004) 'Booms, Busts and Babies' Health.' *Quarterly Journal of Economics* 119(3): 1091–130.

Doytch, N., Hu, B. and Mendoza, R.U. (2010) 'Public Spending, Governance and Human Development Outcomes Revisited.' New York: UNICEF.

Ferreira, F. and Schady, N. (2008) 'Aggregate Economic Shocks, Child Schooling and Child Health.' Policy Research Working Paper 4701. Washington, DC: World Bank.

Frankenberg, E., Thomas, D. and Beegle, K. (1999) 'The Real Costs of Indonesia's Economic Crisis: Preliminary Findings from the Indonesia Family Life Surveys.' Labor and Population Working Paper Series 99-04. Santa Monica, CA: RAND.

Friedman, J. and Schady, N. (2009) 'How Many More Infants Are Likely to Die in Africa as a Result of the Global Financial Crisis?' Policy Research Working Paper 5023. Washington, DC: World Bank.

Grosh, M., del Ninno, C., Tesliuc, E. and Ouerghi, A. with Milazzo, A. and Weigand, C. (2008) *For Protection and Promotion: The Design and Implementation of Effective Safety Nets*. Washington, DC: World Bank.

Haddad, L., Alderman, H., Appleton, S., Song, L. and Yohannes, Y. (2003) 'Reducing Child Malnutrition: How Far Does Income Growth Take Us?' *World Bank Economic Review* 17(1): 107–31.

Heltberg, R. (2009) 'Malnutrition, Poverty and Economic Growth.' *Health Economics* 18(1): S77–88.

Hill, K. and Amouzou, A. (2006) 'Trends in Child Mortality, 1960–2000.' In Jamison, D. et al. (eds) *Disease and Mortality in Sub-Saharan Africa*. 2nd Edition. Washington, DC: World Bank.

ILO (2009) 'Brazil Extends Bolsa Família during the Economic Crisis.' Geneva: ILO.

Jalan, J. and Ravallion, M. (2003) 'Does Piped Water Reduce Diarrhea for Children in Rural India?' *Journal of Econometrics* 112(1): 153–73.

Lawn, J., Cousens, S. and Zupan, J. (2005) '4 Million Neonatal Deaths: When? Where? Why?' *The Lancet* 365(9462): 891–900.

Loayza, N. and Raddatz, C. (forthcoming) 'The Composition of Growth Matters for Poverty Reduction.' *Journal of Development Economics*.

Lustig, N. (2000) *Shielding the Poor: Social Protection in the Developing World*. Washington, DC: Brookings Institution Press.

Macinko, J., Marinho de Souza, M.F., Guanais, F.C. and da Silva Simoes, C.C. (2007) 'Going to Scale with Community-based Primary Care: An Analysis of the Family Health Program and Infant Mortality in Brazil, 1999-2004.' *Social Science and Medicine* 65(10): 2070–80.

Mendoza, R.U. (2009a) 'Responding to the Food, Fuel and Financial Crises of 2009: A Case for Pro-poor Stabilization Policy.' VoxEU.org Policy Portal.

Mendoza, R.U. (2009b) 'Aggregate Shocks, Poor Households and Children: Transmission Channels and Policy Responses.' *Global Social Policy* 9(1): 55–78.

Mendoza, R.U. (forthcoming) 'Why Do the Poor Pay More? Exploring the Poverty Penalty Concept.' *Journal of International Development.*

Miller, G. and Urdinola, P. (2007) 'Time versus Money in Child Health Production: The Case of Coffee Price Fluctuations and Child Health Survival in Colombia.' CID Working Paper. Cambridge, MA: Harvard University.

Paxson, C. and Schady, N. (2005) 'Child Health and Economic Crisis in Peru.' *World Bank Economic Review* 19(2): 203–23.

Pritchett, L. and Summers, L. (1996) 'Wealthier is Healthier.' *Journal of Human Resources* 31(4): 841–68.

Rajkumar, A.S. and Swaroop, V. (2008) 'Public Spending and Outcomes: Does Governance Matter?' *Journal of Development Economics* 86(1): 96–111.

Ravallion, M. (2008) 'Bailing out the World's Poorest.' Policy Research Working Paper 4763. Washington, DC: World Bank.

Rose, E. (1999) 'Consumption Smoothing and Excess Female Mortality in Rural India.' *The Review of Economics and Statistics* 81(1): 41–9.

Rukumnuaykit, P. (2003) 'Crises and Child Health Outcomes: The Impact of Economic and Drought/Smoke Crises on Infant Mortality and Birthweight in Indonesia.' East Lansing, MI: Michigan State University.

Schady, N. and Smitz, M.F. (2010) 'Aggregate Economic Shocks and Infant Mortality: New Evidence for Middle-income Countries.' *Economics Letters* 108(2): 145–8

Shrimpton, R.C., Victora, C., de Onis, M., Costa Lima, R., Blössner, M. and Clugston, G. (2001) 'Worldwide Timing of Growth Faltering: Implications for Nutritional Interventions.' *Pediatrics* 107: 75–81.

Soares, F.V. (2009) 'Do CCTs Lessen the Impact of the Current Economic Crisis? Yes, But...' One Pager 96. Brasilia: IPC-IG.

UNDESA (2008) *The Social and Political Economy of Care: Contesting Gender and Class Inequalities.* New York: UNDESA.

UNDP (2007) *Human Development Report 2007/2008, Fighting Climate Change: Human Solidarity in a Divided World.* New York: Palgrave MacMillan.

UNICEF (2008) *State of the World's Children 2009.* New York: UNICEF.

Vreeland, J. (2006) *The International Monetary Fund: Politics of Conditional Lending.* London and New York: Routledge.

WHO (2000) 'Effect of Breastfeeding on Infant and Child Mortality Due to Infectious Diseases in Less Developed Countries: A Pooled Analysis.' *The Lancet* 355(9202): 451–5.

4

Education and Health Spending Patterns through the Business Cycle: An Empirical Analysis

Nadia Doytch, Bingjie Hu and Ronald U. Mendoza

Introduction

Social policy as part of the countercyclical response to crises has become much more urgent in the context of the food price volatility and global economic slowdown that started in 2008. A growing number of development practitioners have argued that, without the appropriate pro-poor policies, economic recovery is not necessarily going to be inclusive, nor will its benefits trickle down automatically to the poor. Disruptions in critically important investments in human capital for the vast majority of the low-income population in many countries could also result in long-lived human and economic costs. If their most pernicious effects are unmitigated, not only could crises plunge individuals and families into poverty, but they could also cripple countries' long-run growth prospects.[1] One key question, then, relates to whether governments do in fact adjust their social spending to buffer the difficult adjustments implied by troughs in the business cycle.

The principal aim of this chapter is to examine the empirical link between indicators of the business cycle – that is, the output gap and economic growth – and social spending, with a main focus on subcomponents of the latter in education and health. These are possible barometers of the supply of public social services over the business cycle. The recent focus on boosting cash transfers during crises focuses mostly on the demand side (that is, boosting families' budgets), which is important, but it may suggest an imbalance if the supply side (that is, boosting social sector budgets) is not strengthened (Mendoza, 2010).

The chapter first reviews the literature in this area, and then it undertakes an empirical analysis of the pattern of public spending on education and health services for a sample of 51 industrial and developing countries. The focus is on historical data prior to the aggregate shocks that began in 2008, in an effort to try to draw lessons from longer historical patterns covering past business cycles. The approach of disaggregating social spending into its education and health spending components could also help in identifying potentially distinct patterns across different country income groups. The chapter concludes with main policy messages.

Review of the empirical literature

There is now a rich literature examining the cyclicality of public spending in both industrial and developing countries. Typical empirical studies here use annual aggregate data to examine the link between some measure of government spending (for example, the budget balance) and some measure of the business cycle (for example, the output gap). The crux of the evidence in this area suggests that fiscal policy is countercyclical in industrial countries, whereas in developing countries it is procyclical or acyclical. The two main theories are as follows:

(1) International credit markets are imperfect and they prevent countries from borrowing in bad times (in turn, leading to a lack of capacity to undertake countercyclical policy).
(2) Political economy issues amplify the tendency for fiscal profligacy and rent-seeking activities (for example, strong domestic interest groups push for higher spending in some sectors during boom times, and some have a weaker voice, notably the poor, so that, during periods of contraction, programmes benefiting them are vulnerable to cuts).[2]

Ilzetski and Vegh (2008) critique earlier approaches, outlining possible problems of reverse causality. That is, the expansionary effect of fiscal policy could be misidentified, leading to a spurious empirical finding. The authors address this issue through a battery of empirical tests and identification techniques, including instrumental variables,[3] generalised method of moments (GMM), simultaneous equations and time series methods (for example Granger causality and impulse response methods), using quarterly data for 49 (27 developing and 22 industrial) countries, going as far back as 1960 for some. Their general finding is that developing countries do indeed exhibit procyclical fiscal policies – that is, government spending is linked positively to an exogenous expansionary business cycle shock. However, for industrial countries, findings are mixed.

The focus of this chapter is on a more specific strand of the literature which examines social spending patterns as a potentially distinct element from the overall fiscal stance. In practice, overall public sector spending could be increasing even as social spending is decreasing, and social spending could be increasing, even as overall public sector spending is contracting (for example through a reprioritisation of social sector spending and investments).[4]

But why boost social spending during downturns? There are at least two possible rationales for maintaining a countercyclical social spending policy. One is rooted in social justice and/or human rights arguments to protect the most vulnerable (and often also the least culpable in the context of a financial or economic crisis); the other is based on a human development and growth rationale. Because crises could undermine human capital accumulation, it is possible to advance an argument that seeks to preserve if not boost investments in this area, on social and economic recovery grounds. Countercyclical policies targeting poor and low-income segments of the population could also make the quality of the recovery much more effective. These groups are more likely to spend rather than save additional resources, and also they are more likely to face the greatest immediate need to boost their consumption, suggesting that the stimulus effect may be much larger and much more effective if targeted at this group (Ravallion, 2008).

These arguments could underpin pro-poor stabilisation policies or, put differently, 'countercyclical safety nets'.[5] Have countries followed this strategy? What does the empirical evidence suggest? Unlike the abovementioned literature on fiscal policies, the literature examining the cyclicality of social spending more specifically is less extensive. Darby and Melitz (2008) are among the few to analyse formally the pattern of government spending over the business cycle. They examine both aggregated and disaggregated government social spending data for Organisation for Economic Co-operation and Development (OECD) countries and find that age- and health-related social expenditures react to the business cycle in a stabilising manner. Their empirical findings suggest an elasticity of total social spending to the output gap equal to 0.5, implying that social spending could act as part of the automatic stabiliser.

In addition, Furceri (2009) uses data on 23 industrialised countries from the period 1980–2003 in order to examine the extent to which social spending could help absorb shocks to GDP. Essentially, he estimates the percentage of shocks to GDP smoothed through different channels (for example international net transfers of income factors, consumption smoothing and government spending) and, more specifically, items of social spending. He finds evidence that social spending could be used to smooth anywhere from 12 per cent to 23 per cent of a shock to GDP. The stabilising effect of social spending is also larger in countries with more extensive social spending. Although the study does not examine this aspect, it is also possible that lower-income families are more likely to spend rather than save, facilitating a more robust stimulus effect.

The literature on crisis responses suggests that the social and economic impacts of stabilisation programmes themselves are chequered.[6] Anecdotal evidence from past crises suggests the social sectors have typically been among those remaining stagnant or being retrenched at precisely the time when more people have been falling into poverty and the already existing poor have been falling deeper into destitution. For instance, Cutler et al. (2002: 280) note a key policy paradox during Mexico's 'tequila crisis' in the mid-1990s: 'Countries experiencing economic crises have found that they reduce the ability to provide social services to the poor, just as the needs of the poor increase.' Per capita public health expenditures in Mexico fell by about 15 per cent during the period 1994–96.

Ravallion (2002) examines Argentina's budget trends in the 1980s and 1990s – periods of economic volatility – and finds evidence that non-social sector spending tended to be better protected than social spending against cuts during downturns. Spending on targeted social assistance and employment programmes was also much more vulnerable than more universal social services to aggregate spending cuts. Social spending in general, and that targeted at the poor in particular, typically have been cut during periods of fiscal austerity.

A political economy explanation would emphasise that programmes targeted at the poor are vulnerable to cuts because the poor are often those with the weakest political voice. The middle-income segment of society, which often shoulders the brunt of the tax burden, is relatively more influential in political discourse. The latter group would tend to support protecting programmes that benefit them more (or perhaps cutting taxes that fall more heavily on the middle class, in turn leaving fewer resources for social programmes). To shed light on whether government programmes targeted specifically at the poor are more vulnerable to cuts, Ravallion (2002) also examines the pattern of expansion and contraction in funding for Argentina's *Trabajar* programme, whose aim is to reduce poverty by providing relatively low-wage work on community projects in poor areas.[7] He finds evidence that the programme expanded into poor areas when the budget increased but retreated from poor areas when it was cut. Ravallion's analysis thus suggests a possible 'catch-22' in terms of better-targeted and explicitly pro-poor programmes: while they clearly offer stronger benefits for the poor, they are also much more vulnerable to the vicissitudes of political deliberations, notably during periods of contraction.

Governance issues are at the core of effective macroeconomic policies, and decision-making on and execution of the budget at various levels of government are no exceptions. Whether and to what extent governments manage fiscal space well and decide to deploy this space for investments in the social sectors are therefore among the key issues that need to be examined. The literature on the political economy of debt policy is illustrative in this regard. According to contributions to this strand of work, political uncertainty could be associated with higher levels of external debt (for example, governments will think simply of the immediate term), and corruption could lead to procyclicality in public spending and windfall revenues (for example, windfall revenues open the door for opportunities for more rent seeking).[8] For instance, Arezki and Bruckner (2010) examine the impact of commodity price shocks on external debt management in a sample of 93 countries spanning the period 1970–2007. They find evidence that positive commodity price shocks are associated with reduced external debt in democracies,[9] whereas in autocracies there is less evidence that windfalls are translated into lower external debt levels. This suggests that countries with weaker governance may tend to be in a perennial position of having relatively less capacity to undertake countercyclical and crisis-response policies.[10]

Empirical analysis

Methodology and data

In order to complement the still largely anecdotal evidence on this topic, we analyse empirically a dataset of education and health spending covering up to 51 industrial and developing countries. The final sample depends on the model specification and the scarcity of some data points. We turn to the following empirical model, which builds on earlier approaches in the literature:

$$s_{it}^{k} = \beta_0 + \beta_1 g_{i,t-1} + \beta_2 g_{i,t-1} q'^{j}_{it-1} + \beta_3 x_{it} + \beta_4 D^{t} + \mu_i + \varepsilon_{it}$$

$$\mu_i \sim i.i.d(0, \sigma_{\mu_i}),\ \varepsilon_{it} \sim \text{i.i.d.}(0, \sigma_\varepsilon), \text{ and } E[\mu_i \varepsilon_{it}] = 0$$

where s_{it} is public social expenditures and $g_{i,t-1}$ is the lagged output gap.[11] The term $g_{i,t-1}q'^{j}_{it-1}$ is a cross term of the lagged output gap (or the lagged real per capita GDP growth) $g_{i,t-1}$ and a quality of governance variable. The superscript k stands for a *social expenditure index* (k = public spending on education and health care), the superscript j stands for a quality of governance index (that is, control of corruption, government stability and bureaucracy quality) and the subscripts i and t describe the cross-sectional and time dimensions of the panel data, respectively. The row vector x_{it} consists of the most commonly used control variables in the literature, comprising a quality of governance variable, foreign aid expressed as a share of GDP, net transfers from abroad expressed as a share of GDP, foreign portfolio investment (an aggregate for equity and bond investment) expressed as a share of GDP and tax revenue expressed as a share of GDP. D^t is a row vector of 29-year dummy variables and μ_i is a country fixed-effect term. Thus, the main variables of interest included:

- **Indicators of the business cycle:** The output gap is the main indicator of interest, and it is defined as the difference between the trend GDP and actual GDP. We follow the convention in the literature for estimating trend GDP using the Hodrick-Prescott filter. The second indicator is economic growth. In the main analysis, we turn to the model specifications using lagged output gap (or lagged real GDP growth) in order to address potential endogeneity issues.[12]
- **Quality of governance:** Both stylised facts and empirical evidence (Gupta et al., 1999) suggest that quality of governance may affect the fiscal decision government makes. For example, in countries with weaker indicators of governance, public expenditure may be biased towards sectors that are more conducive to rent seeking or subject to more intense lobbying. The social sectors may tend to receive relatively less emphasis, particularly if poor and low-income people are unable to organise themselves to lobby more effectively for better quality and quantity of public services. Weak institutional capacity and corruption can also diminish the effectiveness of any given

amount of resources allocated to the social sector (Deles et al., 2009). Quality of governance is based on indicators in the Inter-country Risk Guide published by the Political Risk Group.[13]

- **Determinants related to fiscal space:** The approach controls for other economic factors that affect fiscal space or the scope and ability of governments to implement their fiscal policies. These factors include foreign aid as a share of GDP, portfolio investment in bonds and equity as a share of GDP, net foreign transfers from abroad as a share of GDP and tax revenue as a share of GDP. Among these control variables, foreign transfers may not only have an income effect on the fiscal capabilities of the recipient country, but they may also influence the prioritisation of public spending. For instance, Hagen and Hatlebakk (2002) find that the most generous bilateral donors have a significant impact on the budget shares of social sectors using targeted aid.

Apart from the above factors, it is likely that there are other economic or political determinants of fiscal choice, such as regime and political transitions. The fixed effects method is expected to account for these context-specific factors that vary across countries.

Empirical results

Tables 4.1 and 4.2 present the results for the fixed effects regressions, with public spending in education and in health, respectively, as the dependent variables. The regression results for the full set of variables suggest that the lag of the output gap is linked negatively to public spending in education and health (see first column in Tables 4.1 and 4.2). Nevertheless, a note of caution is appropriate, given that the significance of this coefficient is sensitive to the model specification.[14] The interaction term between the lag of the output gap and the lag of the corruption control variable is positive and significant in both cases, even as the significance of this coefficient appears sensitive to the model specification and the addition of other control variables for fiscal space. There is only weak evidence that better-governed countries tend to follow more countercyclical spending in education and health.

The empirical results for low-income countries (second column in Tables 4.1 and 4.2) indicate that public education spending is procyclical, whereas public health spending is acyclical. The interaction term between lagged output gap and lagged corruption control has a positive and statistically significant coefficient only in the public education spending regressions, with no evidence of statistical significance

Table 4.1 Dependent variable – public education spending, fixed effects methodology

Variable	Full sample	Low income	Lower middle income	Upper middle income	High income
Lag of output gap	−3.59e−11*	−1.32e-09***	2.41e−14	−1.38e−10	−2.88e−11
	(−1.91)	(−12.34)	(0.00)	(−1.32)	(−1.04)
Lag of output gap * lag of control of corruption	8.89e−12*	7.29e−10***	−4.26e−12	2.16e−11	7.20e−12
	(1.98)	(5.16)	(−0.41)	(0.66)	(1.03)
Control of corruption	−0.0759742	−0.2296261	0.6048546**	−0.2120757	0.0813243
	(−0.68)	(−1.34)	(2.22)	(−1.61)	(0.38)
Aid (% of GDP)	0.0038798	−0.2243773	0.0190866*	0.0553017	−0.0148056
	(0.42)	(−0.60)	(2.05)	(1.18)	(−1.47)
Portfolio investment (% of GDP)	1.217632***	13.45282	1.851282	−1.022451*	1.144538***
	(3.51)	(0.38)	(0.26)	(−1.89)	(3.53)
Net transfers (% of GDP)	5.369945*	−0.756204	9.442275	−7.554246	−19.067
	(1.91)	(−0.07)	(0.91)	(−1.73)	(−0.53)
Revenue (% of GDP)	0.0091767	0.0585903	0.0107166	−0.0063577	0.0187284
	(0.28)	(1.34)	(0.09)	(−0.26)	(0.40)
Constant	4.864409***	3.715757***	0.9375037	4.705199***	4.923864***
	(4.78)	(3.46)	(0.66)	(4.09)	(3.29)
Observations	318	40	69	89	120
Countries	50	7	14	12	17
R-squared within	0.2259	0.8160	0.6890	0.5749	0.4052

Note: Robust t-statistics in parentheses. *** $p < 0.01$, ** $p < 0.05$, * $p < 0.1$.

in the public health spending regressions. The evidence that control of corruption in low-income countries tends to be associated with more countercyclical public spending in either education or health appears mixed, and these are sensitive to model specifications. The evidence on the links between public education and health spending, respectively, and various indicators of fiscal space is also generally mixed. These are kept in the model mainly to control for the possible influence of available fiscal space for implementing social spending policies.

The results for lower- and upper-middle-income countries suggest public education spending is acyclical and health spending procyclical. This is the reverse of the pattern observed in low-income countries (see columns 3 and 4 in Tables 4.1 and 4.2). There are several possible explanations for these differences. One is that, on average, the private–public balance of the education and health sectors (that is, the shares of total services accounted for by private and public providers, respectively)

Table 4.2 Dependent variable – public health care spending, fixed effects methodology

Variable	Full sample	Low income	Lower middle income	Upper middle income	High income
Lag of output gap	−1.61e−11***	−1.79e−10	−2.28e−11***	−5.87e−10**	−1.61e−11
	(−3.20)	(−0.95)	(−3.89)	(−2.39)	(−1.63)
Lag of output gap * lag of control of corruption	3.94e−12***	1.00e−10	5.72e−12***	1.66e−10**	3.98e−12
	(2.94)	(1.05)	(3.60)	(2.34)	(1.64)
Control of corruption	0.0270783	0.0757737	0.1302178**	−0.328824*	0.1982589
	(0.30)	(0.60)	(2.75)	(−1.91)	(1.54)
Aid (% GDP)	0.006967*	−0.3877129	−0.0012237	−0.0075051	0.0069562*
	(1.75)	(−1.73)	(−0.36)	(−0.56)	(1.79)
Portfolio investment (% GDP)	−0.0794434	4.336766	−0.3775778	2.269843***	−1.193469
	(−0.12)	(0.34)	(−0.23)	(4.09)	(−1.25)
Net transfers (% GDP)	0.2780908	−1.78972	5.581463	−3.940984	−1.988837
	(0.06)	(−0.45)	(1.58)	(−0.55)	(−0.06)
Revenue (% GDP)	0.0152038	0.0411518	0.0902748**	0.002741	0.0612919*
	(0.60)	(1.67)	(2.45)	(0.08)	(1.79)
Constant	3.738927***	0.9185	0.5398988	5.154663***	3.49474***
	(5.83)	(1.67)	(0.91)	(5.09)	(3.00)
Observations	365	45	83	96	141
Countries	51	8	13	13	17
R-squared within	0.1848	0.5995	0.6927	0.3499	0.6404

Note: Robust t-statistics in parentheses. *** $p < 0.01$, ** $p < 0.05$, * $p < 0.1$.

differs substantially across country income groups. This is unsurprising, as different countries' political and economic systems imply different state-market balances. The private–public mix, in turn, may influence the extent and manner of public sector countercyclical spending and investments in these sectors. If the private sector were larger, it could be boosted through cheaper credit or perhaps tax breaks, which would be different from support through direct government spending. Crises could be opportunities to fine tune public sector spending and support policies, and it is this overall combination or balance of support that is critical.

As to the difference of pattern between education and health, it is also possible that the political economy behind public education spending is different from that behind public health spending. In poorer countries, with possibly less progress in promoting education access, the sector may be much more vulnerable to fiscal consolidation. However, in less poor countries which have achieved relatively more progress in promoting education (including among the more politically active generation), resistance to public education spending cuts may be stronger, more organised and possibly more effective.

The regressions involving high-income countries appear to show acyclical public education and health spending patterns. These results do not fully conform to our expectation that more industrialised (and possibly better-governed) countries will likely exhibit stronger countercyclical public spending policy in education and health. A possible explanation is that more developed access to financial and insurance services in richer countries could help alleviate the need for a much stronger public sector response to downturns. Essentially, people could continue to opt for privately provided education and health services, to the extent that insurance mechanisms cover temporary income shocks. Similarly, boom periods may not necessarily lead to excessive increases in public spending due to stronger institutions and fiscal restraint. Another potential explanation is that, in industrial countries, direct public spending is not the only policy lever governments can turn to in order to mount a more pro-poor policy response. More indirect support to the social sectors could include tax breaks that augment the capability of (notably poorer) households to continue to invest in education and health.

Finally, it is also possible that demographic and technological trends in more industrialised countries have helped elevate public sector spending trends, notably in health. This sets the stage for some cost cutting during crisis situations when affordability issues come to light. Unlike in developing countries, where the principal challenge is to expand the health safety net and boost access to basic health care, in industrial countries, health care spending has been skyrocketing and it is expected to continue to climb. The challenge for these countries is to try to curb the steep rise in health spending, finding ways to make higher technology and more advanced care much more affordable (IMF, 2010a). This does not mean that industrial countries no longer undertake pro-poor countercyclical spending policies. Instead, we note that the public spending aggregate figure may need to be disaggregated to tease out the pro-poor countercyclical response. The issue could become one of reallocation rather than resource augmentation.

As a robustness check, we also run regressions using the economic growth variable in lieu of the output gap variable. These also turn to a wider set of governance indicators, spanning control of corruption, bureaucracy quality and government stability. This adjustment does not materially change the main findings for developing countries, and the results are no longer reported here. Overall, the developing countries still appear to exhibit either acyclical or procyclical public spending patterns in the areas of education and health. On the other hand, the regressions using economic growth do produce results suggesting that high-income countries follow countercyclical public education and health spending policies. The latter is consistent with earlier studies that have used similar approaches.

Conclusion

Interesting patterns emerge in the empirical analysis of the cyclicality of public education and public health spending across industrial and developing countries. The results suggest that in low-income countries, education spending is procyclical and health spending acyclical – a pattern that is reversed when one examines the results for lower- and upper-middle-income countries. High-income countries tend to exhibit acyclical patterns for public education and health spending. While the results are tentative, this assessment is presented here based on a pattern that seems to emerge from a series of reasonable model specifications.

There are important differences across industrial and developing countries' education and health spending patterns. Countries with lower incomes and poorer governance indicators tend to display more procyclical results. These results cohere with the earlier literature and anecdotal evidence on the political economy behind budget cuts in developing country settings. Spending on the poor tends to suffer, notably in countries with weaker governance. It is also possible that spending on education and health is a casualty of broader public sector retrenchment during economic downturn in these countries. In such cases, the problem may not just be political, but it also could be linked to poor public finance management through the business cycle. This latter point seems to be present in Eastern European countries, which appear to have been the worst hit by the 2008–10 crisis. These countries had much weaker fiscal conditions prior to the crisis, setting the stage for their difficulties in preserving (let alone boosting) education and health spending during this period.[15]

As for the acyclical findings for industrial countries, there are several factors worth considering. Better-developed complementary markets (for example health insurance) and other policy levers could afford these countries a less pronounced public spending response to crisis situations. But, even more cogent for the health sector, it is possible that excessive and unsustainable spending on higher technology care (exacerbated by ageing trends) could imply a tendency towards a cost-cutting response during crises.[16] It is therefore possible that the pro-poor countercyclical response we are looking for has been dominated instead by this effect.

A causal review of the deep fiscal cuts witnessed in many industrialised countries in 2010–11 does appear to support this observation. Initially, industrial (and some developing) countries responded to the global economic slowdown with strong fiscal stimuli. However, as the recovery tapered out, the crisis may have accentuated already glaring sustainability and affordability issues, notably in countries with already high public sector spending. Thus, in the immediate aftermath of the global economic slowdown during the 2010–11 period, a number of industrial countries undertook severe austerity measures. These measures included raising the retirement age (France) or cutting pension benefits (Greece) to be able to make pensions more sustainable; retrenching significant numbers of public sector employees (UK) or cutting civil servants' wages (Spain) to lower the profile of the public sector; and cutting defence spending and public works programmes (Germany, US) to rationalise spending and investments in these sectors. Clearly, what began as a countercyclical response was replaced by austerity strategies as soon as longstanding weaknesses in the sustainability of public sector programmes surfaced. Nevertheless, and as noted earlier, efforts to improve fiscal sustainability need not result in sacrificing government's equity objectives. A pro-poor countercyclical response is still possible, with adequate reallocation of resources into programmes that provide stronger benefits to poor and low-income people who have less access to alternative (private) health care service providers.

Boosting social services during an economic downturn – be this in education or in health – remains an important challenge yet to be met in many countries, developing and industrial alike. Public spending in education and health care are historically procyclical in different parts of the developing world. These appear acyclical in industrial countries. As noted earlier, the recent focus on boosting cash transfers during crises signals an increasing focus on boosting the demand side of social spending and investments. By providing cash to poor families (in some cases targeted at women), the necessary spending and investments could be made in child and maternal health, as well as in education, food and other goods and services critical to human development. During a crisis, this relaxation in the budget constraints of poor families could spell the difference between life and death, notably for the most vulnerable children. While efforts to boost demand are welcome and helpful, it is also critical to consider adequate provision on the supply side of social services, especially in places where the market malfunctions or where it excludes the bulk of the poor and low-income population. Providing cash to poor families, while at the same time allowing social services such as education and health to weaken, will be unlikely to achieve the objective of protecting children and safeguarding gains in human development during a crisis.

In future research, these results could be compared with more contextualised studies of public education and health spending over the business cycle, particularly during boom periods and downturns. There are several main areas for further exploration. First, the findings in this chapter point to the possibly different patterns across various subcomponents of social spending. It is possible that education and health services (that is, the supply side) are being retrenched even as cash transfers to ensure better education and health investments in children are being pursued (that is, the demand side). The net impact of these policies on outcomes for children will be ambiguous, given that the former policy may undermine the latter. More holistic analysis of social sector support needs to be undertaken. On this point, it might be crucial to analyse the specific policy instruments that allow countries to stabilise financing through the business cycle.[17]

Another angle to consider relates to the role of the public sector in the different subsectors of total social spending. As mentioned earlier, it is possible that the private–public balance varies across sectors and across countries, and also across country income groups. Industrial countries, for example, may have much more developed private sector providers of education and health services. The data on this balance are still quite limited, preventing their consideration in the present chapter. Nevertheless, some country-specific indicators do exist. For instance, a recent study in Pakistan points to the large and growing share of private schools charging low fees and serving low-income families and children. By one estimate, a little over one-third of all children in primary school in the country were in these types of schools (Andrabi et al., 2008).[18]

It would also be critical to analyse the subcomponents of social spending, to help ensure that both the demand and the supply sides are boosted adequately according to country context and need. After the 2008–10 crisis erupted, spending on social protection was boosted in a number of countries (see Box 4.1), and it is not clear whether this is linked directly to budgets for public education and public health spending. It is likely that the bulk of it is not, and thus a fuller analysis

Box 4.1 Selected social protection policies initiated in 2008–9

A review of selected social protection responses to the 2008–10 crisis suggests that many developing countries are boosting such programming not just in response to the crisis, but also with a long-term view of the transformative, poverty and inequality reduction and safety net aspects of their social protection systems.

- **Brazil** has boosted its *Bolsa Família* programme by increasing cash transfers to existing poor beneficiaries by some 10 per cent and expanding coverage to include an additional 1.3 million families.
- **Guatemala** initiated a CCT programme in 2008, *Mi Familia Progresa*, which will provide monthly health and nutrition transfers to families with children under 6, and additional transfers for education to families with at least one child between the ages of 6 and 15 attending primary or preschool. Visits to health care centres and use of a basic package of nutritional and preventative maternal and child health care services, as well as regular school attendance, are required. The programme was expected to cover 45 priority municipalities in 2008 and 125 of the country's 333 municipalities (that is, 500,000 families) by the end of 2009.
- **Nepal** has continued to build on its existing social protection initiatives by providing a monthly allowance to ethnic groups at risk, persons of low caste, single women and people of the mountainous Karnali zone above the age of 60, as well as all other citizens above the age of 70. The government is also in the process of piloting a child grant programme and continuing its work with donors and development agencies to build towards a more comprehensive social protection policy.
- **Pakistan** initiated a domestic policy discourse on the crisis culminating in a report titled 'Economic Stabilisation with a Human Face'. In addition to economic reform recommendations, the report pushed for a more robust social protection response to the crisis. The latter includes an employment guarantee scheme in poor districts, increasing microfinance and housing access for the poor and increasing coverage of the Benazir Income Support Programme, which was slated to cover 1.8 million poor families in 2009 and later to expand to cover 5 million families in 2010.
- **The Philippines** has expanded its key social protection programmes, such as the Pantawid Pamilyang Pilipino Program (4Ps), which provides cash grants under particular conditions to poor households, with a goal of reaching 700,000 households in 2009; the Self-Employment Assistance Kaunlaran, which provides capital assistance and capacity-building for livelihood projects; and the Food for School Programme, which provides rice allocations to elementary school children.
- **Senegal** has boosted its social protection for mothers and young children by creating a cash transfer programme for vulnerable mothers of children under age five, accompanied by a strong communication campaign on maternal and child nutrition; designing a community-driven nutrition strategy involving growth monitoring for children under two, nutrition education for mothers, provision of iron and vitamin A supplements,

de-worming and supply of insecticide-treated bed nets; and providing support to sectoral and national nutrition policies, encompassing periodic distribution of micronutrient supplements and supervision of nutrition services.

- **Vietnam** nearly doubled its social safety net budget in 2009 compared with 2008. Its array of crisis responses includes one-off additional financial assistance to poor households, housing support for the poor and a boost to existing social assistance programmes, such as its programme for poverty reduction in ethnic minority and mountainous areas (Programme 135) and its health insurance programme for the poor and near poor.

Source: Excerpted from Mendoza (2010).

should necessarily include it. Further data and analyses on social protection financing are therefore necessary. These and other policy developments in recent years signal the growing emphasis on undertaking countercyclical social spending and policies in the developing world.

All of this suggests that the earlier literature and the 'received wisdom' for social spending policies cannot be taken as a given: patterns of public social spending may be changing in important ways in both industrial and developing countries. Further research in this area could yield more insights as to the design of more effective and sustainable policy interventions.

Notes

For very helpful comments, the authors thank participants at the 26th Conference of the American Committee for Asian Economic Studies, 'Asia after the Crisis', held 5–6 March 2010 in Kambai-kan Hall, Doshisha University, Kyoto, Japan.

1. See, among others, Alderman and Haque (2006); Mendoza (2009a; 2009b); Ravallion (2008).
2. See, among others, Alesina et al. (2008); Gavin and Perotti (1997); Talvi and Vegh (2005).
3. For instance, in addition to other possible instrumental variables, they use the weighted gross domestic product (GDP) growth of countries' trading partners as an instrument for GDP.
4. These statements could be interpreted in various ways, including when measuring these variables in real terms, as a share of total public spending or as a share of GDP. In this chapter, our focus is on scaling as a share of GDP in order to arrive at some sense of the total magnitude of spending relative to the size of the economy, which is the convention in the literature. This is coherent with our focus on the political economy of public spending allocations. Our main interest is in how much of the total pie the social sectors receive.

5. See, among others, Alderman and Haque (2006).
6. For a detailed discussion see, for example, Vreeland (2006) and evaluations produced by the Independent Evaluation Office (IEO) of the International Monetary Fund (IMF) (www.ieo-imf.org/).
7. Under the *Trabajar* programme, the central government covers the wage costs and local or provincial governments cover other costs.
8. See, among others, Alesina and Tabellini (1989); Alesina et al. (2008).
9. For more on measuring democracies using the Polity IV database, see www.systemicpeace.org/polity/polity4.htm.
10. In a related paper, Arezki and Ismail (2010) examine evidence suggesting that oil price busts were not accompanied by a commensurate decline in the real exchange rate. The authors attribute this to possible political pressures skewing policy choices towards increases in public expenditures during boom times rather than cutting these during periods of decline, thus leading to the real effective exchange rate remaining elevated, even after a decrease in commodity prices.
11. As a robustness check, we also run the same regression using lagged real GDP per capita growth as an alternative indicator of the business cycle, replacing the output gap variable.
12. The output gap could trigger public spending adjustments, and public spending could also be linked to the output gap itself.
13. See www.prsgroup.com/icrg.aspx.
14. Indeed, some caution is necessary in interpreting all the results, given this sensitivity to model specification. We can take some comfort in the battery of specifications (some of which are not reported in this chapter due to space constraints) to try and establish some robustness in the results.
15. See IMF (2010b) and an analysis of medium-term public spending cuts across regions by Ortiz et al. (2010).
16. Public spending on health care has increased by about 4 percentage points of GDP since 1970, accounting for roughly half the overall increase in non-interest spending (IMF, 2010a). It is expected that in the next 20 years health care costs will continue to increase due to technological expenses and other factors.
17. See Gonzalez and Paqueo (2003) on 'rainy day funds' in the US and Mendoza (2009c) for a review of financial stability instruments and proposals that aid in countries' stabilisation and pro-poor countercyclical spending efforts.
18. The interested reader may wish to turn to Lindert (2004) and Moreno-Dodson and Wodon (2008) for a discussion of the private–public balance in various contexts, notably the social sectors.

References

Alderman, H. and Haque, T. (2006) 'Countercyclical Safety Nets for the Poor and Vulnerable.' *Food Policy* 31(4): 372–83.

Alesina, A., Campante, F. and Tabellini, G. (2008) 'Why is Fiscal Policy Often Procyclical?' *Journal of the European Economic Association* 6(5): 1006–36.

Alesina, A. and Tabellini, G. (1989) 'External Debt, Capital Flight and Political Risk.' *Journal of International Economics* 27(3–4): 199–220.

Arezki, R. and Bruckner, M. (2010) 'International Commodity Price Shocks, Democracy and External Debt.' Working Paper 10/53. Washington, DC: IMF.
Arezki, R. and Ismail, K. (2010) 'Boom-Bust Cycle, Asymmetrical Fiscal Response and the Dutch Disease.' Working Paper 10/94. Washington, DC: IMF.
Cutler, D., Knaul, F., Lozano, R., Méndez, O. and Zurita, B. (2002) 'Financial Crisis, Health Outcomes and Ageing: Mexico in the 1980s and 1990s.' *Journal of Public Economics* 84(2): 279–303.
Darby, J. and Melitz, J. (2008) 'Automatic Stabilizers.' *Economic Policy* 23(56): 715–56.
Deles, P., Mendoza, R. and Vergara, G. (2009) 'Social Budgeting Initiatives and Innovations: Insights Using a Public Finance Lens.' Working Paper. New York: ANSA-EAP, Fordham University and UNICEF.
Furceri, D. (2009) 'Stabilization Effects of Social Spending: Empirical Evidence from a Panel of OECD Countries Overcoming the Financial Crisis in the United States.' Working Paper 675. Paris: Economics Department, OECD.
Gavin, M. and Perotti, R. (1997) 'Fiscal Policy in Latin America.' *NBER Macroeconomics Annual*. Cambridge, MA: NBER.
Gonzalez, C. and Paqueo, V. (2003) 'Social Sector Expenditures and Rainy-Day Funds.' Policy Research Working Paper 3131. Washington, DC: World Bank.
Gupta, S., Verhoven, M. and Tiongson, E. (1999) 'Does Higher Government Spending Buy Better Results in Education and Health Care?' Working Paper 99/21. Washington, DC: IMF.
Hagen R. and Hatlebakk. M. (2002) 'Foreign Aid and Social Sector Spending in Developing Countries.' Mimeo.
Ilzetski, E. and Vegh, C. (2008) 'Procyclical Fiscal Policy in Developing Countries: Truth or Fiction?' Working Paper 14191. Cambridge, MA: NBER.
IMF (2010a) 'Macro-Fiscal Implications of Healthcare Reform in Advanced and Emerging Economies.' Washington, DC: IMF.
IMF (2010b) 'Europe: Building Confidence.' IMF Regional Economic Outlook. Washington, DC: IMF.
Lindert, P. (2004) *Growing Public*. Cambridge: Cambridge University Press.
Mendoza, R. (2009a) 'Aggregate Shocks, Poor Households and Children: Transmission Channels and Policy Responses.' *Global Social Policy* 9(1): 55–78.
Mendoza, R. (2009b) 'Responding to the Food, Fuel and Financial Crises of 2009: A Case for Pro-Poor Stabilization Policy.' VoxEU.org on Policy Portal.
Mendoza, R. (2009c) 'A Review of Financial Stability Instruments for Emerging Market Economies.' *CESIfo Economic Studies* 55(2): 353–97.
Mendoza, R. (2010) 'Inclusive Crises, Exclusive Recoveries and Policies to Prevent a Double Whammy for the Poor.' Mimeo.
Mendoza, R. and Rees, N. (2009) 'Infant Mortality during Economic Downturns and Recovery.' Social and Economic Policy Working Paper. New York: UNICEF.
Moreno-Dodson, B. and Wodon, Q. (eds) (2008) *Public Finance for Poverty Reduction: Concepts and Case Studies from Africa and Latin America*. Washington, DC: World Bank.
Ortiz, I., Chai, J., Cummins, M. and Vergara, G. (2010) 'Prioritizing Expenditures for a Recovery for All.' Social and Economic Policy Working Paper. New York: UNICEF.

Ravallion, M. (2002) 'Are the Poor Protected from Budget Cuts? Evidence from Argentina.' *Journal of Applied Economics* 5(1): 95–121.
Ravallion, M. (2008) 'Bailing out the World's Poorest.' Policy Research Working Paper 4763. Washington, DC: World Bank.
Talvi, E. and Vegh, C. (2005) 'Tax Base Variability and Pro-cyclical Fiscal Policy in Developing Countries.' *Journal of Development Economics* 78(1): 156–90.
Vreeland, J. (2006) *The International Monetary Fund: Politics of Conditional Lending.* London and New York: Routledge.

Part II

Emerging Evidence on the Impact of the 2008–10 Crises

5

Simulating the Impact of the Global Economic Crisis and Policy Responses on Children in West and Central Africa

John Cockburn, Ismaël Fofana and Luca Tiberti

Introduction

The increasing integration of West and Central African (WCA) countries into the global economy has been a source of significant economic growth in recent years, but this exposure has also made their economies more vulnerable to global crises (World Bank, 2008). Integration is still relatively weak, which meant that they were initially sheltered from the effects of contagion when the financial crisis broke out in 2008. However, the ensuing economic crisis has affected them directly, particularly through the channels of international trade, investment, foreign aid and remittances.

Overall, the global financial and economic crisis has threatened recent growth and poverty reduction achievements in many developing countries. Indeed, economic growth rates in Sub-Saharan Africa (SSA) declined from an average 7 per cent in 2007 to 1.3 per cent in 2009 (IMF, 2009b). This has exacerbated the impacts of the energy and food crises that preceded the global financial crisis in 2007.

Designing practical and appropriate policies in developing countries to stimulate growth and protect vulnerable population groups, in particular children, from the harmful short- and long-term effects of the crisis requires an understanding of the likely magnitude and nature of these effects. As real-time data on child wellbeing are not available to guide the rapid implementation of policies to protect children from the impacts of crisis, we develop a predictive model that anticipates the impacts of the crisis, and possible policy responses, on various essential dimensions of child welfare in three WCA countries: Burkina Faso, Cameroon and Ghana. The dimensions studied include monetary poverty; hunger; school and work participation and access to health services. Burkina Faso is a low-income country with a per capita gross domestic product (GDP) estimated at \$480 in 2008. The average growth of GDP was 5.3 per cent in real terms between 2005 and 2008, with the IMF projecting this to fall to 3.5 per cent in 2009 (IMF, 2009b). The economic slowdown in 2009 was owed largely to difficulties faced in agriculture, in particular the cotton sector, as a result of a fall in output prices and reduced access to trade credit.

With an average economic growth rate of about 4 per cent annually over the past half-decade and a per capita income of \$1,150 in 2008, Cameroon's GDP growth rate fell to 1.6 per cent in 2009 according to IMF (2009a) forecasts. The deterioration of the foreign account, resulting mainly from a substantial fall in the prices of its main export commodity (that is, oil and petroleum products), and the deterioration of its fiscal account, which went from a surplus equal to 2 per cent of GDP in 2008 to a 1 per cent deficit in 2009, are identified as the main causes of this slowdown.

Although the crisis has affected Ghana's exports less severely than it has those of many other countries, given persistent strong export prices for gold and cocoa (the country's two main exports), private remittances are falling, foreign direct investment (FDI) appears to be lower and access to global credit has suffered a setback. These developments have had a direct impact on the balance of payments, domestic demand and economic growth. At the same time, currency pressures have triggered higher inflation, requiring tighter monetary policy, with further adverse impacts on economic activity. The International Monetary Fund (IMF) Regional Economic Outlook in October 2009 forecast a 4.5 per cent GDP growth rate in Ghana, representing a reduction of 2.8 percentage points compared with its 2008 performance (IMF, 2009b).

Methodology and hypothesis

In contrast with industrialised and emerging economies, which faced the direct effects of the financial crisis, it has been the ensuing global economic crisis that has most affected developing countries, including WCA. Understanding the nature and the extent of the effects of the crisis in these countries requires a rigorous analysis of the main transmission mechanisms at both macro and micro levels.

The global economic recession has affected demand for and prices of commodities traded by these countries, as well as foreign aid, FDI and remittances. These changes have large and complex impacts on product markets, factor markets, government finances and international trade at the macro level. Meanwhile, in order to track the varying impacts of these changes on individual households and, in particular, their children, and to be able to design appropriate policy responses, the macro-level analysis needs to be complemented by a micro investigation. The methodology followed to capture the macro impacts and to link them to the micro model of child wellbeing outcome variables is described in detail in Bibi et al. (2010a).

The impact of the global economic crisis is captured in terms of the four main channels – external trade, private remittances, FDI and international aid – that link these three WCA economies to the global economy (Table 5.1). Recent trends are highlighted and hypotheses are developed concerning the impacts of the economic crisis on these channels over the 2008–11 period studied. Throughout our simulations, government expenditures are assumed to remain constant, and the increase in the government deficit, induced by the fall in domestic tax revenue and foreign aid inflows, is assumed to be compensated for through increased domestic borrowing.

The IMF in 2009 predicted stabilisation by early 2010 and recovery beginning in the second half of 2011. On this basis, the chapter simulates the shocks introduced by the global crisis according to the following general scenario: crisis in 2008–9, stabilisation in 2009–10 and beginning of recovery in 2010–11. The crisis period in 2008–9 is characterised by a macro contraction. Changes in world import prices are observed in IMF databases and affect each country differently according to the structure of their external trade. Hypotheses are made on the changes in the other macro variables based on official reports published by the IMF (for export prices and volumes) (IMF, 2009b); the World Bank (for international remittances) (Ratha et al., 2009); the European Commission (EC) (for foreign aid) (European Report on Development, 2009) and the UN Conference on Trade and Development (UNCTAD) (for foreign investment) (UNCTAD, 2009).

With stabilisation in 2009–10, all macro variables are assumed to remain at their 2008–9 levels with the exception of import prices, which are expected to increase, as it is currently being observed in most commodity markets.

Table 5.1 Channels of impact (variations in per cent)

	Burkina Faso			Cameroon			Ghana		
	2009	2010	2011	2009	2010	2011	2009	2010	2011
Baseline scenario									
World price of imports	0.0	0.0	0.0	0.0	0.0	0.0	0.0	0.0	0.0
Export volume	4.0	3.6	3.3	5.0	4.6	4.7	12.3	12.0	11.4
Foreign investments	10.5	9.6	8.9	0.0	0.0	0.0	11.0	9.9	9.0
Foreign aid	7.4	6.9	6.5	0.0	0.0	0.0	2.7	2.7	2.6
Private remittances	7.5	7.0	6.5	0.0	0.0	0.0	7.0	6.4	5.8
Crisis scenario									
World price of imports	–18.1	4.9	4.9	–9.4	1.3	0.0	–19.2	10.1	10.2
Export volume	–6.5	0.0	3.3	0.2	3.6	3.2	5.0	0.0	11.4
Foreign investments	–42.0	0.0	8.9	–35.0*	–15.0*	5.0*	–42.0	0.0	9.0
Foreign aid	–12.7	0.0	6.5	–5.0	–9.0	–6.0	–14.0	0.0	2.6
Private remittances	–11.6	0.0	6.5	–12.5	–20.0	20.0	–11.6	0.0	5.8

Note: *Foreign reserves.

Source: Authors' calculation.

The world economy is assumed to begin recovery from the global economic crisis in 2010–11. In our simulations, this translates into an increase in import prices, export demand, foreign investments, development aid and private transfers, following their long-term growth rates observed during the pre-crisis period.[1]

Results drawn from the simulated crisis scenario are compared with a simulated scenario without crisis, called the baseline or 'Business as Usual' (BaU) scenario. This assumes that all four channels follow their respective pre-crisis historical trends throughout the simulation period.

Simulating the impact of the global economic crisis

Our simulations indicate that the crisis slows growth in Burkina Faso, Cameroon and Ghana between 2009 and 2011 (Table 5.2). GDP growth

Table 5.2 Annual real GDP growth rates (per cent)

	Burkina Faso			Cameroon			Ghana		
	BaU	Crisis	*Variation**	BaU	Crisis	*Variation**	BaU	Crisis	*Variation**
2009	5.3	4.1	*−1.1*	4.2	1.9	*−2.3*	7.3	5.1	−2.3
2010	5.0	4.0	*−1.0*	4.2	3.1	*−1.1*	7.3	3.8	−3.5
2011	4.9	4.4	*−0.4*	4.4	3.4	*−1.0*	7.4	6.5	−1.0

Note: *Percentage points (rounding).

Source: Authors' calculation.

rates fall between 1.1 and 2.3 percentage points relative to our BaU (no global economic crisis) scenario.

Burkina Faso is least affected by the crisis, losing only around 1 percentage point or less of growth each year. Cameroon and Ghana both suffer from a 2.3 percentage point reduction in growth in 2009. Recovery comes quicker in Cameroon than in Ghana. For the latter, the second year of the crisis appears to be even more damaging for the economy, with a 3.5 percentage reduction in the growth rate. This result can be traced to the assumed increase in import prices in 2010, given Ghana's greater import dependency.

Monetary poverty

Burkina Faso has a child monetary poverty rate in the base year equal to 32.7 per cent, Cameroon 50.2 per cent and Ghana 33.7 per cent[2] (Figure 5.1). First, while Cameroon and Burkina Faso show an inverse-U shaped profile of child monetary poverty over the period 2009–11, with a peak in 2010, in Ghana, child monetary poverty shows a continuously increasing trend. Indeed, Ghana is where children are predicted to suffer most from the global crisis (in both absolute and relative terms), with monetary poverty increasing by more than 6 percentage points in 2010 and 2011 relative to the base year.

Table 5.3 disaggregates the contribution to the observed poverty impacts of the different price and income channels affecting household real expenditure. In Ghana, the deterioration is driven primarily by a reduction in consumer purchasing power, (as high import dependency results in strongly rising consumer prices) and a large drop in income in the non-agriculture sector. Increases in agricultural incomes somewhat offset the increase in child monetary poverty. In contrast, child poverty in Burkina Faso is affected mainly by a fall in incomes in the agriculture sector. In Cameroon, the impacts are more diffuse. Changes in consumer prices and a reduction in income from

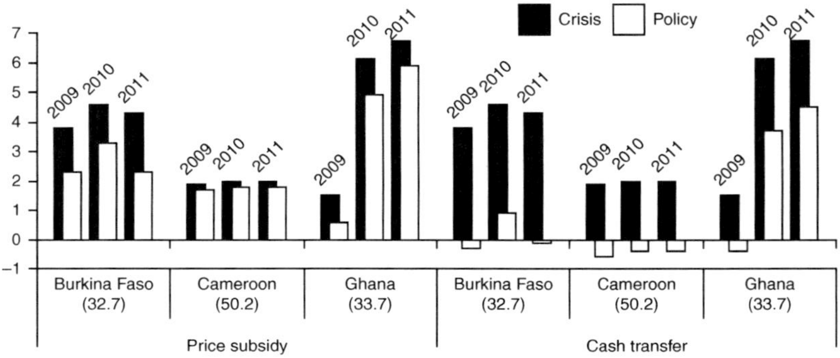

Figure 5.1 Effects of policy responses on child monetary poverty: food subsidy and targeted cash transfer (variation in percentage points relative to base year rates)

Note: Numbers in brackets refer to base year values.

Source: Authors' calculation.

Table 5.3 Simulated impacts of the crisis on child monetary poverty, by channel

	Burkina Faso			**Cameroon**			**Ghana**		
	32.66 (year)			**50.20 (year)**			**33.73 (year)**		
Absolute rate (base year)	**2009**	**2010**	**2011**	**2009**	**2010**	**2011**	**2009**	**2010**	**2011**
With crisis (% change to base year)	3.79	4.67	4.36	1.85	2.04	2.01	1.52	6.10	6.65
Contribution to child poverty changes after crisis by different channels (% change to base year)									
Consumer prices	0.28	0.65	1.12	0.67	0.62	0.59	2.12	4.44	5.04
Agriculture sector	2.85	3.23	2.33	0.37	0.39	0.44	−1.77	−1.64	−2.37
Non-agriculture sector (self-employment)	0.00	0.00	0.01	0.53	0.56	0.64	1.11	2.99	3.63
Salaries and wages	0.02	0.02	0.01	0.30	0.29	0.30	−0.08	0.08	0.07
Formal	0.00	0.01	0.01	0.01	0.01	0.23	0.00	0.00	0.01
Informal	0.02	0.01	0.00	0.29	0.28	0.28	−0.08	0.08	0.05
Other incomes	0.54	0.74	0.77	0.02	0.09	0.03	0.20	0.21	0.19

Notes: As changes in poverty status linked to the different channels do not necessarily affect all individuals, the sum of the changes in each component does not exactly equal the total change. Base years are 2003, 2007 and 2005/06 for Burkina Faso, Cameroon and Ghana, respectively. No changes in the micro data between the base years and 2008 (the starting year for the simulations) were thus assumed.

Source: Authors' calculation.

the non-agriculture sector are the major contributors to the increase in child poverty. The fall in wages affects child poverty relatively more in Cameroon, representing roughly one-sixth of the total child monetary poverty increase.

Finally, reductions in wages, which are not a major source of income in the region, contribute only slightly to the deterioration in monetary poverty, especially in Burkina Faso. It is noteworthy that changes in the informal wage sector affect children relatively more than those in the formal sector, with the exception of Cameroon for 2011. Remittances also do not seem to play a crucial role in the predicted increase in child monetary poverty, as relatively few households rely on international remittances. Only in Burkina Faso, where 6 per cent of individuals live in households receiving remittances (of which more than a quarter are poor), does this channel play much of a role, accounting for roughly one-sixth of the total change in child monetary poverty (in 2011).

Differences emerge in regional and urban/rural impacts within the three countries. In Ghana, urban areas are more affected by the economic crisis than rural areas. This is due to the rise in agricultural incomes in rural areas, which partly offsets the fall in other incomes and the rise in consumer prices. In Cameroon, absolute changes in child urban poverty rates over the simulated crisis period are around 1 percentage point larger than in rural areas, but high population in rural areas makes its absolute contribution to national poverty stronger. In Burkina Faso, the crisis mainly affects children living in rural areas.

Hunger

As Figure 5.2 shows, only Ghana is predicted to experience a serious increase in child hunger rates as a result of the crisis, a situation that worsens continuously over the period 2009–11 such that hunger rates are a full 7 percentage points higher in 2011 in comparison with the base year (2008). This is due to the fact that, in Ghana, food prices are predicted to increase much more than non-food prices, whereas in both Burkina and Cameroon food prices decrease in comparison with non-food prices. In Cameroon, this difference between food and non-food price changes is such that hunger rates under the crisis are even slightly lower than those observed in the base year.

School and work participation

Younger school-age children (ages 6–10) are predicted to be somewhat more affected by the crisis in terms of school participation and child labour (Figures 5.3 and 5.4). Children in Burkina Faso are the

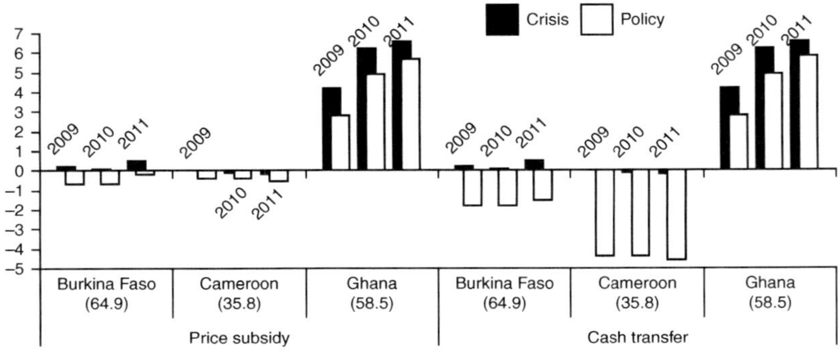

Figure 5.2 Effects of policy responses on child hunger: consumer price subsidy and targeted cash transfer (variation in percentage points relative to base year rates)

Note: Numbers in brackets refer to base year values.

Source: Authors' calculation.

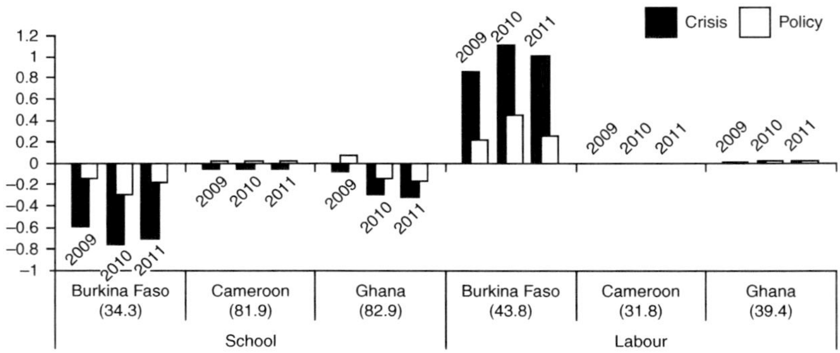

Figure 5.3 Effects of cash transfer on school participation and child labour for children age 6–10 (variation in percentage points relative to base year rates)

Notes: For Burkina Faso, the sample is 7–10 years old. Numbers in brackets refer to base year values.

Source: Authors' calculation.

most affected, with a reduction of up to 0.8 percentage points in school participation and an increase of their involvement in work of nearly 1.2 points. In breaking down these results, the situation is even worse: the fall in school participation is driven entirely by a reduction in the 'school/no work' alternative, while the rise in child work is the result of an increase in the 'no school/work' alternative. In Ghana, while school participation is reduced by the economic crisis (fall of up to 1

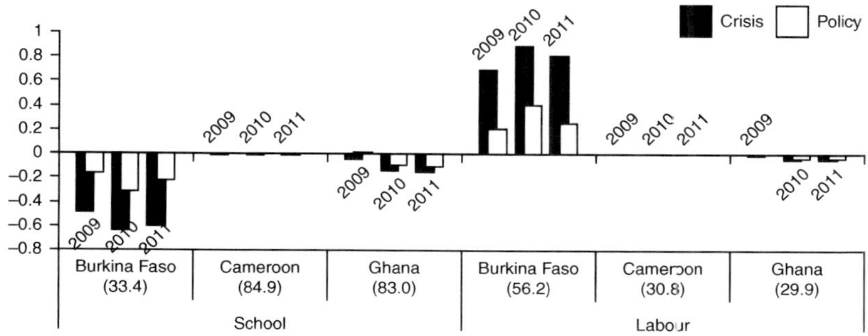

Figure 5.4 Effects of cash transfer on school participation and child labour for children age 11–14 (variation in percentage points relative to base year rates)

Note: Numbers in brackets refer to base year values.

Source: Authors' calculation.

percentage point), the impacts on child labour are much less. School and labour impacts are practically nil in Cameroon with or without a policy response. This suggests that, even more than in the other two countries, interventions should focus more on supply-side policies in order to try to reach the relatively small number of children currently out of the school system.

Access to health services

Ill children are less likely to access health services as a result of the crisis (Figure 5.5). In Burkina Faso, the likelihood falls by up to 1.2 percentage points, whereas the impact is more modest, albeit still substantial, in Cameroon and Ghana. An additional effect of the crisis is the diversion from higher- to lower-quality health services, such as traditional healers, and greater recourse to self-care. In Burkina Faso, services supplied by health and social promotion centres (CSPS), which represent the most popular type of health facility for Burkinabe children, are hardest hit; in Ghana and Cameroon, it is hospital-provided health services that fall most.

Simulating child welfare impacts of policy responses

The chapter quantifies the impact of two stimulus programmes aiming to protect children from the negative effects of the global economic crisis:

- Food subsidies – actually consumption tax cuts (value-added tax (VAT) or tariff) on food products;

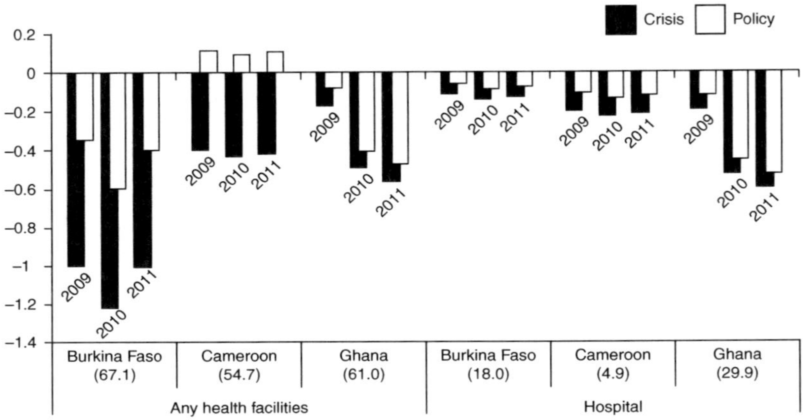

Figure 5.5 Effects of cash transfer on access to health services (variation in percentage points relative to base year rates)

Note: Numbers in brackets refer to base year values. Categories of health facilities consulted by ill children.

Source: Authors' calculation.

- Cash transfers targeted at children/households predicted to be poor using a proxy means test approach. We assume this transfer is pooled with other household income and shared equitably among household members. The effectiveness of a universal cash transfer is also discussed.

The total amount transferred under each programme is fixed arbitrarily at 1 per cent of national GDP in 2008. This amount is by assumption financed entirely from external sources (international aid). The proposed stimulus packages have few notable macroeconomic effects; consequently, our analysis in the next section focuses solely on the effects on child wellbeing.

Monetary poverty

Among the policy responses proposed to counteract the negative effects of the crisis on child welfare, a targeted cash transfer is by far the most effective, particularly in Burkina Faso and Cameroon (Figure 5.1). With the same overall budget, food subsidies have smaller effects, as they do not specifically target the poor or children. Indeed, a large share of food consumed by poor people is own-produced.

The effectiveness of both policies differs across the countries. The food subsidy, while still much less effective than a cash transfer, has significant and positive effects in Burkina Faso, reducing monetary poverty by 2 percentage points by 2011 after the crisis. In Ghana, effectiveness falls to 1.2 points in 2010 and in Cameroon its impact is nil.

Large differences also emerge in terms of the impacts of the cash transfer policy. In Burkina Faso, a targeted cash transfer fully offsets the negative effect of the crisis (with only a minor exception in 2010). Similar results are found for Cameroon where, in all the three years simulated, child poverty rates are even lower than those simulated in the baseline scenario, albeit in a context in which the impacts of the crisis are smaller. In Ghana, due to the strong predicted effects of the economic crisis on child poverty in 2010 and 2011, the cash transfer is not enough to fully offset them, although poverty is still reduced by more than 2 points in each year.

Weaker performance in Ghana is also a result of the fact that the amount of the cash transfer represents only around 5 per cent of both the poverty line and the consumption of predicted poor children, whereas for Burkina Faso it is around 10 per cent and 9 per cent, respectively, and for Cameroon it is around 7 per cent of both. The cash transfer also has more impact in Burkina Faso because a much larger number of children receiving the cash transfer live in poorer households compared with Cameroon and Ghana, so the total amount received by poorer households tends to be higher.

A final factor in determining the effectiveness of these two policy responses is the targeting performance of the cash transfer programme, which is based on a proxy means prediction of income based on easily observable household characteristics. Here, we find that Cameroon has the lowest rate of under-coverage (10.7 per cent nationwide), that is, of poor children excluded erroneously from the programme by the proxy means test. Cameroon also has the lowest rate of leakage. As the amount of transfer per child is equal to the total budget (1 per cent base year GDP) divided by the number of predicted poor children, leakage to non-poor children reduces the amount received by poor children, whereas under-coverage excludes them completely. There is a trade-off between minimisation of under-coverage (exclusion) and leakage (inclusion) errors.

Targeted cash transfers require time, money (not included in our analysis) and institutional capacity to administer. Universal targeting is relatively easier to carry out and, at least in a first phase, may represent a more cost-effective alternative, particularly where some wealthier households self-exclude by deeming the amount of the transfer too small to collect. Table 5.4 reports child monetary poverty rates when a universal transfer (with the same total budget as the targeted transfer discussed above: 1 per cent of GDP) is provided to *all* children under the age of six. We assume this transfer is pooled with other household income and shared equitably among household members, as is the case for the targeted transfer.

As the total population of children under age six turns out to be smaller than the population of children age 0–14 that are predicted to be poor (and thus targeted), the total amount transferred to each individual child is larger: French West African Franc (FCFA) 11,200 in Burkina Faso, FCFA 29,300 in Cameroon and ¢30.6 in Ghana (under the targeted scheme, the individual transfer in Burkina Faso is FCFA 8,628, in Cameroon FCFA 20,479 and in Ghana ¢19.8). When the whole child population is analysed, providing a universal cash transfer to all children under age six is very effective in reducing poverty rates after the crisis and gives results that are very close (and only slightly higher) to the scenario in which we simulated a targeted cash transfer collected by all children predicted as poor. This good performance is due to the combination of a higher individual transfer and the elimination of under-coverage errors from the targeted approach. The case for a

Table 5.4 Child monetary poverty rates under targeted and universal transfer (per cent), by different age groups

	0–14 years old			**0–5 years old**		
	Crisis	**TT 0–14**	**UT 0–5**	**Crisis**	**TT 0–14**	**UT 0–5**
Burkina Faso	*Base year poverty rate: 32.7%*			*Base year poverty rate: 29.8%*		
2009	36.5	32.4	32.9	33.8	29.6	29.2
2010	37.3	33.6	33.9	34.6	30.7	30.3
2011	37.0	32.6	33.0	34.3	29.7	29.3
Cameroon	*Base year poverty rate: 50.2%*			*Base year poverty rate: 47.4%*		
2009	52.1	49.6	50.1	49.4	46.9	46.5
2010	52.2	49.8	50.2	49.5	47.0	46.6
2011	52.2	49.8	50.0	49.5	47.1	46.5
Ghana	*Base year poverty rate: 33.7%*			*Base year poverty rate: 31.3%*		
2009	35.2	33.3	33.4	32.6	30.7	30.0
2010	39.8	37.4	37.4	37.4	34.9	33.9
2011	40.4	38.2	38.2	37.7	35.7	34.9

Notes: TT 0–14 is for targeted cash transfer to all predicted poor children age 0–14 years old; UT 0–5 is for universal transfer for all children age 0–5 years old.

Source: Authors' calculation.

universal programme is bolstered further if we take into account that it is easier and less costly to administer than a targeted programme.

A universal cash transfer programme could also be integrated with a school feeding programme, which would mean targeting school-age children, starting with the most deprived districts in the country. In the case of Cameroon, a programme of this sort was estimated to cost the government 0.19 per cent of GDP and lead to a decrease in both national monetary poverty and hunger rates for children by 0.6 and 2.6 percentage points, respectively (Bibi et al., 2010b). A programme in Burkina Faso would have a smaller impact, as school participation there is still very low.

Hunger

The cash transfer is also very effective in reducing hunger rates, especially in Burkina Faso and Cameroon. In Ghana, there are no substantial differences between the impacts of food subsidies and a targeted cash transfer (Figure 5.2).

School participation and child labour

As for the child welfare dimensions analysed above, a cash transfer appears to be relatively more effective in combating the impacts of the crisis (Figure 5.3). This is particularly true for Burkina Faso, where school participation for children age 7–10 years old increases by up to 0.5 percentage points (entirely through the 'school/no work' alternative) in comparison with participation during the crisis, whereas child labour participation rates fall by up to 0.8 percentage points. In Ghana, thanks to the cash transfer, school participation for children age 6–10 years old increases by up to 0.2 percentage points in comparison with the results under the crisis. Finally, in Cameroon, school and labour participation are not affected significantly by the crisis or policy responses, as income is not a major determinant in these decisions.

However, these and other demand-side policies would likely be much more effective in the presence of complementary improvements on the supply side.[3]

As for older children (age 11–14), the effects are somewhat smaller, but generally follow the same pattern (Figure 5.4).

Access to health services

A targeted cash transfer policy is found to be very effective in offsetting the impact of the crisis on the use of health services in Burkina Faso and Cameroon (Figure 5.5). The impact is much weaker in Ghana, given the smaller relative size of the transfer and less sensitivity to income levels. In terms of choice of health services, cash transfers counteract the movement in favour of less formal health services engendered by the crisis. In Burkina Faso, cash transfers more than halve the increase in recourse to traditional healers, which is roughly 1 percentage point in 2011, and instead diverts most of these children towards the more formal CSPS system.

Conclusion

The global financial and economic crisis, which exacerbated the impacts of the energy and food crises that immediately preceded it, has spread to developing countries, endangering recent gains in terms of economic growth and poverty reduction. The effects of the crisis are likely to vary substantially between countries and between individuals within the same country, with children among the most vulnerable. Especially in least developed countries (LDCs), where social safety net programmes are missing or perform poorly, and where public fiscal space is extremely limited, households with few economic opportunities are at a higher risk of falling into (monetary) poverty, suffering from hunger, removing children from school and putting them into work and losing access to health services.

This chapter simulated the impacts of the global economic crisis and alternative policy responses on different dimensions of child welfare in WCA over the period 2009–11. It based these on country studies for Burkina Faso, Cameroon and Ghana, which broadly represent the diversity of economic conditions in WCA countries. In order to capture the complex macroeconomic effects of the crisis and the various policy responses on trade (investment, remittances, aid flows and goods and factor markets), and then to trace their consequences in terms of child welfare (monetary poverty, hunger [caloric poverty], education, child labour and access to health services), a combination of macro and micro analysis was adopted.

Benefits from falling import prices only partially offset the negative effects of reduced export prices and volumes, FDI, remittances and foreign aid. Different patterns emerge across the countries under analysis. While Cameroon's growth rate is predicted to have begun to recover in 2010, according to our simulations we need to wait until 2011 to see economic growth start to recover in Burkina Faso and Ghana.

Ghana is the country where children are predicted to suffer most from the global crisis, with monetary poverty rates increasing by more than 6 percentage points, which translates into around 630,000 additional children in poverty. Impacts in Burkina Faso and Cameroon are more modest, at roughly 4 and 2 percentage points, respectively (around 259,000 and 173,000 additional children, respectively, predicted to fall into monetary poverty as a result of the crisis).

Children in Ghana are also the most severely affected in terms of hunger, with increases of almost 7 percentage points (corresponding to around 620,000 additional children), compared with negligible effects in Burkina Faso and Cameroon. This is primarily because of the greater monetary poverty impacts already noted and because in Ghana food prices are predicted to increase much more than non-food prices.

In addition, the model adopted in the analysis predicts a reduction in school attendance of around 0.8 percentage points for 7–10-year-old children in Burkina Faso (12,000 additional 7–10-year-old children out of school) and an increase in participation in labour activities by 1.1 percentage points (18,000 more 7–10-year-old working children). In Cameroon and Ghana, the effects of the crisis on school participation and child labour are predicted to be negligible.

Finally, the crisis also affects children's access to health services, particularly in Burkina Faso, where the consultation rate for any kind of health facility is simulated to decline from 67.1 per cent of sick children using health facilities in the base year (preceding the crisis) to 65.9 per cent in 2010, the year when the effect on access is predicted to be the highest. This reduction corresponds to an approximate increase in the number of sick children not seeking health assistance by 4,000.

Among the policy responses examined to counteract the negative effects of the crisis on children, a targeted cash transfer to children predicted (based on a proxy means test approach) to be poor is by far the most effective programme, particularly in Burkina Faso and Cameroon. With the same overall budget, which we assume to be financed by foreign aid and to be equal to 1 per cent of GDP, food subsidies have smaller effects, on average.

The cash transfer is most effective in Burkina Faso where, as in Cameroon, it is able to fully offset the negative effects of the crisis on child monetary poverty. This policy is also very effective in reducing hunger among children in Burkina Faso and particularly Cameroon. Indeed, this policy is even able to reduce hunger by 3–4 percentage points in these countries relative to levels predicted in the absence of the crisis. In absolute terms, due to this policy, in Burkina Faso around 256,000 and 120,000 children would escape monetary poverty and hunger, respectively, after the crisis; in Cameroon, these figures would be roughly 200,000 and 390,000, respectively. As we put no limits on the number of beneficiary children living in the same (poor) household, it follows that a cash transfer targeted at children is a progressive policy response, as households with more children, which are usually poorer, benefit proportionately more.

We should highlight that designing and implementing a cash transfer programme requires time and cannot represent an immediate response to the crisis. Only Ghana may be in a position to rapidly implement a cash transfer programme, as it can build on the existing Livelihood Empowerment Against Poverty (LEAP) programme. Other interventions (or a mix of policies) might be more cost-effective in the short run. A combination of a universal or regionally targeted (starting with those regions where child poverty is most widespread) cash transfer programme for children age 0–5 years old, together with a school feeding programme for school-age children, might represent a more effective way to intervene quickly to improve child wellbeing. Given the same budget, a cash transfer provided to all children under six years of age is estimated to lead to child monetary poverty rates that are substantially similar to the case in which a cash transfer is targeted to all children (0–14 years old) predicted as poor. It also has the advantage of favouring younger children, who are the most vulnerable, and avoiding erroneously excluding poor children, as occurs in the targeted approach.

In general, a note of caution regarding these results is in order, given that cash transfers and other demand-side policies will be most effective in the presence of complementary improvements from the supply side.

Notes

Our sincere thanks to Barbara Bentein and Anthony Hodges (UNICEF West and Central Africa Regional Office); Leonardo Menchini and David Parker (UNICEF Innocenti Research Centre); Ronald Mendoza (UNICEF Division of Policy and Practice); Theodore O. Antwi-Asare and Daniel K. Twerefou (University of Ghana); Lacina Balma and Samuel Kaboré (Université de Ouagadougou); Sami Bibi (Université Laval); Edgar F.A. Cooke (Sussex University); Massa Coulibaly (Groupe de Recherche en Economie Appliquée et Théorique, Mali); Christian Emini (Université de Yaoundé II) and Paul Ningaye (Université de Dschang) for their support and contributions to this study. We also thank Pa Lamin Beyai, Pedro Conceição, Emanuele Ferrari, Wei Ha, Sarah Martelli, Leonardo Menchini, Anthony Ngororano, Isiyaka Sabo, Lisa Singh and Felicite Tchibindat for reviews and helpful comments.

This chapter draws largely on Cockburn et al., (2010). The research was conducted between June 2009 and December 2009, as part of a study commissioned by the UN Children's Fund (UNICEF) and conducted by the African office of the Poverty and Economic Policy (PEP) Research Network (www.pep-net.org) in collaboration with UNICEF's Innocenti Research Centre.

1. The pre-crisis period is the period ending in 2006 when the energy crisis began, followed by the food crisis and then the global economic crisis.
2. It is noteworthy that, when a relative poverty line (equal to 50 per cent of the median value of consumption) is used, child monetary poverty rates are 13.9 per cent in Burkina Faso, 30.6 per cent in Ghana and 20.8 per cent in Cameroon. If an absolute international (extreme) poverty line equal to $1.25 2005 purchasing power parity (PPP) is used, child monetary poverty rates are 46.8 per cent in Burkina Faso, 12.2 per cent in Ghana and 16.0 per cent in Cameroon. When an absolute poverty line equal to $2 2005 PPP is used, child monetary poverty rates are 72.3 per cent in Burkina Faso, 31.6 per cent in Ghana and 40.8 per cent in Cameroon. Although the two international absolute poverty lines proposed by the World Bank are widely debated, it emerges clearly that Burkina Faso has adopted a national absolute poverty line which is far below both and which thus needs to be revised, whereas Ghana has adopted an (upper-bound) absolute poverty line very close to $2 2005 PPP, which also happens to be close to the relative poverty line of above 50 per cent of median consumption value. Cameroon's poverty line is closer to the $1.25 standard.
3. This result is widely confirmed by Kakwani et al. (2006), who assess the impact of cash transfers for school-age children in 15 African countries, even when a huge (and unrealistic) budget is devoted to this aim.

References

Bibi, S., Cockburn, J., Fofana, I. and Tiberti, L. (2010a) 'Impacts of the Global Crisis and Policy Responses on Child Well-being: A Macro–Micro Simulation Framework.' Working Paper 2010-06. Dakar and Florence: UNICEF WCA Regional Office and UNICEF Innocenti Research Centre.

Bibi, S., Cockburn, J., Emini, C.A., Fofana, I., Ningaye, P. and Tiberti, L. (2010b) 'Incidences de la Crise Economique Mondiale de 2008/09 et des Options de Politiques de Réponse sur la Pauvreté des Enfants au Cameroun.' Working Paper 2010-04. Dakar and Florence: UNICEF WCA Regional Office and UNICEF Innocenti Research Centre.

Cockburn, J., Fofana, I. and Tiberti, L. (2010) 'Simulating the Impact of the Global Economic Crisis and Policy Responses on Children in West and Central Africa.' Working Paper 2010-01. Dakar and Florence: UNICEF WCA Regional Office and UNICEF Innocenti Research Centre.

European Report on Development (2009) *Overcoming Fragility in Africa: Forging a New European Approach.* Fiesole: Robert Schuman Centre for Advanced Studies, European University Institute.

IMF (2009a) 'World Economic Outlook.' IMF World Economic and Financial Survey. Washington, DC: IMF.

IMF (2009b) 'Regional Economic Outlook: Sub-Saharan Africa.' World Economic and Financial Survey. Washington, DC: IMF.

Kakwani, N., Soares, F. and Son, H.H. (2006) 'Cash Transfers for School-age Children in African Countries: Simulation of Impacts on Poverty and School Attendance.' *Development Policy Review* 24(5): 553–69.

Ratha, D., Mohapatra, S. and Silwal, A. (2009) 'Outlook for Remittance Flows 2009-2011: Remittances Expected to Fall by 7-10 Percent in 2009.' Migration and Development Brief 10. Washington, DC: Migration and Remittances Team, Development Prospects Group, World Bank.

UNCTAD (2009) 'Assessing the Impact of the Current Financial and Economic Crisis on Global FDI Flows.' Geneva: Division on Investment and Enterprise, UNCTAD.

World Bank (2008) 'Lessons from World Bank Research on Financial Crises.' Policy Research Working Paper 4779. Washington, DC: World Bank.

6
Child Poverty in South Africa and the Global Financial and Economic Crisis

Ramos Mabugu, Servaas van der Berg, Debra Shepherd, Margaret Chitiga-Mabugu, Bernard Decaluwé, Hélène Maisonnave, Véronique Robichaud and Dieter von Fintel

Introduction

Poverty in South Africa is much higher than one might expect for a country with its level of per capita gross domestic product (GDP), given high inequality and the fact that child poverty is much higher than that among adults. Child poverty prevents children from developing to their full potential and leads to poor human capital and lower productivity in later life, thus creating the risk of a vicious circle of poverty. To ensure that upward mobility is possible for those born into poor families, we need to create circumstances that will minimise this phenomenon.

The global economic crisis has again put child poverty on the global agenda. This chapter reports on a study that links a macroeconomic computable general equilibrium (CGE) model to microeconomic analysis to identify the channels through which economic performance may impact on child poverty. It estimates the possible impact such a global crisis may have had on child poverty and assesses whether policies to deal with child poverty (particularly the Child Support Grant [CSG]) have had the desired effect. The full results of this study have been reported elsewhere (Chitiga et al., 2010); this chapter reports on child poverty only.

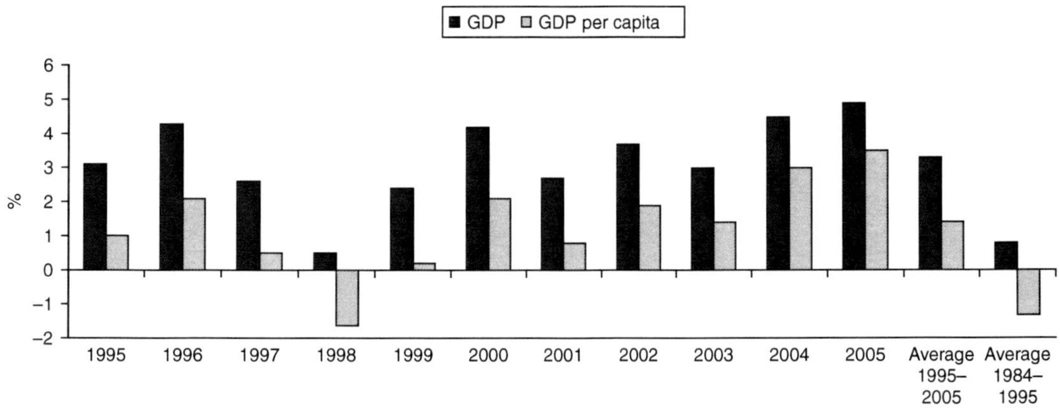

Figure 6.1 GDP and GDP per capita growth rates (constant 2000 prices) (per cent)

Source: South African Reserve Bank (SARB) database (www.reservebank.co.za).

The economic crisis

The global financial crisis and resulting economic crisis had serious impacts on developing countries. South Africa did not escape these impacts. The economy started to emerge from recession in 2009 but employment did not recover. Salary increases remained smaller than anticipated, despite stubbornly high inflation, and house prices have not yet fully returned to positive growth.

To the extent that South Africa's historical economic growth rate has been very closely linked to that of the world economy since 1993–4, reduced prospects for the world economy imply reduced domestic growth.

In this context, it is likely that poverty has been increasing and that this has affected children. The concern is for the extent to which the crisis has undermined gains in child wellbeing in recent years, as well as the achievement of child-related targets in Vision 2014 and the Millennium Development Goals (MDGs). It is important to consider how these effects are mediated via mechanisms that may partly protect children from such shocks.

Child poverty in South Africa

To derive a profile of child poverty, a poverty line is set at the 40th percentile of household per capita income in the 2005 Income and

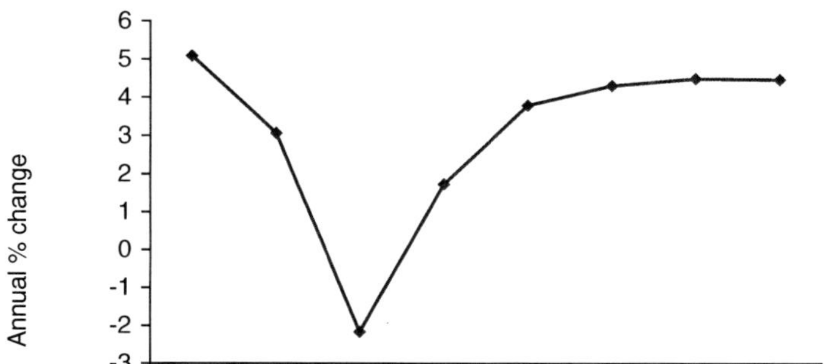

	2007	2008	2009	2010	2011	2012	2013	2014
Annual % change	5.098	3.062	-2.171	1.739	3.815	4.325	4.494	4.484

Figure 6.2 Growth projections for South Africa (annual per cent change)

Note: Estimates start after 2008.

Source: IMF World Economic Outlook Database, October 2009.

Expenditure Survey (IES) of 2005. Such a line is arbitrary, but accords with what has been used by a number of other authors. Streak et al. (2009) conclude that the child poverty profile is little affected by the use of any adult equivalent scale and that there is stochastic poverty dominance across most dimensions;[1] that is, an alternative poverty line or a measure other than the headcount ratio would not much affect the broad poverty profile. Thus, the use of per capita income here rather than adult equivalent income reflects that our findings on the insensitivity of the child poverty profile to the choice of adult equivalence scale support the argument of Woolard and Leibbrandt (2006) that one may as well use the simple per capita method for profiling poverty in South Africa and testing its robustness to alternative poverty lines.

Table 6.1 presents the profile of child poverty. As poor households tend to be larger, the poverty headcount for the population as a whole is 52.9 per cent. But poorer households contain a disproportionate number of children: 11.8 million or 65.5 per cent of children are among the poor versus only 45.2 per cent of the adult population. Similar differences between adult and child poverty apply for the depth and severity of poverty. In fact, proportional differentials are larger, indicating that children's share of the poverty headcount rises if lower poverty lines are used, due to more severe poverty among children.

Table 6.1 illustrates that the poverty headcount is highest for the youngest age cohort, followed by children age 5–14 and 15–17, but differences are small and the ordering changes for poverty depth and severity. Given that the CSG did not extend to the oldest group at the time of the survey, one would have expected households containing only older children to experience more poverty. The profile also confirms the racial dimension of child poverty, with headcount, depth and severity of poverty much higher among black children. There is little gender difference in child poverty, but it is still more prevalent, deeper and more severe in rural areas: nearly two-thirds of children identified as poor live in rural areas. This is the most prominent feature of child poverty in South Africa, especially when depth and severity of poverty are considered: the rural poor are further below this poverty line than the urban poor, and the share of the rural child poverty headcount thus rises as the poverty line is set lower.

There is also large variation in child poverty across provinces. Although poverty incidence is highest in Limpopo, the poverty *share* of more populous provinces is larger, with Kwazulu-Natal and the Eastern Cape together containing 46 per cent of poor children. Rankings for

Table 6.1 Poverty profile for children and adults

	Child poverty (0–17 years)					Adult poverty		
	P_0 Poverty head count rate			P_1 Poverty depth measure	P_2 Poverty severity measure	P_0 Poverty headcount rate (%)	P_1 Poverty depth measure	P_2 Poverty severity measure
	Rate (%)	Share (%)	No.					
Age								
0–4	66.1	26.0	3,066,509	0.336	0.213			
5–14	65.7	56.5	6,681,507	0.343	0.202			
15–17	63.8	17.5	2,067,609	0.332	0.203			
0–17 (all children)	65.5	100.0	11,822,544	0.328	0.205			
18+ (all adults)						45.2	0.213	0.126
Racial group								
Black	72.5	93.9	11,100 826	0.375	0.232	54.4	0.261	0.156
Coloured	41.3	5.3	623,412	0.167	0.093	30.1	0.110	0.057
Asian	24.2	0.7	76,137	0.093	0.052	13.7	0.049	0.027
White	2.0	0.2	18,081	0.012	0.008	1.2	0.006	0.004
Gender								
Girls	65.4	49.1	5,819,410	0.336	0.204	39.7	0.238	0.142
Boys	65.6	50.9	5,985,265	0.332	0.206	49.9	0.184	0.109
Urban/rural								
Rural	82.8	63.3	7,376,451	0.446	0.280	69.0	0.344	0.209
Urban	48.6	36.7	4,442,491	0.226	0.133	31.7	0.139	0.080
Province								
Western Cape	37.9	5.0	587,580	0.153	0.085	25.1	0.094	0.048
Eastern Cape	77.9	20.1	2,378,696	0.415	0.258	59.8	0.292	0.174
Northern Cape	69.1	2.0	235,269	0.333	0.195	48.5	0.219	0.126
Free State	63.6	5.9	695,166	0.294	0.171	44.2	0.193	0.110
Kwazulu-Natal	75.0	25.2	2,975,734	0.413	0.266	53.8	0.279	0.175
Northwest	66.2	8.1	962,355	0.345	0.216	49.3	0.239	0.143
Gauteng	41.3	9.6	1,138,511	0.186	0.110	26.0	0.111	0.065
Mpumalanga	66.4	7.2	846,494	0.322	0.187	48.6	0.218	0.123
Limpopo	78.0	16.9	2,002,739	0.400	0.242	65.6	0.313	0.183

Source: Authors' calculations using IES 2005 data.

poverty severity measures are slightly different from those for depth and headcount measures, indicating that stochastic poverty dominance does not always hold.

Testing the sensitivity of the child poverty profile to the selection of the poverty line resulted in the findings that race, gender and urban/rural dimensions are robust. In the poverty-relevant range, there is clear first-order dominance in each of these cases, implying that poverty rankings are invariant to the poverty line chosen and invariant to whether the poverty measure used is P_0, P_1 or P_2. The same does not apply to poverty between provinces, where some rankings are sensitive to the choice of poverty line or poverty measure, as was the case for age group of children.

Trends in child poverty and the role of social grants

There is evidence that poverty declined substantially after 2000, caused largely by the expansion of social grants, in particular the CSG. Non-comparability between surveys obscures the measurement of poverty trends, but a non-money metric measure, child hunger, as reported by respondents in large annual household surveys, was on a consistent downward trend until 2007. This also applies to the severity of reported hunger: the more severe measures, of always or often experiencing hunger, also dropped strongly (Figure 6.3). Importantly, the turnaround in the trend in reported hunger in 2008 following the advent of the global crisis is in line with expectations and strengthens one's confidence in this social indicator.

The CSG was introduced after the political transition and it expanded dramatically in scale and as a proportion of total spending on social grants. By April of 2001, approximately 1 million people received it; this had increased more than eight-fold by April of 2008. Figure 6.4 confirms that the CSG is the most rapidly growing grant type.

It is thus worth investigating the role of the grants system in driving down poverty. Table 6.2 and Figure 6.5 show coverage has expanded in two ways. On the one hand, coverage of those in the age-eligible group has grown over time; on the other hand, age eligibility has increased from initially being those below eight years of age to cover those below 15.[2] There was a continuous upward trend in the percentage of age-eligible children receiving the CSG (that is, in the coverage rate), from 27.0 per cent to 45.6 per cent, between 2003 and 2006. The coverage rate was more than 50 per cent in 2006 in Eastern

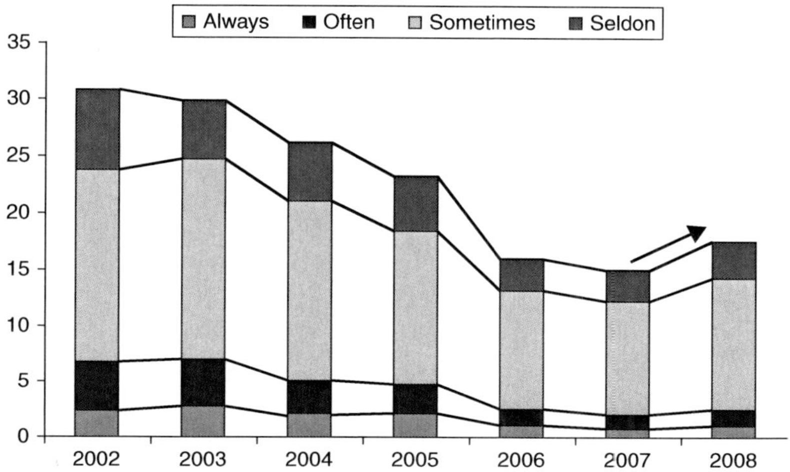

Figure 6.3 Households that reported that children went hungry in the past year (per cent)

Source: Authors' calculations from General Household Surveys (GHSs).

Cape, Mpumalanga and Limpopo, but the lowest in Western Cape and Gauteng, reflecting differences in poverty prevalence. Coverage in provinces containing most poor children was initially low due to slow rollout, but it rose very rapidly (from less than 26 per cent to over 56 per cent in Eastern Cape). Amazingly, the programme also succeeded in expanding coverage to be greater in rural areas than in urban areas, something seldom achieved in social programmes in developing countries.

Figure 6.6 shows that targeting was fairly good (a far higher proportion of age-eligible children received the grant in the poorest deciles) and that progressiveness increased with increased rollout over time. However, there were still major errors of exclusion: many age-eligible children in the lowest income deciles did not receive the grant.

More than 50 per cent of CSG recipients come from households headed by females. Coverage rates for households headed by males and females are quite similar, implying that the latter constitute the majority of households with age-eligible children.

It has been shown that expansion of the social grant system, in particular the CSG, was instrumental in reducing poverty in the period after 2000 (van der Berg et al., 2008). However, policymakers fear

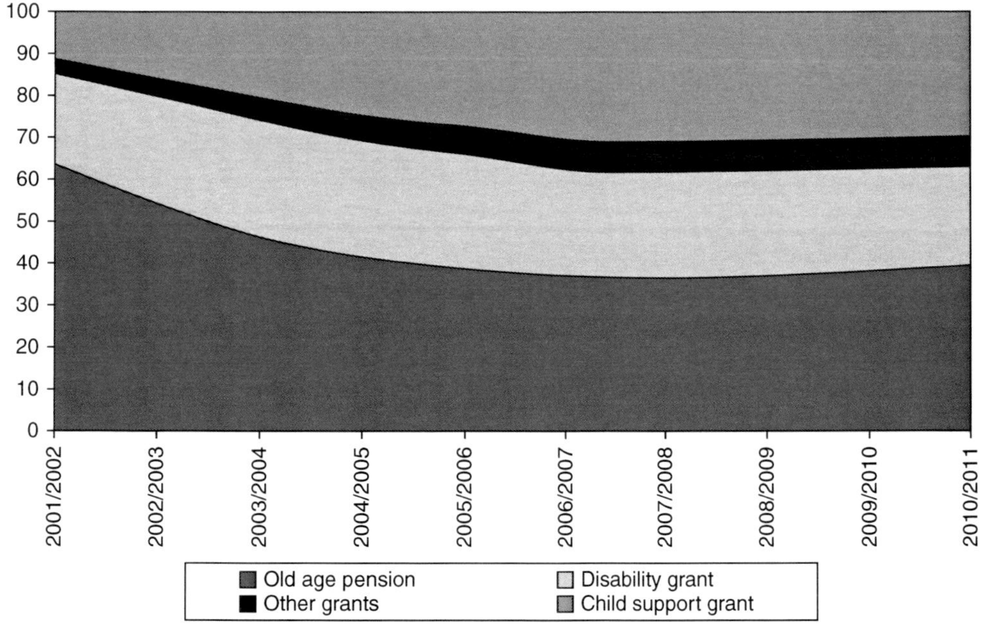

Figure 6.4 Contribution of spending on each social grant type to total spending on social grants (per cent)

Source: National Treasury website (www.treasury.gov.za/).

Table 6.2 Number of individuals and households receiving the CSG

	Eligible age	Recipients: Of eligible age [A]	Recipients: Not of eligible age [B]	Recipients: Total [C]	Population of eligible age [D]	Coverage rate [A]/[D]
Individuals						
2003	0–8	2,241,760	321,534	2,563,294	8,299,039	27.01%
2004	0–10	4,201,481	175,526	4,377,007	11,100,241	37.85%
2005	0–13	5,702,793	139,043	5,841,836	14,052,170	40.58%
2006	0–13	6,459,760	265,579	6,725,339	14,152,509	45.64%
GHS	**Eligible age**	**No. of households containing at least one child of eligible age**	**No. of households containing no children of eligible age**	**Total**	**No. of households containing at least one child of eligible age**	**Coverage rate**
Households						
2002	0–6	845,577	79,725	925,302	4,329,616	19.53%
2003	0–8	1,830,602	42,599	1,873,201	5,141,072	35.61%
2004	0–10	2,776,295	29,621	2,805,916	6,054,697	45.85%
2005	0–13	3,289,555	20,455	3,310,010	6,701,973	49.08%
2006	0–13	3,504,585	35,843	3,540,428	6,884,332	50.91%

Source: Authors' calculations from GHSs.

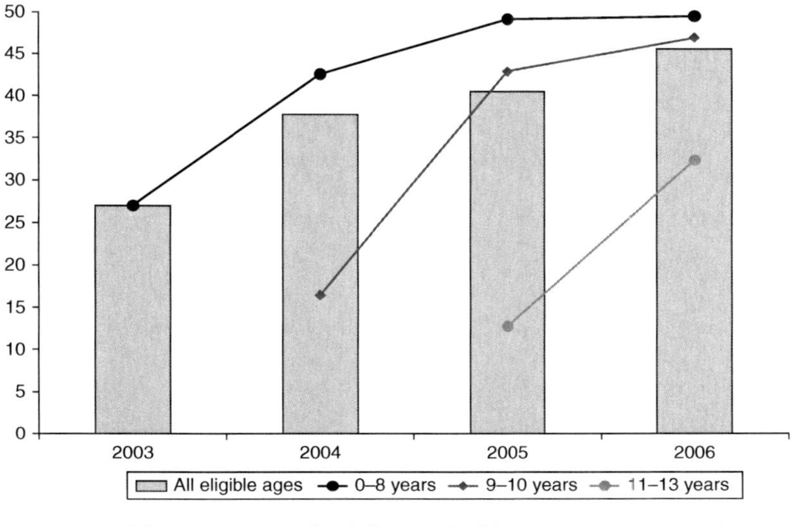

Figure 6.5 CSG coverage rates for different eligible age groups (per cent)
Source: Authors' calculations from GHSs.

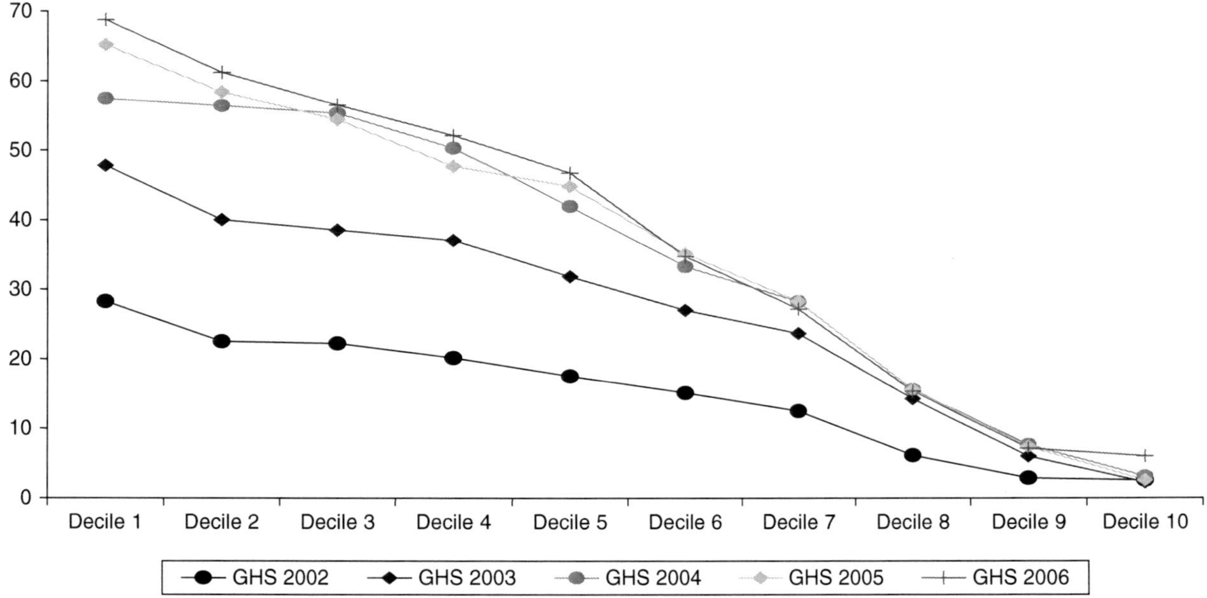

Figure 6.6 Progression over time in CSG coverage rates in households (per cent)

Note: Deciles arranged by earnings decile of the employed.

Source: Authors' calculations from GHSs.

Table 6.3 Eligible children receiving the CSG by demographic characteristics (per cent)

	GHS 2003	GHS 2004	GHS 2005	GHS 2006
All	**27.0**	**37.9**	**40.6**	**45.6**
Province				
Western Cape	23.5	26.6	25.4	27.5
Eastern Cape	25.8	34.0	46.8	56.3
Northern Cape	14.0	34.6	37.2	39.0
Free State	34.3	42.9	47.0	49.4
KwaZulu-Natal	21.6	33.5	38.4	43.5
North West	29.6	45.9	40.6	48.4
Gauteng	19.3	26.8	29.1	32.2
Mpumalanga	38.3	48.4	47.9	54.8
Limpopo	39.7	55.9	51.4	54.2
Area type				
Urban	21.9	29.9	n/a	n/a
Rural	31.7	44.7	n/a	n/a
Gender				
Male	26.6	37.4	40.4	45.1
Female	27.4	38.4	40.9	46.2
Race				
Black	30.8	43.0	45.5	51.1
Coloured	16.0%	24.1%	25.0%	26.6%
Indian	2.3%	5.8%	12.6%	16.6%
White	0.8%	0.3%	0.8%	0.8%

Note: Area type is no longer available from GHS 2005.

Source: Authors' calculations from GHSs.

that the CSG could also potentially create important perverse incentive effects that may undermine its beneficial influence on poverty. Incentives related to the grant structure and rules could affect work effort, household formation, location of children (in situations where households are often loosely structured) and even fertility, while social grants have a large fiscal cost. Although some doubt the magnitude of these perverse incentive effects, and there is conflicting evidence, at least on labour supply (Ardington et al., 2009; Klasen and Woolard 2008), it is nevertheless important to consider such potential effects. A simple way of illustrating this is to imagine what would happen if the grant were 10 times or 20 times as large as it is currently. In the context of substantial poverty, there can be little doubt that this would indeed increase fertility in some contexts. Thus, the question is not whether grants *can* have such perverse incentive effects, but rather how large these are and whether possible negative incentive effects outweigh their positive impact on child poverty. Our assessment, based on the available literature, is that the grants have strong beneficial effects, but one must doubt the fiscal sustainability of attempts to expand them further.

The grants have been reducing poverty in a time of good economic growth. Attempts to measure their effects on non-money metric child outcomes have not been very convincing, due to data issues and because their relatively small size limits the impact and makes its measurement difficult. Measured effects include earlier school enrolment (Case et al., 2005), although this may be specific to the rural area studied, as most school-age children are enrolled in school (Agüero et al., 2006), and weak evidence on nutritional outcomes (ibid.; Coetzee, 2010).

However, the disruption to growth and the world economic crisis may have reversed some of the poverty improvement, as the figure on child hunger above illustrates. A hypothesis of this chapter is that the grants also provide a measure of protection against economic shocks. Social grants offer a form of income diversification and, like all forms of such diversification, some protection for beneficiaries against risks of income loss, for example from losing a job. Thus, one might consider the CSG an important factor assisting those affected by the economic crisis to cope.

The next part of the chapter turns to the macroeconomy, to assess how great the impact of the economic crisis may have been on GDP, employment and consumption. This is then linked to the labour market, to assess the full impact on poverty and specifically child poverty. It should be remembered that this modelling was undertaken while the crisis was still in full swing, with its outcome, severity and duration not yet known. It also attempts to isolate the effects of the global crisis from the effect of any possible other shocks.

Modelling the economic impact of the crisis against the Business as Usual simulation

The main data used for the economy-wide modelling came from the Social Accounting Matrix (SAM). This is a presentation of the national accounts in a condensed matrix form with the important property that the sum of the row elements is equal to the sum of the corresponding column elements. It provides a consistent quantitative macroeconomic data framework representing flows between different sectors and institutional units within an economy, therefore describing the general equilibrium of an economy. The selected SAM was for South Africa for 2005, updated from 2001. It had 54 activities and 54 commodities; two broad factors (labour and capital); four institutional sector accounts (households, enterprises, government and rest of the world); and two saving and investment accounts (change in inventories and gross domestic fixed investment (GDFI)). Trade, demand, industry production and household demand parameters were borrowed from other sources and unemployment rates from the Labour Force Survey. Import penetration and export intensity rates reflected existing trade patterns.

To evaluate the impacts of the crisis on South Africa, we used the dynamic Poverty and Economic Policy (PEP 1-t) standard model by Decaluwé et al. (2009), changing several assumptions to better reflect the South African economy. A full description of the model and the methodology is provided elsewhere; Figure 6.7 gives the value-added structure.

South Africa faces high unemployment but unions are very strong. As a result, wages and salaries are strongly rigid downwards. To take this into account, we assumed that wages could not decline. Thus, if production decreased, producers would not have been able to decrease their wages below initial levels, and would therefore have had to retrench some workers.

As the model did not take into account financial flows, it cannot directly capture the financial consequences of the crisis for the South African economy. However, the economic consequences of the global

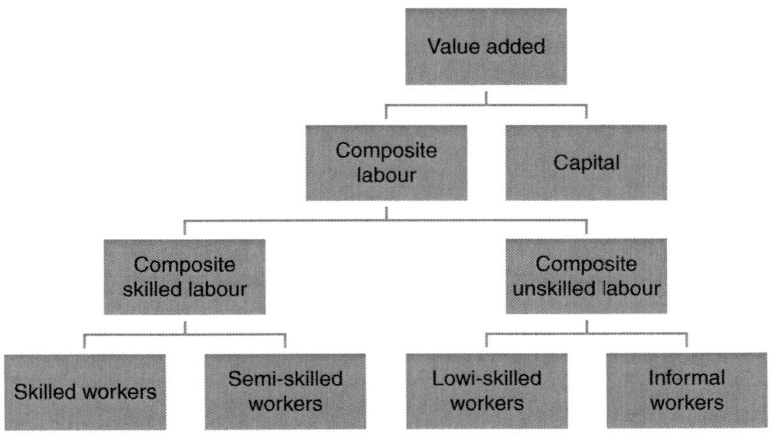

Figure 6.7 The value-added structure
Source: Authors' model.

slowdown were captured through the real side of the CGE model. The main transmission channels of the crisis to developing countries were decreased export demand and export prices, decreased foreign direct investment (FDI) and tightened capacity to finance a current account deficit, decreased remittances from abroad and a drop in tourism revenues. The latter two channels are not relevant to South Africa, as the country did not receive substantial remittances from abroad and tourism did not decrease. Thus, we focused on external trade and foreign financing of domestic firms.

The Business as Usual (BaU) simulation used consensus growth forecasts by economists of around 4.5 per cent of GDP growth for 2005 and beyond. In technical terms, we generated a BaU that fits with 4.5 per cent GDP growth, allowing the total factor productivity parameters to adjust. Because the model is recursive dynamic, it was solved over a ten-year time horizon. Other data requirements related to GDP, population and labour force growth and capital stock. Statistics of South Africa estimates that the population will grow at around 1 per cent annually. Calibrating the BaU on these 'real' data, capital grows faster than labour, so the BaU reflects a decrease in unemployment. Moreover, as production factors become more efficient, prices decrease (in real terms). These pieces of information are important to understanding the results.

An innovation of this study was that we split the economy into four different groups of activities, defined by their degree of dependence/exposure to the crisis:

- **Unaffected sectors (Group 1):** It was assumed these sectors would not face a reduction in foreign demand or in international prices (gold, food and beverage commodities).
- **Weakly affected sectors (Group 2):** These sectors were not heavily dependent on foreign trade and not closely related to other sectors (agriculture, clothing, wood).
- **Mildly affected sectors (Group 3):** These sectors were also not heavily dependent on foreign trade but were linked closely to other sectors. Such sectors reacted to a reduction in consumption, investment expenditures or demand for intermediate goods (most transport products, trade, construction).
- **Strongly affected sectors (Group 4):** These sectors were linked closely to international markets through either exports or imports (fossil fuels, other mining, machinery and equipment).

Mildly affected sectors represented around 60 per cent of total output, while strongly and mildly affected sectors together represented 80 per cent of total exports.

Over and above the BaU scenario, two scenarios are presented that were distinguished by the magnitude of the recession (severe or moderate) (Table 6.4). The moderate scenario was consistent with the fact that growth began to pick up, albeit moderately, from the end of 2009. We also modelled a severe scenario, which reflected a protracted slow global growth era and implied tight public budgets for some time to come. It was important to investigate what impact this scenario might have on the sustainability of interventions to protect children and poor families and to obtain an indication of how its magnitude compares with that of the beneficial impact of grants.

Results from the macroeconomic modelling

The various simulations had differential impacts on industries' output, modified the entire price structure and consequently caused factor reallocation. Impacts on households depended on their factor endowments and their consumption patterns. These effects were different in the short run compared with the long run; this is partly why dynamic analysis was called for.

GDP falls in the short run (2008–10) but rises gradually to its BaU trend in the long run (2011–15) (Figure 6.8), when the shock of the crisis is expected to have petered out and capital is mobile. The magnitudes

Table 6.4 Assumptions for moderate and severe scenarios

	Changes in world prices of exports and imports	**Changes in world demand for exports**
Moderate scenario		
Weakly affected	–2% in 2008 and 2009	
Mildly affected	–3.5% in 2008–9 and +2.1% in 2010	–2% in 2008–9 and +2.1% in 2010
Strongly affected	–5% in 2008–9 and +2.1% in 2010	–2% in 2008–9 and +2.1% in 2010
Severe scenario		
Weakly affected	–10% in 2008 and 2009	
Mildly affected	–15% in 2008 and 2009	–10% in 2008–09 and +1% in 2010
Strongly affected	–20% in 2008 and 2009	–10% in 2008–09

Source: Authors' assumptions.

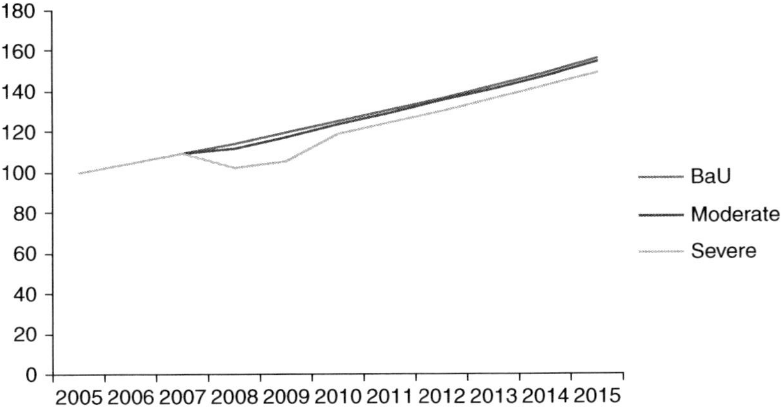

Figure 6.8 Evolution of real GDP in BaU, moderate and severe scenarios
Source: Authors' calculations.

involved are small in the moderate scenario because of the nature of the shock but quite pronounced in the severe scenario.

Results on unemployment were quite surprising (Table 6.5). For high-skilled labour, the initial level of unemployment was very small (1 per cent), so a small nominal decrease translated into a large proportional increase in unemployment. All types of labour were likely to have been affected, but for highly skilled workers, from 2010 in the moderate scenario and 2011 in the severe scenario, the economy returns to a skills shortage. Impacts on employment of low-skilled labour were quite large.

As expected, the effects of the crisis on the South African economy were really quite harsh, even in the moderate recession scenario, in both the short run and the long run. Indeed, the decrease of world prices combined with the drop in world demand led to a decrease in production and labour demand for many sectors. Even if the crisis itself lasted only two years (2008 and 2009), its effects relative to BaU lasted much longer, notably because of the permanent impact of the drop in investment.

Extrapolating from the macroeconomic impact to child poverty

The impacts described above were used in conjunction with a micro model of the economy to estimate the likely impact of the crisis on South African child poverty. The methodological approach for the

Table 6.5 Impact on total labour demand (per cent change from BaU)

	High-skilled		Skilled and semi-skilled		Low-skilled	
	Moderate	Severe	Moderate	Severe	Moderate	Severe
2008	–4.40	–20.73	–4.90	–19.57	–5.86	–23.87
2009	–2.36	–20.82	–3.96	–20.50	–4.23	–24.65
2010	0	–5.49	–1.33	–7.86	–1.04	–8.24
2015	0	0	–1.21	–6.59	–0.99	–5.28

Source: Authors' calculations.

micro simulations drew on the work of Cockburn et al. (2010) and Bibi et al. (2009; 2010). Essentially, the micro modelling aimed to estimate the impact of the economic changes simulated by the CGE model on households. Essentially, three channels were modelled:

- Changes in prices, taken to apply across the board to all households, differences arising only from the composition of their spending. Note that adult equivalence scales were also applied to allow for differential spending needs of different households;
- Changes in wages in different skill categories;
- Changes in employment for the three formal labour market categories.

A possible fourth channel was not modelled: possible changes in non-labour earnings on household poverty.

Price and wage changes were relatively small and they had little impact on poverty in the models. By far the major impact came from changes in employment. Probit models of the probability of employment for each employed and unemployed worker for jobs in various skills categories were estimated. These were then used to identify those employed workers in each skill category most likely to lose their jobs when employment declined relative to the labour force. Wages of employed workers were assumed to remain as they had been recorded.

The dataset used for the micro simulations was the 2008 National Income Dynamics Survey (NIDS). Data were taken to reflect the approximate situation in 2007 before the crisis, and the modelling was then applied to these data to arrive at simulations. Because the micro simulations essentially dealt with a static model, projections were not attempted beyond 2011. As is shown, by that time poverty would have returned almost to its usual course under both scenarios.

Results of the micro model

Child poverty in 2007, that is, before the crisis, was estimated at 52.6 per cent using the moderately low poverty line of R250 per capita per month in 2000 rand (or R377 in January 2008 rand to apply to NIDS data), a poverty line often quoted in the literature. In the absence of an economic crisis, this headcount rate of child poverty would have been declining by a small percentage every year, based on linking the macro and micro simulations. Thus, BaU would have meant a slow but continuing decline in child poverty to 51.8 per cent in 2011. The most severe effects were simulated for 2008 and 2009. The choice of scale in Figure 6.9 is intended to allow a visual inspection of the different impacts and accentuates the stark difference between severe and moderate scenarios, but note the fairly small range.

The impact of the moderate scenario for the crisis on the child poverty headcount was quite small in 2008 – increasing by 0.1 percentage

Table 6.6 Trends in child poverty under three scenarios

		BaU	% change	Moderate scenario	% change from 2007	Severe scenario	% change from 2007
2007	P0	0.526	0.0				
	P1	0.205	0.0				
	P2	0.107	0.0				
2008	P0	0.522	−0.8	0.527	0.2	0.549	4.4
	P1	0.205	0.0	0.230	12.2	0.294	43.4
	P2	0.106	−0.9	0.137	28.0	0.208	94.4
2009	P0	0.519	−1.3	0.522	−0.8	0.545	3.6
	P1	0.204	−0.5	0.219	6.8	0.304	48.3
	P2	0.106	−0.9	0.125	16.8	0.215	100.9
2010	P0	0.519	−1.3	0.518	−1.5	0.536	1.9
	P1	0.203	−1.0	0.203	−1.0	0.238	16.1
	P2	0.105	−1.9	0.105	−1.9	0.145	35.5
2011	P0	0.518	−1.5	0.518	−1.5	0.529	0.6
	P1	0.201	−2.0	0.202	−1.5	0.228	11.2
	P2	0.104	−2.8	0.104	−2.8	0.135	26.2

Note: Per cent change is shown relative to BaU in 2007.

Source: Authors' projections.

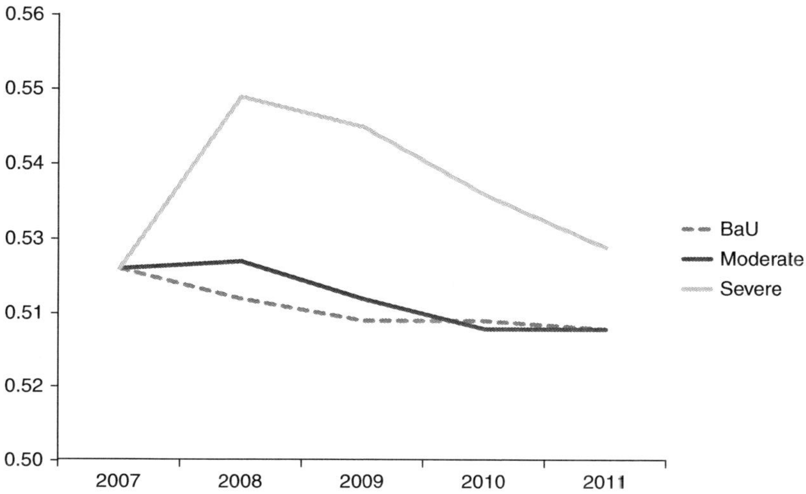

Figure 6.9 Poverty headcount ratio under three scenarios
Source: Authors' calculations.

points or 0.2 per cent only – but there was a 12 per cent increase in the child poverty gap ratio and a 28 per cent increase in the child poverty severity ratio. This indicates that much of the change in the economic situation in 2008 under the moderate scenario occurred at lower income levels, that is, quite some way even below this relatively low poverty line. Thus, those deepest in poverty were also the most affected. Under this scenario, child poverty actually started improving in 2009: the headcount ratio dropped to 52.2 per cent, only 0.3 per cent above the level of poverty that would have applied under BaU and below the initial poverty headcount ratio. Yet some impact on the poverty gap ratio as well as the poverty severity ratio for children remained. This indicates that, although fewer children were in poverty according to the modelling than in 2007, changes at the bottom of the distribution had worsened the situation for the worst-off children. If the poverty line had therefore been drawn at a lower level, the poverty headcount would have risen more.

In the more severe scenario, the child poverty headcount ratio was expected to rise by 4.4 per cent (2.3 percentage points) to 54.9 per cent in 2008 relative to 2007, the poverty gap ratio by 43 per cent and the poverty severity ratio by 94 per cent. This again illustrates the severe consequences for children at the bottom of the income distribution, far below conventionally used poverty lines. Clearly, under the severe economic scenario, very poor children would have been greatly affected by the crisis in 2008. There was little further change in poverty ratios in 2009.

Figure 6.10 shows the effect of the moderate scenario in 2008 and 2009 against the initial situation, in terms of cumulative density functions (CDFs) or poverty incidence curves. If one CDF line lies clearly above another, it reflects more poverty by any of the conventional measures, irrespective of the poverty line chosen. Such a situation is referred to as stochastic poverty dominance. The three lines depicting the initial situation and the moderate scenarios in 2008 and 2009 are barely distinguishable, except at extremely low-income levels, where there is clear poverty dominance. In contrast, the child poverty situation would have been much worse if there had been no CSG: the line depicting that situation lies well above all three other lines. Thus, the moderate scenario for the economic crisis had too small an impact to

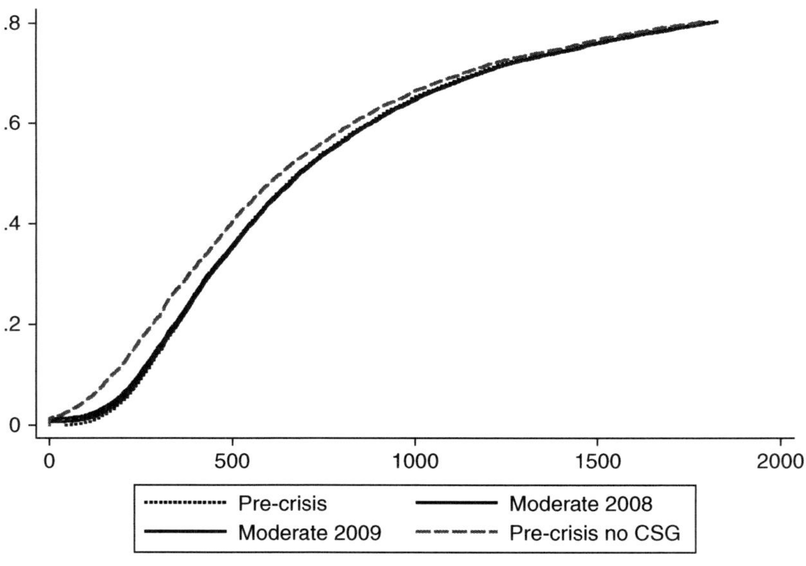

Figure 6.10 CDFs for child poverty, under a moderate scenario, and a comparison with beneficial effects of CSG

Source: Authors' calculations.

undo the beneficial effects for children of the earlier introduction and expansion of the CSG.

Figure 6.11 compares the 2007 situation with the modelled impact of the severe scenario in 2008 and 2009. Here, the impact of the crisis was much clearer and there was complete poverty dominance: irrespective of the poverty measure or line chosen, except for very high poverty lines, there was a large (and probably statistically significant) effect on poverty. Among the very poor, it was even larger than the beneficial effects of the CSG had been.

In summary, then, the CDFs indicate that the effect of the crisis according to our moderate simulation was not all that large. In contrast, the impact of the severe scenario was large, particularly at lower levels; clearly, these poverty impacts would have most affected the poorest.

Using a lower poverty line confirms what the CDFs and the magnitude of the impacts on P1 and the P2 relative to P0 had already intimated, that the major impact of the crisis was among the very poorest.

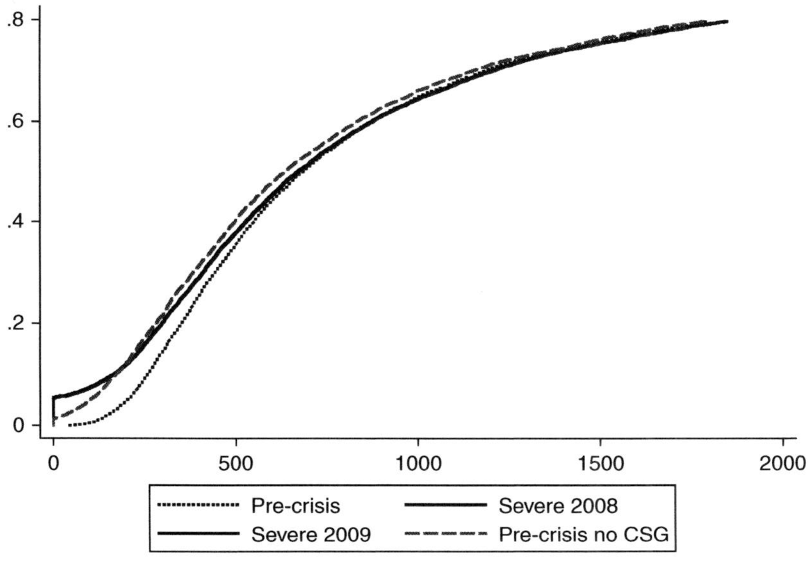

Figure 6.11 CDFs for child poverty, under a severe scenario, and comparison with beneficial effects of CSG

Source: Authors' calculations.

At the lower line, the severe scenario had a greater impact on the poverty headcount ratio.

Breaking down the impacts on child poverty in urban and rural areas takes this analysis further. Poverty among children is generally more severe in rural areas than in urban areas. In 2007, before the crisis, poverty among children in urban areas was 44.9 per cent versus 58.7 per cent in rural areas. The crisis may have had a similar effect in terms of who crossed the poverty line in urban and in rural areas, as the rise in P0 is quite similar. However, the crisis affected already poor children in rural areas much more: under the severe scenario, P2 would have risen by 55 per cent in urban areas and by 136 per cent in rural areas by 2009, and under the moderate scenario, all urban poverty measures would even have improved, while P2 would have deteriorated by 31 per cent in rural areas. Even the price effects, which tend to moderate the difference at lower incomes and in rural areas, could not overcome the greater impact of the negative labour market impact in rural areas.[3]

The greater impact of the crisis at lower income levels and in rural areas may at first glance seem counterintuitive. However, although much of the income loss was likely to occur in urban areas and even among skilled workers, such people were better protected against job losses because they often formed part of households that had a greater variety of other income sources, for example additional earners and non-earnings income. Apart from social grants, which had a similar effect of diversifying income among the poor, the poor and rural dwellers were in many cases quite weakly protected against job loss. It would thus not be surprising if they were pushed below, or further below, the poverty line when losing their jobs.

Conclusion on money-metric poverty impact

What does all of this mean for the children's situation? In the first place, it is clear that the extent of the impact on child poverty depends on the economic scenario one assumes. The moderate scenario, which allowed for a quick return to economic growth, would have had far less severe child poverty impacts. On the other hand, the severe crisis scenario saw quite a strong impact on child poverty, particularly among the very poorest children.

It is worth returning to the poverty impact of the CSG. As it has been indicated, this reduces child poverty both because of good targeting and because children are often concentrated in poor households. The beneficial impact of the grant exceeded the negative impact of even the severe crisis. Without the CSG, the child poverty headcount ratio would have been 61.5 per cent in 2007 rather than the 52.6 per cent recorded.[4] This implies a 16.9 per cent increase in the headcount ratio, a 65 per cent increase in the poverty gap ratio and a 119 per cent increase in the poverty severity ratio. Clearly, the grant is most effective for those deepest in poverty.

In contrast, with the grant, the severe crisis would have increased the poverty headcount to 54.0 per cent in 2009, although this is still a much better situation than had there been no CSG. Thus, the impact of the CSG outweighs that of the economic crisis, and it may even have reduced that of the crisis by keeping people out of poverty, even if their other incomes alone would have placed them in poverty. This is effectively the same as the typical behaviour found in responding to crises, namely, trying to diversify income, thus reducing vulnerability. Although here this does not result from individual effort, but rather from state policy, such income diversification for the poor has a very positive effect on their ability to deal with crises of this nature.

Impact on non-money metric poverty

Lack of money as a result of the economic crisis may spill over into other spheres of life, with potential consequences for other dimensions of child poverty. Three areas stand out: education, health and welfare services.

Access to education up to secondary level is now close to universal. The poor do not suffer exclusion, although education is often of extremely poor quality. Figure 6.12 shows that almost all children age 7–17 are enrolled in schools. Given such universal access and policies to support access for the poor (for example free education for children in the poorest three quintiles of schools), the economic crisis and resultant money-metric poverty probably had little effect on enrolment. However, there may have been negative implications for school attendance, a much more pervasive problem. School-related costs (uniforms, some books and, in some cases, excursions and extra-curricular activities) can make it difficult and sometimes embarrassing for poor children to attend school, although school feeding programmes may dampen such effects. Another dampening effect may have been the fact that few school-age children have realistic options of participating successfully

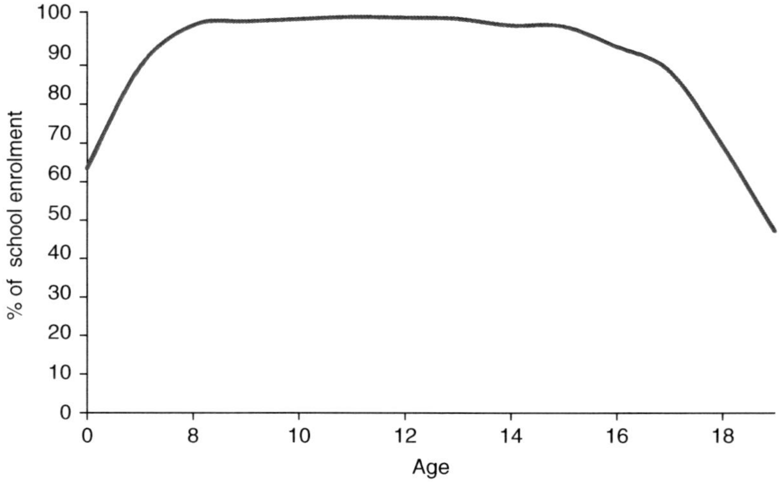

Figure 6.12 School enrolment ratio by age for children age 6–19, 2008
Source: Authors' calculations from GHS 2008.

in the labour market or being engaged in subsistence agriculture, due to the small size of this sector.

Health access has improved considerably since the political transition, but severe quality problems remain. Most people, even the poor, visit private health facilities when their ailment is serious enough or when financial resources permit. Figure 6.13 shows that access to *quality* health services is highly dependent on economic status, as in the case of education. It is likely that the crisis forced some poor children back into visiting public rather than private health facilities, despite a preference for the latter.

Social welfare services in South Africa are inadequate and mainly urban-based, as they depend to a large extent on private welfare organisations, with some partly subsidised by the state. Child abuse is quite common, particularly in some of the poorest communities. Although this phenomenon is not linked directly to money-metric poverty, increased economic stress levels could exacerbate such problems in circumstances in which they are already common. Thus, the economic crisis may have contributed to this.

Conclusion

Child poverty has already long been a source of concern in South Africa, thus progress in the past decade through expanding the CSG

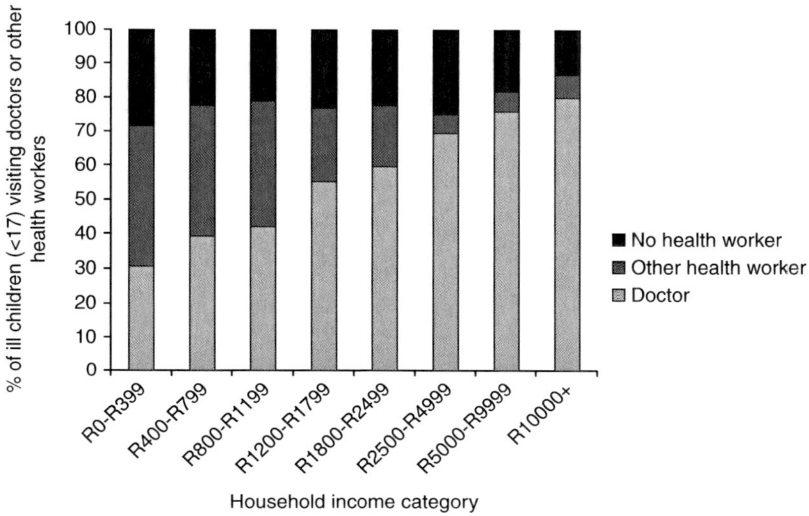

Figure 6.13 Health visits to doctors and other health workers by ill children, 2008

Source: Authors' calculations from GHS 2008.

system has been very important. The combination of macro and micro modelling in this chapter shows that the impact of the economic crisis was not large enough to completely reverse the positive impact of these grants. Nevertheless, the crisis did indeed have an impact on monetary poverty, and this was felt most by the poorest. The CSG provides some protection against the effects of the economic crisis, *ex ante*, by reducing poverty and vulnerability. The income diversification the grant offers is particularly valuable to the poorest and those in rural areas, precisely those whose ability to diversify their sources of income is most constrained.

The macro model attempted specifically to isolate the effects of the economic crisis, separate from the earlier but perhaps enduring effects of the international fuel and food crises. Thus, actual outcomes may be worse than modelled. Current knowledge suggests that the moderate scenario better reflects the course the international economy took than the severe scenario, although the employment effects appear considerably worse than in this scenario. This may result from even greater wage rigidities (wage increases during an economic crisis) than allowed for in the macro model.

The time period observed and modelled did not really allow for an anti-poverty policy. Such responses are slow to implement and require use of existing institutions. The CSG was a major instrument to this end, as it was already in place and protected the vulnerable both before the crisis and during it. In principle, it would be possible to use it to expand transfers to households, although the constellation of fiscal forces in South Africa (the fact that grants are already being expanded very rapidly) and the relatively short duration of this crisis reduced its potential role here.

This chapter did not consider household and individual responses to poverty, which may have unknown impacts on actual poverty outcomes, particularly for children, who cannot protect themselves from impacts. Intra-household behaviour, for instance the extent to which households allocate resources to shield children from the crisis, is of particular importance. Meanwhile, household formation, dissolution and fracturing can all occur in response to changing economic situations. To some extent, the CSG mitigates the possible impact of such behaviour on children, as it makes it more attractive to have them as part of the household.

Finally, the short section on non-money metric poverty illustrates that South Africa is better equipped than many other countries against the impact of an economic crisis on children. Access to public social services is not highly dependent on income, although the quality of such services needs more attention.

Notes

This chapter was much informed by participation in a UNICEF/Overseas Development Institute conference on the same topic held in London in November 2009. This chapter forms part of work undertaken for UNICEF South Africa on the impact of the global financial crisis on child poverty in South Africa. The full results, including the methodology, are presented elsewhere and are only summarised here.

1. The exception is in the case of provinces: there is no stochastic poverty dominance across this dimension, thus poverty ranking of some provinces would change if another poverty line or measure were used.
2. CSG age eligibility rules have changed in gradual steps. When it was introduced, caregivers who met the means test criteria could receive the grant until the child turned seven. This was expanded to children under nine years in 2003, 11 years in 2004, 14 in 2005 and 15 in 2009. According to data from the GHS, coverage of individual children in the age-eligible group increased from 27 per cent in 2002 to 46 per cent in 2006; for households with age-eligible children, coverage increased from almost 20 per cent to 51 per cent in the same period. Higher coverage with an unchanged means test in nominal terms (implying an increasingly strict means test in real terms over the period concerned) meant the expansion resulted

largely from increased rollout of the grant to a growing proportion of the eligible.
3. In retrospect, modelling price effects did not contribute greatly to the model. Poverty lines were set for each cluster of observations in the initial sample based on price ratios which appeared to apply in those clusters.
4. This, of course, ignores possible behaviour effects, such as work seeking, which may have resulted from the CSG, or changes in family composition with regard to the location of both the child and the caregiver. It simply subtracts the CSG from existing incomes.

References

Agüero, J.M., Carter, M. and Woolard, I. (2006) 'From Flows to Stocks: The Impact of Unconditional Cash Transfers on Human Capital.' Conference on Reducing Poverty and Inequality: How Can Africa Be Included. Oxford, 20 February–1 March.

Ardington, C., Case, C. and Hosegood, V. (2009) 'Labor Supply Responses to Large Social Transfers: Longitudinal Evidence from South Africa.' *American Economic Journal: Applied Economics* 1(1): 22–48.

Bibi, S., Cockburn, J., Fofana, I. and Tiberti, L. (2010) 'Impacts of the Global Crisis and Policy Responses on Child Well-being: A Macro–Micro Simulation Framework.' Working Paper 2010-06. Dakar and Florence: UNICEF WCA Regional Office and UNICEF Innocenti Research Centre.

Bibi, S., Cockburn, J., Tiberti, L. and Coulibaly, M. (2009) 'The Impact of the Increase in Food Prices on Child Poverty and the Policy Response in Mali.' Working Paper 09/66. Florence: UNICEF Innocenti Research Centre.

Case, A., Hosegood, V. and Lund, F. (2005) 'The Reach and Impact of Child Support Grants: Evidence from KwaZulu-Natal.' *Development Southern Africa* 22(4): 467–81.

Chitiga, M., Decaluwé, B., Mabugu, R., Maisonnave, H., Robichaud, V., Shepherd, D., van der Berg, S. and von Fintel, D. (2010) 'The Impact of the International Economic crisis on Child Poverty in South Africa.' Working Paper 13/2010. Stellenbosch: Department of Economics, Stellenbosch University.

Cockburn, J., Fofana, I. and Tiberti, L. (2010) 'Simulating the Impact of the Global Economic Crisis and Policy Responses on Children in West and Central Africa.' Working Paper 2010-01. Dakar and Florence: UNICEF WCA Regional Office and UNICEF Innocenti Research Centre.

Coetzee, M. (2010) 'Finding the Benefits: Evaluating the Impact of the South African Child Support Grant.' Master's dissertation, Stellenbosch University.

Decaluwé, B, Lemelin, A, Maisonnave, H and Robichaud, V. (2009) 'PEP-1-t. Standard PEP Model: Single-country, Recursive Dynamic Version.' PEP Research Network. Quebec: Université Laval.

Klasen, S. and Woolard, I. (2008) 'Surviving Unemployment without State Support: Unemployment and Household Formation in South Africa.' *Journal of African Economies* 18(1): 1–51.

Streak, J., Yu D. and van der Berg, S. (2009) 'Measuring Child Poverty in South Africa: Sensitivity to the Choice of Equivalence Scale and an Updated Profile.' *Social Indicators Research* 94(2): 183–201.

van der Berg, S., Louw, M. and Yu, D. (2008) 'Post-transition Poverty Trends Based on an Alternative Data Source.' *South African Journal of Economics* 76(1): 58–76

Woolard, I, and Leibbrandt, M. (2006) 'Towards a Poverty Line for South Africa.' Background Note. Cape Town: Southern Africa Labour and Development Research Unit, University of Cape Town.

7

Lessons from the Financial Crisis: Remittances and Social Assistance among Left-Behind Children and Women in Mexico

Jerónimo Cortina

Introduction

For the first time since the Great Depression, an economic recession has been felt simultaneously in developed and developing countries, without much selectivity. Meanwhile, although economic indicators seem to suggest that the recession is over, the extent and nature of the fiscal burden facing countries and their citizens as a result of the worldwide economic downturn has yet to be estimated. It is likely that the effects, particularly on emerging economies and less developed countries, will be felt for months, possibly years, to come.

This chapter explores some of the potential impacts of the crisis on international migrants' families back home. Using Mexico's 2006 and 2008 National Household Income and Expenditure Survey (ENIGH), a national representative survey of more than 25,000 households, it investigates the impact of remittance flows on governmental social assistance. In particular, it seeks to answer the following questions: In light of the financial crisis, were remittance-recipient households more or less likely to have received social assistance before the crisis or one year after it began? Is the responsiveness of social assistance conditional on remittances?

The results suggest that remittance-recipient households were more likely to receive governmental social assistance in the form of cash transfers a year after the start of the economic crisis compared with a year before the crisis became evident. Moreover, after controlling for the determinants of social assistance receipts, remittances are found to be related inversely to governmental cash transfers. Overall, a decrease in remittance income is associated with an increase in demand for social assistance in order to smooth the liquidity constraints generated by the economic crisis.

These findings hold important implications for families left behind and for national governments. First, they put into question recent studies that conceptualise remittances as an insurance mechanism against bad economic times, at least in the short run. Second, they raise interesting questions about children's prospects for upward mobility, as well as about limited governmental responses under a potential fiscal crisis.

Previous research suggests that during economic crises remittances, as a result of a negative income shock, tend to increase as a share of private consumption and as a by-product of domestic currency devaluation (Kapur, 2005).[1] In other words, remittances work as an alternative insurance mechanism, allowing households to maintain the same consumption levels as prior to the economic downturn and shielding them against the negative income effects associated with an economic crisis.

Under this premise, the implications of remittances as an alternative insurance mechanism are important for several reasons. At the household level, an increase in remittance flows during bad economic times in the home country may prevent children from having to enter the labour market, since these funds can be used as compensatory income in response to a negative income shock (Jacoby and Skoufias, 1997; Morduch, 1995). This coping mechanism will in theory reduce the probability of persistent poverty resulting from a negative income shock and its subsequent effects on human capital formation (Gaiha and Deolalikar, 1993; Jalan and Ravallion, 1998).

At the national level, an increase in remittance flows may help remittance-recipient countries narrow their balance of payments, and they may also provide foreign exchange-thirsty countries with much-needed currency to keep their domestic monetary system afloat. Most importantly, remittances supply national governments with a free safety net – which is of particular value to fiscally strained governments.

As the global economic crisis has illustrated, financial downturns do not always occur unilaterally in the developing world. The duality of the crisis has, almost inevitably, highlighted the need to examine carefully the implications of remittance flows and governmental social assistance. It is necessary to take into account, at least theoretically until new data are available, that during global economic crises remittances may not function as an alternative safety net: the amount and timing are strongly related to migrant workers' employment and the conditions of the sectors in which they work (Chami et al., 2008). Migrants are overrepresented in construction, manufacturing, leisure and hospitality and services, which tend to be the sectors that shrink first. A contraction in these sectors will thus determine to some extent migrant workers' prospects of employment and the amount and timing of remittances they send back home.

Rising unemployment rates among migrant workers necessarily decrease their capacity to send money back home. This may in turn force remittance-receiving households to cut back on expenses such as children's education and non-emergency health-related expenses in order to cover basic needs (Lustig, 2000). As a by-product, remittance-recipient households' demand for governmental social assistance may increase significantly as a way to help them cope with the loss of income. Developing countries may not be able fiscally to increase their safety net coverage unless, through some fiscal mechanism (that is, a tax rate increase) they can make funds available to cover the rise in demand for social assistance by these households.

Migration, social protection and remittances

At the outset, it is important to situate this chapter within the broader literature on migration and remittances and their link with social protection. Migration theories are not new: since Ravenstein's 'Laws of Migration' (1885), scholars have attempted to explain why people migrate.[2] People move in search of better wages or as an attempt to maximise their household's expected income, while minimising the risks they face, primarily due to market failures. They also move as a consequence of global environmental change, civil war, ethnic and political violence, etc.

Even though there are as many explanations as to why people migrate as there are international migrants, the common denominator is that people move due to differences between countries of origin and destination, differences in economic opportunities, differences between war and peace and differences between fertile and desertified lands, among others. However, few studies have addressed the role the state plays in stimulating migration through the creation of (or the lack of) the necessary conditions for its citizens to stay in the home country and thus make migration a choice rather than a survival strategy (see de la Garza and Cortina, 2009).

The role of the state is not neutral to emigration (Evans et al., 1985); it can stimulate or dampen population movements through its actions (de la Garza and Cortina, 2009), especially those related to social protection in the form of promotive and protective measures.[3] For example, in addition to economic reasons, the failure of the state to improve the real incomes and capabilities of its citizens or the lack of protective measures in the form of public assistance that guarantee relief from deprivation may be factors influencing the decision to migrate.

In this context, remittances play an important role as alternative protective and/or promotive social protection. On the one hand, they allow households to gain, maintain or increase their access to certain measures relevant to poverty reduction, such as health and education, and on the other hand, they shield them against the negative income effects associated with the lack of state action in the provision of and transfer of resources to groups considered eligible due to deprivation.

The impact of remittances on those who receive these funds depends to some extent on the motivations for sending money back home. Although there is no systematic explanation of remitter motivations (Lucas and Stark, 1985), there are three bodies of literature that address this subject. The first sees remittances as interfamilial transfers for family maintenance. The second considers remittances as insurance against bad economic times affecting those left behind. The final perspective views remittances as a community-oriented investment in the home country.

Interfamilial transfer theories assume the underlying motivation migrants have for sending money home is an unselfish one. Lucas and Stark (ibid.: 902) argue that the most obvious motive for remitting is a kind of 'self-contractual arrangement between migrant and family' in which migrants and members of a household act collectively to maximise expected income and migrants remit with the sole purpose of helping to support the household economy.

A variant of this approach stipulates that since households in migrant-sending countries are likely to be unbanked, that is, they do not have access to financial institutions that insure them against bad economic times, they send money home in order to assure those who stayed behind that 'in the event that economic conditions at home deteriorate and productive activities there fail to generate sufficient income, the household can rely on migrant remittances for support' (Massey, 1999: 36). Backing this argument is research indicating that when risks are present, the likelihood of and the amount remitted increases (Amuedo-Dorantes and Pozo, 2002).

A second approach views remittances as investments in human capital or in capital goods such as land, houses or agricultural inputs. Human capital is increased by using remittances on health and education expenses, which are an important element of development in migrant-sending countries (Durand et al., 1996).

A third argument is that immigrants send money home to support community-oriented projects involving public works infrastructure, social services and economic development in order to prepare for their return home and to help out those who were left behind. Chami et al. (2008), in an attempt to summarise the vast literature, suggest that remittance flows could be seen as 'compensatory' rather than 'opportunistic'. They are sent back home to improve the wellbeing of those left behind by allowing them not only to smooth out or increase their consumption patterns, but also to increase the family's stock of wealth and alleviate liquidity constraints.

Remittances' impact on the household varies with how the money is spent. Remittances are spent primarily on basic consumption, education and health.[4] Some gender differences exist: women tend to prioritise particular family needs, such as food, clothing, education and health; men often channel remittances towards saving and investments to generate future gains (Cortes, 2007).

While a consensus has been 'reached' regarding how remittances are spent, the literature on their impact on the economy and on families left behind has generated diverse perspectives, yielding a wide array of competing theories. On the one hand, there are those who argue that remittances are beneficial for migrant-sending societies, since these monies seem to be a stable and less volatile capital source (Ratha, 2003). Others argue that an increase in the number of international migrants in a country can reduce the percentage of the population living in poverty (Adams and Page, 2003). Similarly, in exogenous growth models, and under the assumption that remittances increase the savings rate of those who receive them, remittances 'will increase the level of per capita capital stock and therefore per capita output' (Drinkwater et al., 2002: 21).

In a similar vein, some studies suggest that remittances stimulate economic activity in the home country through a multiplier effect which results when households use remittances to increase consumption, stimulating local economies into higher levels of employment, investment and income. This in turn improves the recipient's material wellbeing, and in some instances, the accumulation of assets (Adams, 1998; Durand et al., 1996). The literature suggests furthermore that immigrant remittances are used to increase recipients' consumption and stock of wealth. However, as argued by Chami et al. (2003), this does not necessarily increase the overall economy's stock of wealth. Moreover, the expenditure of remittances and the consequent multiplier effect may have different effects on the remittance-recipient's country, such as changing 'relative prices and hence the relative returns of productive factors in the economy' (Stahl, 1988: 371).

In contrast, there are those who argue that, since most of the money sent home is used for consumption purposes and not for investment purposes, remittances do not constitute a developmental tool but only a source of foreign exchange.[5] Moreover, the impact of remittances on development is not definitive: a moral hazard problem coupled with the limited ability of the remitter to direct funds towards developmental projects (Cortina and de la Garza, 2004) could cause remittances to actually have a negative effect on growth (Chami et al., 2003).

A recurring weakness of some of the assumptions made implicitly in the literature is that remittance flows are seen as constant and not as flows whose impact is determined by both the conditions in the home country and the macroeconomic conditions in the host country. For instance, as mentioned earlier, rising unemployment rates among migrant workers will affect the frequency and amount remitted, which in turn will affect the amount spent on consumption, development, education and health.

Figures reported by Mexico's Central Bank (Banco de México, 2010) suggest that, since the financial crisis began in 2007, remittance flows to Mexico have decreased by approximately 23 per cent as a consequence of the macroeconomic conditions in the US. Between 1996 and 2006, remittances grew at an estimated rate of 20 per cent annually, compared with a negative growth rate of 5 per cent between 2007 and the first eight months of 2009. During the first eight months of 2009, moreover, remittances fell approximately 13 per cent in comparison with 2008 (Figure 7.1).

Decreases of such magnitudes have important implications at the national and household level. At the national level, a reduction in remittances implies the government has less room to manage its balance of payments and its floating exchange rate. At the household level, in contrast, it means that households, especially those significantly dependent on these funds, will face a severe negative income shock that will impact their expenditure patterns.

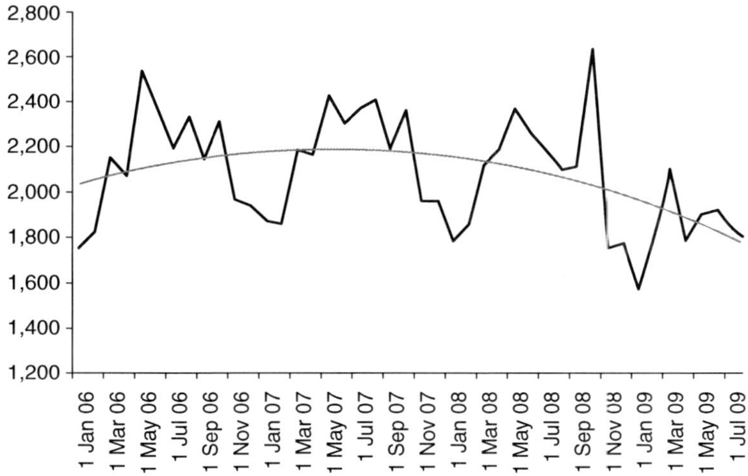

Figure 7.1 Migrant remittance flows ($ millions)

Source: Author's calculation based on data from Banco de México (2010).

So what alternative strategies can remittance-recipient households implement in order to cope with a decrease in remittance income? The first is to adjust their consumption pattern. Remittance-recipient households may be pushed to cut back on expenses such as children's education and non-emergency health-related expenses in order to cover other vital needs. Alternatively, households may increase household members' labour supply to maintain their pre-crisis consumption levels. For instance, children may be driven into the labour market to compensate for loss of income. Finally, remittance-recipient households might turn to the state's safety net, hoping to smooth out some of their liquidity constraints.

Data and methods

Simply put, the two key objectives of this chapter are to predict the likelihood that remittance-recipient households will receive governmental social assistance and to model the responsiveness of social assistance, conditional on remittances. The empirical analysis uses data from the 2006 and 2008 ENIGH and from the National Population Council

(CONAPO) 2000 Migration Intensity Index (IIM). Conceptually, we can think of these data as the product of a natural experiment in which the financial crisis can be seen as an external shock allowing us to contrast its impact in 2008 with a comparison condition in 2006.

ENIGH is a nationally representative survey conducted by Mexico's National Institute of Statistics and Geography (INEGI). Its main objective is to gather data on the amount, origin and destination of Mexican households' income and expenditure. In addition, it collects socio-economic information on household members as well as on their characteristics and their infrastructure. ENIGH allows researchers to make inferences not only at the national level but also at the rural level (areas with fewer than 2,500 inhabitants) and urban level (areas with more than 2,500 inhabitants).

The outcome variable used in this chapter is given by the amount received in social assistance at the household level over a three-month period. For 2006, this variable encompasses two main programmes: *Oportunidades* and *Procampo*. *Oportunidades*, formerly known as *Progresa*, was founded in 1997 and refitted in 2002. It is designed to reduce extreme poverty by providing conditional cash transfers (CCTs) to families who fulfil requirements for school attendance, health checkups and nutritional support. *Oportunidades* targets households experiencing food poverty as well as those with insufficient income levels to be able to invest in human development activities such as education, health and nutrition.

Selection of the target population is completed in two stages. During the first stage, localities are targeted based on their social gap and marginalisation indices. The social gap index is a weighted measure which summarises four social deprivation indicators (education, health, basic services and housing space) into a single index. The marginalisation index summarises four indicators: access to education, household living conditions, monetary income and population distribution in localities with fewer than 5,000 residents. During the second stage, families are targeted based on a household's demographic and socio-economic characteristics, such as income, access to education, health and governmental subsidies, among others (see SEDESOL, 2008). Today, *Oportunidades* covers around 5 million families living in approximately 100,000 marginalised communities, of which 86 per cent are located in rural areas.

Procampo, a federally administered grant programme aimed at agricultural producers, was initiated at the end of 1993 to help modernise the Mexican agriculture sector in response to the adoption of the North American Free Trade Agreement (NAFTA). It was designed so that agricultural producers could choose their crops and means of production freely without creating price distortions, thus allowing them to be competitive with international producers. *Procampo* complements individuals' income with a direct monetary subsidy for each hectare or fraction of a hectare of land that is registered in the programme. The area that is registered voluntarily, regardless of its extension, must be cultivated, destined for an ecological project or exploited for timber or cattle. In order to access the benefits of the programme, agricultural producers need to submit an application and present a series of documents, such as ID and land title or proof that they have the rights to exploit the land for agricultural purposes (a private contract). If the land is not rain-fed, the applicant needs to show they have paid water charges associated with the land.

For 2008, in addition to *Oportunidades* and *Procampo*, the variable covers social assistance to the elderly. *Adultos Mayores* is a cash transfer programme aimed at persons older than 70 years of age living in poverty, focusing on those living in rural areas who are not covered by any other programme.

The main predictor is the amount of remittances received in a particular household over a three-month period. As controls, we include those variables that are used to determine the primary geographic areas of intervention (CONEVAL, 2009). The National Council for the Evaluation of Social Development Policy (CONEVAL), a governmental entity in charge of evaluating Mexico's social policy, uses an index of social development that includes at least eight dimensions to determine areas of primary care: (i) household income; (ii) educational attainment; (iii) access to health services; (iv) access to social policies (outcome variable); (v) basic dwelling characteristics; (vi) access to basic public services; (vii) food security; and (viii) social cohesion. In addition to these key predictors, we include average household employment level, number of women and children living in the household and an indicator for households headed by females. Table 7.1 summarises these data.

Remittances constitute a small component of households' total current income; for those households in the lower part of the income distribution, however, they represent a relatively high percentage of total current income – around 3 per cent in comparison with households in the upper deciles of the income distribution (see left panel of Figure 7.2).

Table 7.1 Descriptive statistics, 2008

Variable	Obs.	Mean	Std. dev.	Min	Max
Receive social assistance	28867	0.23	0.417793	0	1.00
Receive remittances	28867	0.06	0.236976	0	1.00
Number of children <18 yrs	28867	1.47	1.476727	0	21.00
Female-headed households	28867	0.25	0.432303	0	1.00
Remittance income	28867	376.48	2466.054	0	120984.00
Avg. cash transfer ($MP)	28867	552.80	3886.669	0	449153.10
Total current income	28867	37544.47	57950.6	0	4350233.00
Educational attainment	28867	1.30	0.560424	0	10.00
Access to health services	28867	1.18	0.633426	0	2.00
Dirt floor	28866	0.06	0.240612	0	1.00
Avg. no. of bedrooms	28867	1.25	1.013645	0.08	25.00
Access to basic services	28867	0.47	0.83142	0	4.00
Household goods	28867	0.63	0.723221	0	2.00
Food security	18924	2.04	3.166305	0	12.00
Social cohesion	28867	−0.59	2.198125	−12	12.00
Avg. employment	28867	0.44	0.280927	0	1.00
Number of females	28867	2.08	1.314906	0	21.00
% HH receive remittances	28832	4.00	4.454566	0	36.23
% HH with migrants	28832	3.72	4.368402	0	36.27
% HH with circular migrants	28832	0.88	1.131197	0	11.95
% HH with returned migrants	28832	0.77	0.970817	0	8.41

Additionally, the largest share of households that receive remittances is located at the bottom and middle of the income distribution (see right panel of Figure 7.2).

A much more interesting pattern arises when we compare years. Between 2006 and 2008, remittances as a proportion of households' total current income fell 29 per cent on average, while the proportion of households receiving remittances fell by 12 per cent. In other words, amount of remittances as a component of households' total current income and the number of households that receive them have fallen significantly since the crisis began in 2007.

Figure 7.3 shows the proportion of social assistance to total current income (left panel) and the proportion of social assistance recipients (right panel) by income decile. The pattern depicted suggests social assistance disbursements grew considerably between 2006 and 2008,

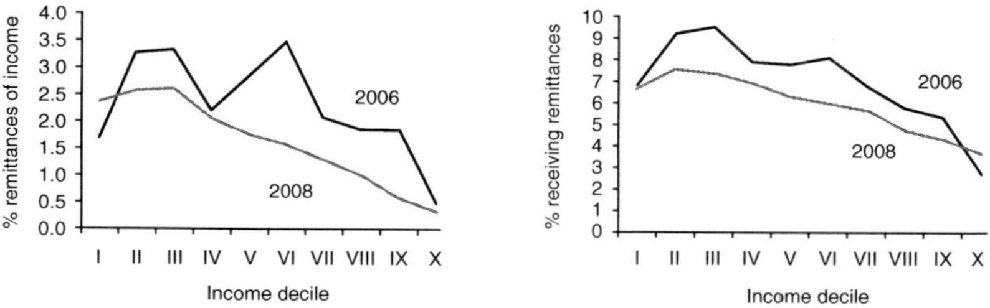

Figure 7.2 Remittances as a proportion of total current income (left panel) and proportion of households receiving remittances (right panel)

Source: Author's calculations based on data from ENIGH 2006 and 2008.

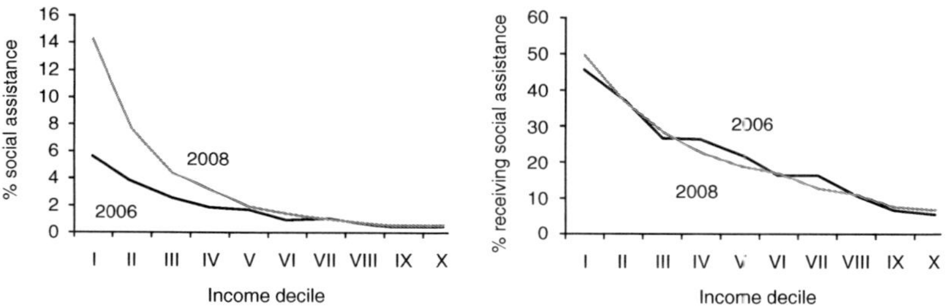

Figure 7.3 Social assistance as a proportion of total current income (left panel) and proportion of households receiving social assistance (right panel)

Source: Author's calculations based on data from ENIGH 2006 and 2008.

which in turns suggests that the share of social assistance in poorer households' total current income also changed and it has become an important component (14 per cent) of households' income. The proportion of social assistance recipients of the total population between 2006 and 2008, in contrast, shows significant changes only at the bottom of the income distribution.

The patterns depicted by Figures 7.2 and 7.3 suggest that remittance-recipient households could turn to the state safety net, hoping to ease some of their liquidity constraints. First, in 2008, fewer households were receiving remittances from abroad, and those who were still receiving these monies were receiving less (see Figure 7.2). Second, households that received social assistance were becoming more dependent on these transfers (proportion of social assistance to the total current income increased from 6 per cent to 14 per cent), while the proportion of social assistance recipients has increased only at the bottom of the income distribution (see Figure 7.3). In order to verify the plausibility of this hypothesis, we need to test it with individual-level data, as detailed in the following paragraphs.

Given that remittances are not randomly assigned within the territory or within the population, we cannot assume their relationship with social assistance policies is going to be independent. A common way of resolving this lack of independence between remittances and social assistance is through the introduction of instrumental variables. The general model uses the following system of equations:

$$x_i = \gamma + \delta z_i + \varepsilon_{1i} \tag{1}$$

$$y_i = \alpha + \beta x_i + \varphi x_i + \varepsilon z_i, \tag{2}$$

where x_i is remittance income, z_i is a vector of instruments (see below for description), y_i is the amount received in social assistance and φ_i is a vector of control variables. This model instruments remittance income using the same four components that make up the Index of Migration Intensity (IIM), which encompasses the most significant characteristics of the migratory phenomenon.

The first component of the IIM is percentage of households that receive remittances in a municipality. The second component of the index is percentage of households in a *municipio* (county) with migrants living in the US between 1995 and 2000. This variable reflects current migratory patterns in a particular *municipio*. The third and fourth components, percentage of households with circular migrants (members of a household who migrated to the US between 1995 and 2000 but at the moment of the Census were living in Mexico) and percentage of households with returned migrants (members of a household who in 1995 lived in the US but returned to Mexico either voluntarily or involuntarily so at the moment of the Census they were counted as residents living in Mexico), measure the extent to which migrant networks may be established in a particular *municipio*. Figure 7.4 illustrates why, for the purpose of this chapter, it is important to use instrumental variables.

As Figure 7.4 shows, migration from Mexico to the US, the main destination country, is not randomly distributed. Migratory flows initially depended on historic worker recruitment programmes, such as the Bracero Programme, and they later became consolidated through social, familial, local and regional networks (Durand, 2005). The west-central

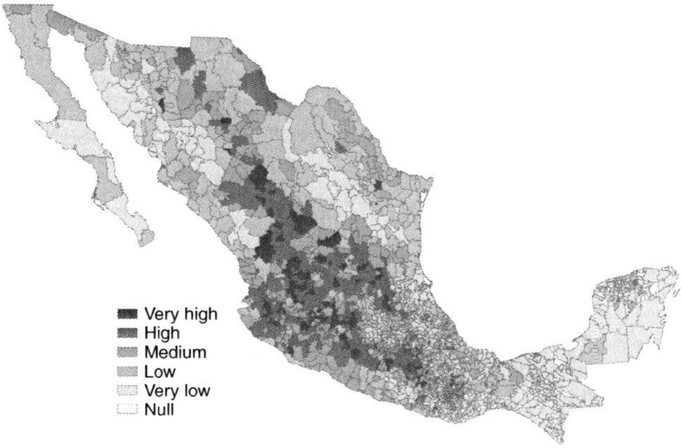

Figure 7.4 Municipal Migration Index, 2000
Source: Author's elaboration based on data from CONAPO (2002).

region, comprising the states of Michoacán, Colima, Jalisco, Nayarit, Guanajuato, San Luis Potosí, Zacatecas, Durango and Aguascalientes, sends the most migrants.

The instruments can be thought of as randomisers in the sense that they affect remittances but they do not directly affect households' social assistance receipts, except through remittances. In other words, they suggest the plausibility that remittances are independently distributed from ε_{1i} and ε_{2i} and that they are dependent on x_i, that is, that we used z_i to determine its value. Given the regional differences depicted in Figure 7.4, the empirical analysis must take into account the different levels of development at the different levels of residency (rural vs. urban). This breakdown allows us to control for the potential differential impacts that remittances and social assistance policies may have among different strata of the population and different levels of development.

Results

Are remittance-recipient households more or less likely to receive social assistance? Figure 7.5 presents the predicted probabilities of fitting a logistic regression model for the relationship between receiving social assistance and remittances for households that are headed by

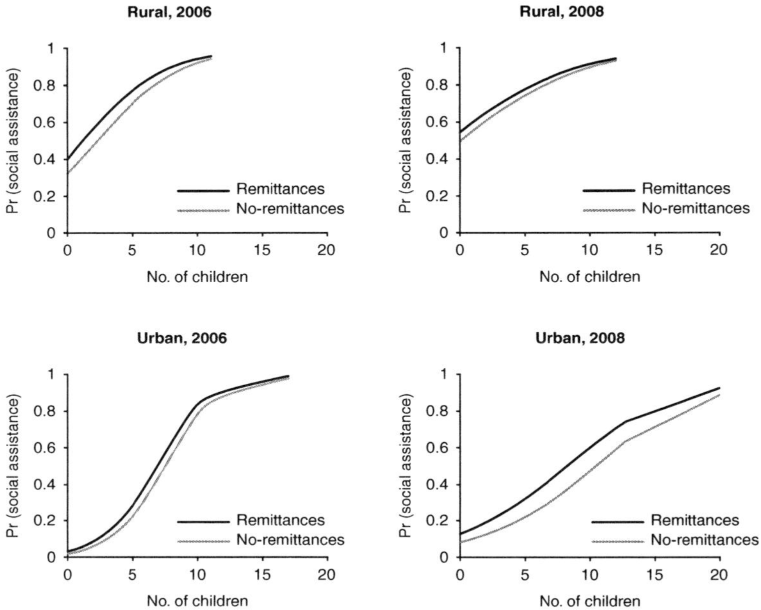

Figure 7.5 Predicted probabilities of receiving social assistance for female-headed households that receive and do not receive remittances, by number of children

Source: Author's calculations based on data from CONAPO (2002).

females with children under 18 years of age.[6] The objective of this analysis is to test an extreme case in which remittances constitute the only source of income for a particular household. We expect that, prior to the crisis (2006), the probability of receiving social assistance for a particular household – whether rural or urban – would be lower than in 2008, when potentially the household would have lost some remittance income as a consequence of the duality of the economic crisis.

Overall, the results confirm this hypothesis. Households headed by females with children under 18 were more likely to receive social assistance in 2008 than in 2006. The most interesting pattern, however, is the one seen between 2006 and 2008. The probability of receiving social assistance increased significantly for rural households headed by females with children under 18 years of age. For instance, in 2006 the probability of receiving social assistance for a rural, remittance-recipient, household headed by a female with four children under 18 was 71 per cent compared with 74 per cent in 2008 – a 4 percentage point increase over a two-year period. For urban, remittance-recipient, households headed by females with four children under 18, the probability increased by 35 per cent – from 20 per cent in 2006 to 27 per cent in 2008 (see Figure 7.5).

Indeed, the results suggest that, in 2008, remittance-recipient households headed by females were more likely to receive social assistance than in 2006. It is important to emphasise that, given the quasi-experimental nature of the data, even if the effect of remittances can be explained by other predictors, the correlations would still be real in the sense of representing real differences between those who receive and who do not receive social assistance. The goal of the second question (Is the responsiveness of social assistance conditional on remittances?) is to test whether social assistance changes are a result of shifts in remittances – after controlling for other covariates – that could affect a household's eligibility for this type of governmental transfer. First, we expect a negative relationship between remittances and social assistance. In other words, as the amount of remittances increases, we expect the amount of social assistance to decrease. The logic behind this mechanism is given by the insurance hypothesis: the more remittances income a household receives – with everything else equal – the less social assistance it will receive, since it would not necessarily qualify for this supplemental income. Second, we expect the impact of remittances on social assistance to be contingent on the level of development and on the size of the locality (rural vs. urban), given the selectivity of the migratory phenomenon.

Table 7.2 presents the results after fitting the two-stage least squares instrumental variables regression as indicated by equations (1) and (2). Overall, the impact of remittances on social assistance varies, contingent on the level of development and the size of locality. The results presented in the first column indicate that, for each additional peso received over a three-month period, the amount received in social assistance decreased by 31 cents. Having more education and access to health services is also correlated with a lower amount of social assistance in the order of $MP373 and $MP100 over three months, respectively. Households headed by females receive on average $MP576 more in social assistance over a three-month period than their male-headed households. In contrast, in less marginalised or more developed rural

Table 7.2 Impact of remittances on social assistance, rural areas, 2008

	(1)	(2)	(3)
Variable	**Low development**	**Medium development**	**High development**
Remittance income	−0.312***	0.127*	0.230
	(0.116)	(0.0772)	(0.148)
Total current income	−0.00176	−0.00364	0.0245
	(0.00293)	(0.00461)	(0.0183)
Educational attainment	−373.7***	−62.08	603.7*
	(93.64)	(142.8)	(314.5)
Access to health services	−103.3**	−460.6***	−461.5***
	(45.73)	(74.39)	(111.8)
Dirt floor	−44.57	42.99	−80.52
	(85.03)	(214.8)	(176.2)
Avg. bedrooms	−26.84	−92.64	30.78
	(144.2)	(227.5)	(261.7)
Access to basic services	14.39	109.6	173.4
	(40.34)	(69.20)	(119.7)
Household goods	−80.04	52.55	−5.618
	(85.56)	(97.22)	(83.13)
Food security	−6.137	21.83	42.95*
	(11.66)	(20.09)	(22.09)
Social cohesion	24.40*	7.182	−25.52
	(14.83)	(22.79)	(45.06)
Avg. employment	434.9	1246***	1343*
	(343.8)	(425.0)	(778.1)
Number of females	164.9***	102.3	20.37
	(35.33)	(65.98)	(90.39)
Number of children <18 yrs.	174.6***	147.2**	275.2**
	(33.44)	(59.58)	(130.0)
Female-headed households	576.7**	−572.2*	−409.9
	(247.9)	(294.4)	(299.0)
Constant	1713***	772.5**	−1498
	(284.0)	(388.9)	(1021)
Observations	2261	969	1478
Wooldridge's score test	7.71	1.98	1.90
	(p = .005)	(p = .159)	(p = .168)
Sragan's & Basmann's χ^2	4.084	.923	6.700
	(p = .253)	(p = .820)	(p = .082)

Note: Robust standard errors in parentheses ***p < 0.01, **p < 0.05, *p < 0.1.

areas,[7] remittances do not have an impact on social assistance at traditional levels of statistical significance. Educational attainment is in the expected theoretical direction, but its impact on social assistance is not significant. Access to health care, on the other hand, decreases social assistance significantly, by $MP460, in both medium and highly developed rural areas over a three-month period.

Discussion

This chapter has found the following patterns:

(i) One year after the economic crisis became apparent, remittance-recipient households headed by females that include children under 18 years of age were more likely to receive social assistance from the government than in 2006, a year before the crisis began.
(ii) Controlling for the determinants of social assistance, rural, remittance-recipient households in low development areas in 2008 were significantly less likely to receive social assistance in comparison with non-remittance-recipient households.

What do these findings mean in the context of the current economic crisis? Given that remittances and social assistance are inversely related, a decline in the former implies an increase in the latter. The decline in remittance flows, moreover, depends on the employment conditions of the migrant – that is, on the macroeconomic conditions of the host country. In addition, the magnitude of the effect in Mexico depends on the current socioeconomic characteristics of each household. When households are affected by a negative income shock, they seek alternate ways to make ends meet, which may include adjusting their expenditure in order to cover their basic needs or incorporating members of the household into the labour market, such as children who might have been previously enrolled in school or seeking the assistance of the government. The results presented in the previous section support the plausibility of this last alternative. Moreover, as de la Fuente (2010) shows, a negative income shock operationalised through a fall in remittances will increase the threat of future poverty for rural households.

What are the implications for the Mexican government and left-behind families? For the government, in addition to the obvious macroeconomic effects mediated through the balance of payments and through foreign exchange, a decline in remittances implies an increase in the fiscal burden, due to growth in the demand for social assistance by remittance-recipient households. These households may not have qualified for such assistance before the crisis under the targeting criteria utilised by *Oportunidades*, the main social assistance programme in Mexico.

Given that around 80 per cent of the amount remitted to families back home is spent on consumption, a substantial decrease in remittances – like the one documented here – will increase the proportion of people living in poverty. In just two years, for instance, this number increased by 6 million. In 2009, half of the population living in food poverty, that is, around 9.8 million, were children under 18 years of age (SEDESOL, 2009). A 2010 study by CONEVAL and the UN Children's Fund (UNICEF) – which did not target households affected by migration – points out that food insecurity between 2008 and 2009 rose due to the economic crisis and the increase in prices. The effects of a financial crisis on remittances, moreover, will be more evident among households that are extremely dependent on remittances and those in non-traditional migrant regions. These latter regions are those where migration is not yet a prevalent phenomenon, as residents are as yet less likely to have robust support networks in the host country to rely on.[8] This increases their exposure to negative macroeconomic conditions and they are therefore more likely to lose their jobs and less likely to send money back home than migrants from more traditional migrant regions.

There is no doubt that the economic crisis has had a significant impact on remittances, which represent an important resource for Mexico and for the families who receive them. Remittances are not a panacea to resolve years of bad economic and social policies, and governments cannot rely on these private transfers as substitutes for the provision of public goods such as education and health care, especially for children and women. The challenge for migrant-sending countries in general, and Mexico in particular, therefore, is to develop creative policies that take into account both sides of the equation. These sides are the determinants of the supply of remittances (immigrants' motivations, macroeconomic conditions of the host country and their own skills) and the demand for remittances (socioeconomic status of those left behind, number of children living in the household, etc.) in order to maximise their benefits, while decreasing their potential negative effects.

Co-development strategies between countries of origin and destination in general and between Mexico and the US in particular, to reduce social, economic, educational and health inequalities between them, should be the basis for incorporating migration, its causes and its consequences into countries' developmental strategies to maximise migration's developmental potential.

Notes

1. A similar argument has been developed to test remittance responsiveness after the occurrence of a natural disaster in migrant-sending countries (Mohapatra et al., 2009; Yang, 2007).
2. For a review, see Brettell and Hollifield (2000) and Massey (1999).
3. Promotive measures aim to improve real incomes and capabilities, whereas protective measures guarantee relief from deprivation (see Sabates-Wheeler and Waite, 2003).
4. Chami et al. (2008); Cortina and de la Garza (2004); Delgado-Wise and Rodrigues (2001); Meyers (2002).
5. Appleyard (1989); Glytsos (1993); Macmillen (1982).
6. Given the sampling design, the data do not allow for modelling the impact of remittances on social assistance for children who have been left behind without a head of household or who are themselves the *de facto* head of the household. In order to be able to do this, it would be necessary to create a special design for hard-to-sample populations.
7. Developed rural areas refer to those with fewer than 2,500 residents which are relatively less marginalised or more developed than other areas in terms of access to education, physical characteristics of the dwelling and goods and services available to the household (CONAPO, 2007).
8. Massey and Zenteno (1999); Massey et al. (1994; 1998); Myrdal (1958); Stark and Taylor (1991).

References

Adams, R.H. (1998) 'Remittances, Investment, and Rural Asset Accumulation in Pakistan.' *Economic Development and Cultural Change* 47: 155–73.

Adams, R.H. and Page, J. (2003) 'International Migration, Remittances and Poverty in Developing Countries.' Working Paper 3179. Washington, DC: Poverty Reduction Group, World Bank.

Amuedo-Dorantes, C. and Pozo, S. (2002) 'Precautionary Saving by Young Immigrants and Young Natives.' *Southern Economic Journal* 69(1): 48–71.

Appleyard, R. (ed.) (1989) *The Impact of International Migration on Developing Countries*. Paris: OECD DAC.

Banco de México (2010) 'Ingresos por Remesas Familiares.' November. Mexico City: Banco de México.

Brettell, C. and Hollifield, J. (eds) (2000) *Migration Theory: Talking across Disciplines*. New York: Routledge.

Chami, R., Barajas, A., Cosimano, T., Fullenkamp, C., Gapen, M. and Montiel, P. (2008) 'Macroeconomic Consequences of Remittances.' Occasional Paper 259. Washington, DC: IMF.

Chami, R., Fullenkamp, C. and Jahjah, S. (2003) 'Are Immigrant Remittance Flows a Source of Capital for Development?' Working Paper 03/189. Washington, DC: IMF.
CONAPO (2002) 'Índice de Intensidad Migratoria México-Estados Unidos, 2000.' Mexico City: CONAPO.
CONAPO (2007) 'Índice de Marginación a Nivel Localidad 2005.' Mexico City: CONAPO.
CONEVAL (2009) 'Evaluación Y Monitoreo De Programas Sociales.' Mexico City: CONEVAL.
CONEVAL and UNICEF (2010) 'La Niñez y la Adolescencia en el Contexto de la Crisis Económica Global: El Caso de México.' Mexico City: CONEVAL and UNICEF.
Cortes, R. (2007) 'Remittances and Children's Rights: An Overview of Academic and Policy Literature.' New York: Division of Policy and Planning, UNICEF.
Cortina, J. and de la Garza, R. (2004) 'Immigrant Remitting Behavior and Its Developmental Consequences for Mexico and El Salvador.' Los Angeles, CA: The Tomas Rivera Policy Institute.
de la Fuente, A. (2010) 'Remittances and Vulnerability to Poverty in Rural Mexico.' *World Development* 38(6): 828–39.
de la Garza, R.O. and Cortina, J. (2009) 'Migración Política: Más Allá de las Redes y la Economía.' In Salazar, R. (ed.) *Políticas Migratorias: Hacia la Gobernabilidad de las Migraciones Transnacionales*. Quito: Universidad Andina Simón Bolívar Corporación Editora Nacional.
Delgado-Wise, R. and Rodríguez, H. (2001) 'The Emergence of Collective Migrants and Their Role in Mexico's Local and Regional Development.' *Canadian Journal of Development Studies* 22(3): 747–64.
Drinkwater, S., Levine, P. and Lotti, E. (2002) 'The Economic Impact of Migration: A Survey.' Conference on European Enlargement: The Impact of East-West Migration on Growth and Employment. Vienna, 6–7 December.
Durand, J. (2005) 'Nuevas Regiones De Origen Y Destino De La Migración Mexicana.' Working Paper 05-02. Princeton, NJ: Center for Migration and Development.
Durand, J., Kandel, W., Parrado, E.A. and Massey, D.S. (1996) 'International Migration and Development in Mexican Communities.' *Demography* 33(2): 249–64.
Evans, P., Rueschemeyer, D. and Skocpol, T. (eds) (1985) *Bringing the State Back In*. Cambridge: Cambridge University Press.
INEGI (2007) 'Encuesta Nacional de Ingresos y Gastos de los Hogares 2006.' Aguascalientes: INEGI.
INEGI (2009) 'Encuesta Nacional de Ingresos y Gastos de los Hogares 2008.' Aguascalientes: INEGI.
Gaiha, R. and Deolalikar, A. (1993) 'Persistent, Expected and Innate Poverty: Estimates for Semi-Arid Rural South India 1975–1984.' *Cambridge Journal of Economics* 17(4): 409–21.
Glytsos, N.P. (1993) 'Measuring the Income Effects of Migrant Remittances: A Methodological Approach Applied to Greece.' *Economic Development and Cultural Change* 42(1): 131–68.
Jacoby, H. and Skoufias, E. (1997) 'Risk, Financial Markets, and Human Capital in a Developing Country.' *The Review of Economic Studies* 64(3): 311–35.

Jalan, J. and Ravallion, M. (1998) 'Determinants of Transient and Chronic Poverty: Evidence from Rural China.' Policy Research Working Paper 1936. Washington, DC: World Bank.

Kapur, D. (2005) 'Remittances: The New Development Mantra?' In Munzele Maimbo, S. and Ratha, D. (eds) *Remittances: Development Impact and Future Prospects*. Washington, DC: World Bank.

Lucas, R.E.B. and Stark, O. (1985) 'Motivations to Remit: Evidence from Botswana.' *Journal of Political Economy* 93(5): 901–18.

Lustig, N. (2000) 'Crises and the Poor: Socially Responsible Macroeconomics.' *Economia* 1(1): 1–19.

Macmillen, M.J. (1982) 'The Economic Effects of International Migration: A Survey.' *Journal of Common Market Studies* 20(3): 245–67.

Massey, D.S. (1999) 'Why Does Immigration Occur? A Theoretical Synthesis.' In Hirschman, C., Kasinitz, P. and de Wind, J. (eds) *The Handbook of International Migration: The American Experience*. New York: Russell Sage Foundation.

Massey, D.S., Goldring, L. and Durand, J. (1994) 'Continuities in Transnational Migration: An Analysis of Nineteen Mexican Communities.' *American Journal of Sociology* 99(6): 1492–533.

Massey, D.S., Hugo, G., Arango, J., Kouaouci, A. and Pellegrino, A. (1998) *Worlds in Motion: Understanding International Migration at the End of the Millennium*. New York: Clarendon Press/Oxford University Press.

Massey, D.S. and Zenteno, R. (1999) 'The Dynamics of Mass Migration.' *Proceedings of the National Academy of Sciences* 96(8): 5328–35.

Meyers, D.W. (2002) 'Migrant Remittances to Latin America: Reviewing the Literature.' In de la Garza, R. and Lowell, L.B. (eds) *Sending Money Home: Hispanic Remittances and Community Development*. Lanham, MD: Rowman & Littlefield.

Mohapatra, S., Joseph, G. and Ratha, D. (2009) 'Remittances and Natural Disasters: Ex-Post Response and Contribution to Ex-Ante Preparedness.' Policy Research Working Paper 4972. Washington, DC: World Bank.

Morduch, J. (1995) 'Income Smoothing and Consumption Smoothing.' *Journal of Economic Perspectives* 9(3): 103–14.

Myrdal, G. (1958) *Rich Lands and Poor: The Road to World Prosperity*. New York: Harper.

Ratha, D. (2003) 'Workers' Remittances: An Important and Stable Source of External Development Finance.' In World Bank *Global Development Finance*. Washington, DC: World Bank.

Ravenstein, E.G. (1885) 'The Laws of Migration.' *Journal of the Statistical Society of London* 48(2): 167–235.

Sabates-Wheeler, R. and Waite, M. (2003) 'Migration and Social Protection: A Concept Paper.' Brighton: Development Research Centre on Migration, Globalisation and Poverty, University of Sussex.

SEDESOL (2008) 'Relgas de Operación para el Programa de Desarrollo Humano Oportunidades Ejercicio Fiscal 2008.' Mexico: SEDESOL.

SEDESOL (2009) 'Intervención del Secretario de Desarrollo Social, Ernesto Cordero Arroyo, en el Marco de la Tercera Mesa Regional en Materia de los Derechos de las Niñas, Niños y Adolescentes, Organizada por el DIF Nacional en Tijuana, Baja California.' Mexico: SEDESOL.

Stahl, C.W. (1988) 'Overview: Economic Perspectives.' In Appleyard, R. (ed.) (1989) *The Impact of International Migration on Developing Countries*. Paris: OECD DAC.

Stark, O. and Taylor, J.E. (1991) 'Migration Incentives, Migration Types: The Role of Relative Deprivation.' *The Economic Journal* 101(408): 1163–78.

Yang, D. and Hwa Jung, C. (2007) 'Are Remittances Insurance? Evidence from Rainfall Shocks in the Philippines.' *World Bank Economic Review* 21(2): 219–48.

8

Children in Crisis in the Philippines: Insights and Evidence from Community-based Monitoring Systems

Celia Reyes, Alellie Sobreviñas, Jeremy de Jesus and Steffie Joi Calubayan

Introduction[1]

Child poverty and deprivation remain a key challenge in the Philippines. Based on official poverty estimates for 2009, about 26.5 per cent of the entire population is considered poor – about 23.1 million people. Moreover, recent trends have been worrisome, with the incidence and magnitude of poverty exhibiting a continuous increase since 2003.

The number of poor families with children was about 3.9 million in 1985, increasing further to 4.1 million by 2006. This translates to about 12.8 million children 0–14 years old (about 44.0 per cent) belonging to income-poor households during the period. This figure is higher by about 1 million than the 2003 figure of 11.8 million and it is almost the same as more than two decades ago. This very high proportion of children and young people living in poverty is very disturbing, given the pernicious and long-lived impact of deprivation on children. Unlike adults, they are still in development, when proper nourishment, among other inputs, is necessary. They are also more vulnerable to diseases and other shocks in their immediate environment.

Many Filipino children already suffer many deprivations. For instance, in recent years, malnutrition prevalence among children 0–5 years old has increased. In particular, the proportion of underweight children increased by 1.6 per cent in 2008 compared with

2005 (based on the National Nutrition Survey). Prevalence of under-height and underweight children also increased during the period. Meanwhile, an increase in the proportion of children not attending school was also recorded. Based on the results of the Annual Poverty Indicators Survey, about 2.2 million children 6–16 years old were not attending school in 2007; the estimate in 2002 was of about 1.8 million. In terms of housing, rapid growth in the number of children in informal settlements was recorded. In fact, the number doubled between 1985 and 2006.

Pre-existing poverty and vulnerability of millions of children in the Philippines served as a backdrop to the crises that erupted in 2008. In many ways, the aftershocks of these crises are continuing to unfold. The food and fuel price shocks of 2008 (with repeated price spikes in 2011) are likely to have affected millions of poor and low-income households, many of which may not have recovered fully from the initial round of price spikes. The subsequent global financial and economic crisis, whose effects were still rippling across the global economy at the time of writing, is also likely to have affected vulnerable sectors in the Philippines. Given that many children suffered from multiple deprivations even prior to these complex crises, there was clearly a high risk that poverty and deprivation among children could worsen as a result.

Conclusive data and evidence on crisis impact may take time to emerge. Yet policymakers need useful information in a timely manner in order to guide policy choices. Macro–micro modelling and simulation methods (see Cockburn et al., Cortina et al. in this volume) are one set of tools that enhance policymakers' understanding of crisis transmission channels and policy options. The recent crises have also spurred the use of rapid and (almost) real-time surveys as another set of tools in policymakers' arsenals to help bridge the information and evidence gap.

This chapter describes the results of one type of rapid survey in the Philippines, using a Community-based Monitoring System (CBMS). While the main objective is to provide evidence on crisis impacts on children in the Philippines, an associated goal is to underscore the importance of platforms for collecting both social and economic indicators in a timely manner. Having these systems in place prior to the onset of a crisis, as in the Philippines, can be quite fortuitous. In this case, it offered policymakers access to credible and timely information and evidence, in turn improving the prospects for more efficient and effective policy choices.

What are Community-based Monitoring Systems?

CBMS is an organised process of data collection and processing at the local level and of integration of data in local planning, programme implementation and impact monitoring. It promotes evidence-based policymaking and programme implementation while empowering communities to participate. It was developed in the early 1990s under the Micro Impacts of Macroeconomic Adjustment Policies Project in the Philippines to provide policymakers and programme implementers with a good information base for tracking the impacts of macroeconomic reforms and various policy shocks. Standard poverty monitoring systems generally rely on income and expenditure surveys, health surveys, population and housing censuses and so on, but these are too costly to be replicated frequently, they are conducted for different time periods, making it impossible to obtain a comprehensive profile of different socio-demographic groups at a specific point in time and they have sampling designs that do not allow for the geographical disaggregation local governments need. Decentralisation policy also creates greater demand for local-level data.

CBMS seeks to address existing data gaps at the local level in diagnosing the extent of poverty, determining its causes, formulating appropriate policies and programmes, identifying eligible beneficiaries and assessing policy and programme impacts. It also supports the decentralisation process by enabling local governments to collect, analyse and use data in local planning and programme implementation.

CBMS has several features that enhance the capacity of local governments to detect and reduce poverty: (1) it is based in local governments while also promoting community participation; (2) it uses existing local government personnel and community volunteers as monitors; (3) it has a core set of indicators; (4) it involves a complete enumeration of all households and (5) it establishes databanks at all geopolitical levels.

CBMS has a number of potentially concrete uses, particularly in the areas of local governance and poverty monitoring, as follows.

- CBMS can be used to further build the capacities of local government units as well as community members to address the needs of their respective localities by maximising the use of existing resources.
- One the most common dilemmas among local authorities is how to efficiently and effectively use and manage meagre financial resources given the many competing projects and programmes that need to be

implemented. CBMS tries to address this issue by providing the necessary information to reveal to decision makers an up-to-date development situation of communities in terms of core areas of welfare.

- CBMS can complement existing databases by providing a regular source of information on the socioeconomic attributes of communities to further enrich the contents and usefulness of existing databases. A number of local government units have been able to obtain funding from international organisations in the past to set up databanks containing information on children, environment and the like. CBMS can help enrich these databases by providing a complete set of household, *barangay* (village), municipality/city and provincial information.
- CBMS data also provide vital baseline information for the preparation of *barangay*, municipality/city and province socioeconomic profiles, annual investment plans, land use plans, infrastructure project proposals and other related development reports.
- CBMS provides disaggregated information that reveals a community's needs, based on the household survey and corresponding explanations for such deficiencies as gathered during the validation forum and supplemented by information gathered from the *barangay* profile questionnaire.
- Through poverty mapping, CBMS aids in identifying the location of municipalities/cities, *barangays* and even households that are in dire need of basic services. It has also been found that local policymakers' and communities' understanding of the poverty situation in their locality is facilitated greatly by the use of maps.
- CBMS can be used as a tool to monitor the Millennium Development Goals (MDGs) at the local level. Through CBMS, MDG indicators can be generated, providing local governments with critical information needed in the effort to attain the MDGs.
- CBMS can provide information on who is benefiting from targeted programmes. Information on leakages and exclusion can be used to refine targeting schemes of programmes.

As of 31 January 2011, CBMS is being implemented in 62 provinces (31 of which are province-wide), 723 municipalities and 44 cities of the Philippines, covering 18,927 *barangays*. The costs of implementation have been borne largely by local government units, indicating that they see the usefulness of the system. This bodes well for its sustainability. In some cases, non-governmental organisations (NGOs), donor agencies and other stakeholders have contributed to implementation.

CBMS has also been pilot tested and/or is being implemented in other countries, including Bangladesh, Cambodia, Indonesia, Laos and Vietnam in Asia; Benin, Burkina Faso, Ghana, Kenya, Nigeria, South Africa, Tanzania and Zambia in Africa and Argentina and Peru in Latin America.

Impact of food and fuel price shocks on children

When the food and fuel price shocks erupted in 2008, CBMS proved useful as one of the first rapid surveys to diagnose their impact.[2] In the Philippines, three sites were selected, including one rural *barangay* (Santa Rita in Capas, Tarlac) and two urban *barangays* (Barangays 51 and 85 in Pasay City). The sites include 1,043 households, representing a total population of 3,729.

During the crisis period, some households adopted a number of food-related coping strategies as the price of food, especially rice, increased significantly. Although some of these actions may not be attributable directly to the price shocks, the soar in food prices is likely to have influenced households' food expenditure during these times.[3]

Data show that about 22.4 per cent of households with children – roughly one in four households with children – in the selected CBMS sites adopted at least one food-related coping strategy, particularly in terms of changing the pattern of food consumption, preparation and purchase (Figure 8.1). The most common was mixing commercial rice with National Food Authority (NFA) rice, which is rice subsidised by the government for poor households (about 8.7 per cent of households). This was followed by eating the same food for several days and combining meals, reported by 7.0 per cent and 6.3 per cent of households, respectively.

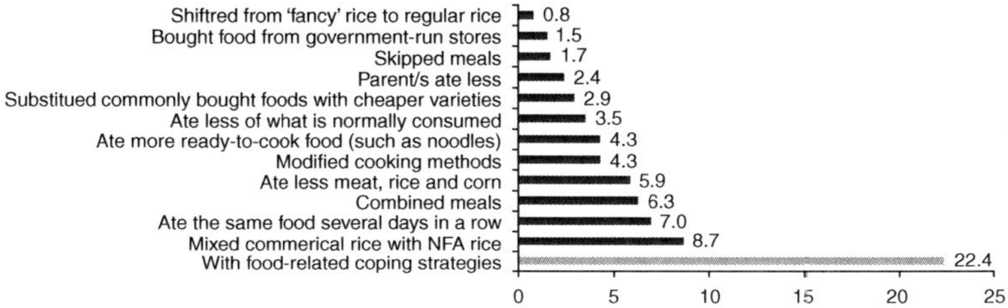

Figure 8.1 Coping strategies adopted by households with children 0–17 years old in relation to food consumption, 2008

Source: CBMS 2008.

Some coping strategies related to changes in food consumption patterns may, in the long run, have an impact on the health and nutritional status of children. The risks of eating the same foodstuff on a daily basis include nutritional deficiencies and calorie intake shortfall. Combining meals and shifting preference to ready-to-cook food entails the same health risks, especially for children and pregnant women. For households that shift to cheaper food or eat less frequently than the usual three meals a day, there is a chance that this may result in malnutrition. In some cases, higher expenditure on rice as a result of higher prices may also reduce expenditure on health and education.

The findings also suggest that the spike in food and fuel prices had a greater influence on the food consumption pattern of urban households, particularly in Barangay 51 (27.7 per cent) and Barangay 85 (23.0 per cent) in Pasay City, than on that of rural households (Sta. Rita – 16.2 per cent). Looking closely at responses from the three *barangays*, differences are apparent in terms of household coping strategies amid soaring prices of food. The household coping mechanism most practised by households with children in Sta. Rita (10.0 per cent) and Barangay 85 (6.3 per cent) was eating less meat and more fish and vegetables, whereas the major strategy adopted by households in Barangay 51 was mixing commercial rice with NFA rice (15.2 per cent). Accessibility of NFA retail stores in Barangay 51 may have influenced the way households coped with the crisis.

Meanwhile, at the individual level, data show that about 23.6 per cent of children 0–17 years old belong to households that modified their food consumption pattern. Again, the most common coping strategy in terms of food consumption was mixing commercial rice with NFA rice (8.5 per cent) (Table 8.1). Other common strategies, such as eating the same food for several days; eating less meat, rice and corn and combining meals may have negative consequences for the health of household members, including children. This again highlights the possibility of these children being malnourished as intake of nutritious food may be limited.

Health-seeking behaviour of households with children also changed during the reference period. In fact, about 26.9 per cent of households reported changes in the way they met their health and medical needs (Figure 8.2). The most common health-related coping strategy was seeking health assistance from government health centres and hospitals instead of private clinics. Santa Rita, which is a rural *barangay*, recorded the highest proportion here (41.2 per cent) of the three CBMS sites. Rural households may have to make adjustments to every aspect of their

Table 8.1 Children 0–17 years old in households that adopted coping strategies related to food consumption, 2008

	Sta. Rita		51		85		Total	
Coping strategy	**No.**	**%**	**No.**	**%**	**No.**	**%**	**No.**	**%**
With at least one food-related coping strategy	**148**	**19.4**	**199**	**28.1**	**62**	**23.5**	**409**	**23.6**
Mixed commercial rice with NFA rice	30	3.9	102	14.4	16	6.1	148	8.5
Ate the same food for several days in a row	31	4.1	91	12.9	0	0.0	122	7.0
Ate less meat, rice and corn and more fish, vegetables and root crops	89	11.6	13	1.8	18	6.8	120	6.9
Combined meals	13	1.7	95	13.4	2	0.8	110	6.3
Ate more ready-to-cook food (such as noodles) and less food requiring more preparation	39	5.1	40	5.7	12	4.5	91	5.2
Modified cooking method	62	8.1	10	1.4	10	3.8	82	4.7
Substituted commonly bought foods with cheaper varieties	34	4.5	23	3.3	8	3.0	65	3.7
Forced to eat less of what household normally consumes	46	6.0	10	1.4	8	3.0	64	3.7
Parent/s ate less	43	5.6	13	1.8	2	0.8	58	3.3
Skipped meals	12	1.6	13	1.8	3	1.1	28	1.6
Bought food from government-run stores	10	1.3	16	2.3	0	0.0	26	1.5
Shifted from 'fancy' rice to regular rice	2	0.3	4	0.6	8	3.0	14	0.8

Source: CBMS 2008.

expenditures including medical/health care needs. Urban households, on the other hand, can still manage to maintain their health-seeking behaviour by tapping other coping strategies available to them.

Data also show that about 31.0 per cent of children 0–17 years old belong to households that adopted coping strategies related to medical and health care (Table 8.2). Again, the data prove that going to government facilities for health-related concerns rather than to private clinics or hospitals is the most common strategy (18.5 per cent). In addition, about 16.3 per cent of children belong to households that decided to

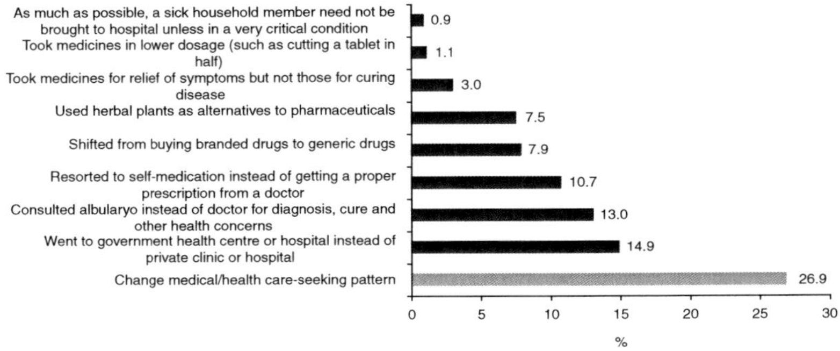

Figure 8.2 Coping strategies adopted by households with children 0–17 years old in relation to health, 2008

Source: CBMS 2008.

consult an *albularyo* (local healer) rather than a licensed doctor. It is also important to note that about 11.8 per cent of the children were living in households that reported resorting to self-medication instead of getting a proper prescription from a doctor (11.8 per cent). Not getting a proper prescription was most common among those living in urban *barangays*. In particular, about 17.7 per cent and 7.6 per cent of children in Barangay 51 and Barangay 85, respectively, belong to households that resorted to self-medication. This strategy may have negatively affected the health of these children.

Results also revealed that some households coped with increasing prices by sacrificing education-related expenses, which could have long-term effects on the poverty situation of the household. Some households decided to withdraw at least one child from school. About 4.1 per cent of children who were previously enrolled had to stop schooling during the reference school year, with Santa Rita recording the highest proportion, at 7.2 per cent. The most common reason for withdrawing children from school was financial limitations: about 36.7 per cent of households said they had no money for education-related expenses.

Impact of the global financial and economic crisis on children

Given its economic openness and strong economic ties with the US (the epicentre of the global financial crisis and the worldwide slowdown in 2009–10), the Philippines was clearly considered among the countries most vulnerable to the crisis impact.

Table 8.2 Children 0–17 years old in households that adopted coping strategies related to health, 2008

	Sta. Rita		51		85		Total	
Coping strategy	**No.**	**%**	**No.**	**%**	**No.**	**%**	**No.**	**%**
Changed medical/health care-seeking pattern	**365**	**47.8**	**144**	**20.9**	**23**	**8.7**	**532**	**31.0**
Went to government health centre or hospital instead of private clinic/hospital	262	**34.3**	51	7.4	4	1.5	317	18.5
Consulted *albularyo* instead of doctor for illness diagnosis, cure and other health concerns	225	29.5	53	7.7	2	0.8	280	16.3
Resorted to self-medication instead of getting a proper prescription from a doctor	60	7.9	122	17.7	20	7.6	202	11.8
Used herbal plants as alternative to pharmaceuticals	153	20.0	9	1.3	1	0.4	163	9.5
Shifted from branded drugs to generic drugs	91	11.9	41	5.9	1	0.4	133	7.7
Took medicines for relief of symptoms but not medicines for curing the disease	8	1.0	47	6.8	8	3.0	63	3.7
Took medicines in lower dosage (such as cutting a tablet into half)	18	2.4	12	1.7	0	0.0	30	1.7
As much as possible, a sick household member need not be brought to the hospital unless he/she is in a very critical condition	6	0.8	10	1.4	8	3.0	24	1.4

Source: CBMS 2008.

The global crisis impact study in the Philippines using CBMS covered a total of 13 *barangays* distributed all over the country to serve as poverty observatories or sentinel sites. These included eight sites in rural areas, four in urban areas outside the National Capital Region (NCR) and one in the urban NCR. Consistent with the CBMS methodology, all households in the selected sites were included in the survey. This translates to about 4,954 households with a total population of 21,454.

Although the impact of the crisis was not as large as initially expected, a modest increase in poverty was observed immediately during the short period of study. Moreover, coupling this with the impact of the food and fuel price shocks in 2008, the effects of recent natural calamities[4] and the commodity price volatility still ongoing at the time of writing, there is still a high risk that poverty incidence could worsen. This is even more worrisome given the recent reversal in poverty incidence observed in 2006, when poverty incidence went up for the first time since 1985.

CBMS results show that the potential impact of the crisis on poverty varies across different groups of households. Certain groups of households or individuals – such as those working in manufacturing or export-oriented firms, or households relying on remittances from overseas workers – were affected more than others. The next sections present the situation of children during the crisis period. The discussion includes a presentation of results for all households, for directly affected households and for panel households. These latter are those with at least one common member in both survey periods (Wave 1 – baseline survey, and Wave 2 – 2009 survey).[5] Panel households were matched for CBMS sites with at least two rounds of CBMS implementation.

Households and children directly affected by the global crisis

CBMS 2009 data show a significant number of children in directly affected households were poor.[6] In particular, about 71.9 per cent of children in affected households were income-poor (Table 8.3). The highest proportion was recorded in urban areas outside NCR, with about 79.5 per cent. Disaggregated data show that a slightly higher proportion of female children among these households were affected.

Based on CBMS 2009, about 3.5 per cent of panel households were affected directly by the global financial crisis (Table 8.4). The highest proportion was recorded in Villa Angeles (14.7 per cent), followed by Gumamela (6.3 per cent). Among those affected, about 79.4 per cent had at least one child member. This translates to about 37.1 of children 0–17 years of age belonging to directly affected households in the panel data. This may also mean that children of these directly affected households may experience worsening conditions as their households adopt coping strategies that can be damaging to their health and economic productivity. Meanwhile, although some households may not be affected directly by the global crisis, they may be affected indirectly.

Income poverty, subsistence poverty and food shortages among children during the crisis

Table 8.5 shows that about 70.0 per cent of households in the selected sentinel sites have at least one child. The highest proportion of households

Table 8.3 Children 0–17 years old in directly affected households, 2009

	Urban NCR		**Urban outside NCR**		**Rural**		**Total**	
	No.	**%**	**No.**	**%**	**No.**	**%**	**No.**	**%**
Income poverty								
Poor	58	26.98	611	79.5	201	40.1	1,068	71.9
Non-poor	157	73.02	158	20.5	300	59.9	417	28.1
Sex								
Male	106	49.3	371	48.2	209	41.7	726	48.9
Female	109	50.7	398	51.8	221	44.1	759	51.1
Total	215		769		501		1,485	

Source: CBMS 2009.

Table 8.4 Directly affected panel households, 2009

	Directly affected		**Directly affected with children**		**Children 0–17 in affected households**	
	No.	**%**	**No.**	**%**	**No.**	**%**
Urban NCR	**33**	**3.9**	**25**	**75.8**	**53**	**34.6**
192	33	3.9	25	75.8	53	34.6
Urban outside NCR	**89**	**0.6**	**70**	**78.7**	**154**	**35.5**
Gumamela	27	6.3	26	96.3	59	41.0
Magbangon	10	3.9	7	70.0	21	36.2
Villa Angeles	52	14.7	37	71.2	74	30.6
Rural	**53**	**2.0**	**44**	**83.0**	**116**	**43.0**
Ando	6	3.4	4	66.7	8	33.3
El Rio	9	3.7	6	66.7	16	35.6
Maligaya	6	0.6	5	83.3	14	51.9
Piglawigan	10	3.7	9	90.0	26	46.4
San Miguel	10	3.7	9	90.0	17	34.0
San Vicente	12	5.3	11	91.7	35	48.6
Total	**175**	**3.5**	**139**	**79.4**	**323**	**37.1**

Source: CBMS 2009.

with children is recorded in the rural sites (that is, about 72.3 per cent), as compared with urban NCR (59.7 per cent) and urban outside NCR (71.9 per cent). At the same time, the poverty rate among households with children is very high, at 40.6 per cent, compared with a poverty rate among households without children of about 19.7 per cent. It can also be noted that poverty incidence among households with children is higher in rural areas than in urban areas. One of the factors that may have contributed to this poverty condition is the occurrence of

Table 8.5 Households with or without children as a proportion of the poor, 2009

	Households with children		Households with children which are poor		Households without children which are poor	
	No.	%	No.	%	No.	%
Urban NCR	**511**	**59.7**	**50**	**9.8**	**7**	**2.0**
192	511	59.7	50	9.8	7	2.0
Urban outside NCR	**1,087**	**71.9**	**404**	**37.2**	**71**	**16.7**
Gumamela	322	74.5	168	52.2	24	21.8
Magbangon	191	73.8	118	61.8	29	42.6
Poblacion III	345	74.0	84	24.4	9	7.4
Villa Angeles	229	64.7	34	14.9	9	7.2
Rural	**1,870**	**72.3**	**954**	**51.0**	**215**	**30.0**
Ando	126	72.4	78	61.9	13	27.1
El Rio	198	81.2	143	72.2	34	73.9
Maligaya	620	66.1	179	28.9	37	11.6
Masikap	152	67.0	25	16.5	6	8.0
Piglawigan	238	87.2	190	79.8	26	74.3
Salvacion	184	77.6	61	33.2	9	17.0
San Miguel	175	65.1	138	78.9	64	68.1
San Vicente	177	78.7	140	79.1	26	54.2
Total	**3,468**	**70.0**	**1,408**	**40.6**	**293**	**19.7**

Source: CBMS 2009.

several shocks in recent years, including economic shocks and natural calamities (although it is difficult to attribute these results solely to such crises).

At household member level, results show that poverty incidence among children is even higher. In fact, about 45.4 per cent (representing 8,094 children) were considered income-poor during the reference period (Table 8.6). Member-level data also confirm that the proportion of income-poor children was higher in rural areas than in urban areas. Moreover, about one-third of children below 18 years of age were living below the food poverty threshold. The proportion of food-poor among children again was highest among those in rural areas. Food shortage was also experienced by about 6.8 per cent of children in the sentinel sites. This rate was even higher among children in rural *barangays*, where about 11.1 per cent belong to households that reported food shortages during the three-month period prior to the survey.

Results reveal that, while about 80.6 per cent of households in Wave 1 have children, the proportion decreased only slightly to 79.4 per cent

Table 8.6 Children under 18 who are income-poor and food-poor and who suffered food shortage, 2009

	Children who are income-poor		Children who are food-poor		Children who experienced food shortage	
	No.	%	No.	%	No.	%
Urban NCR	**254**	**11.6**	**67**	**3.1**	**43**	**2.0**
192	254	11.6	67	3.1	43	2.0
Urban outside NCR	**2,412**	**42.3**	**1,541**	**27.0**	**74**	**1.3**
Gumamela	1,008	57.3	659	37.5	0	0.0
Magbangon	690	65.2	592	55.9	0	0.0
Poblacion III	525	29.4	234	13.1	74	4.1
Villa Angeles	189	17.2	56	5.1	0	0.0
Rural	**5428**	**54.7**	**4319**	**43.5**	**1,097**	**11.1**
Ando	526	68.4	390	50.7	82	10.7
El Rio	759	71.4	622	58.5	424	40.4
Maligaya	877	30.1	613	21.0	6	0.2
Masikap	134	17.4	53	6.9	5	0.7
Piglawigan	1,110	81.2	1,014	74.2	373	27.3
Salvacion	345	36.0	190	19.8	152	15.9
San Miguel	858	81.0	792	74.8	55	5.2
San Vicente	819	80.8	645	63.6	0	0.0
Total	**8,094**	**45.4**	**5,927**	**33.3**	**1,214**	**6.8**

Source: CBMS 2009.

in Wave 2 (Table 8.7). It can also be noted from the panel data that the proportion of poor among these households with children increased from 29.8 per cent in Wave 1 to 31.7 per cent in Wave 2. Comparing the two groups of households according to the presence of a child member, data show that the proportion of poor among households with children is consistently higher than among households without children during the two survey periods.

Looking at the panel households, data show that while about 36.0 per cent of children were income-poor in Wave 1, the proportion increased to 40.2 per cent in Wave 2. This may imply that income poverty among children worsened during the period of the crisis. Moreover, the data show that poverty is more common among male children than among female children. The same trend is observed in both waves. With regard to subsistence, results confirm that food poverty among children increased between Wave 1 and Wave 2 by about 3.8 percentage points. At the same time, the proportion of children who experienced food shortages increased during the period of the crisis: about 4.0 per cent

Table 8.7 Directly affected households that are income poor and with children, Wave 1 and Wave 2

	Wave 1		Wave 2	
	No.	%	No.	%
Households with children	141	80.6	139	79.4
Poor	42	29.8	44	31.7
Non-poor	99	70.2	95	68.4
Households without children	34	19.4	36	20.6
Poor	4	11.8	8	22.2
Non-poor	30	88.2	28	77.8

Source: CBMS 2009.

Table 8.8 Children under 18 who are income-poor and food-poor and suffered food shortages in panel households, Wave 1 and Wave 2

	Wave 1		Wave 2	
	No.	%	No.	%
Income-poor				
Male	65	41.7	71	43.6
Female	48	30.4	59	36.9
All children	113	36.0	130	40.2
Food-poor				
Male	43	27.6	43	26.4
Female	18	11.4	32	20.0
All children	61	19.4	75	23.2
Food shortage				
Male	3	1.9	4	2.5
Female	4	2.5	9	5.6
All children	7	2.2	13	4.0

Notes: Households were asked if in the previous three months they had experienced hunger and not had anything to eat, even once. If the household responded yes, then that household was classified as having experienced a food shortage.

Source: CBMS 2009.

of children suffered food shortages in Wave 2, whereas only about 2.2 per cent experienced food shortages in Wave 1. Although food shortage incidence increased for both groups of children (that is, male and female children), the proportion of food-poor male children increased less, going from 1.9 per cent in Wave 1 to 2.5 per cent in Wave 2. Food shortages are therefore more common among female children than among male children.

Results show that some households adopted coping strategies which, in the long run, could be detrimental to the health of their members, especially children. About 86.2 per cent of households with children reported changing their food consumption pattern during the crisis period (Table 8.9). In addition, about 85.8 per cent of children belong to these households. This means that the health and nutrition status of these children could be affected in the long term. The highest proportion of households with children that adopted food-related coping strategies was recorded in urban NCR (94.7 per cent). The highest proportion of children who belong to households that adopted this strategy was also recorded in urban NCR (94.2 per cent). The most common strategy adopted by households with children was reducing the consumption of expensive food, which was reported by about 43.9 per cent of households (Figure 8.3). Meanwhile, when looking at different groups of households based on location, results show that the most common strategy among households with children in urban areas was reducing

Table 8.9 Households with children age 0–17 that adopted at least one coping strategy related to food consumption, and children who belonged to these households by site, 2009

	Households with children		**Children**	
	No.	**%**	**No.**	**%**
Urban NCR	**484**	**94.7**	**2,070**	**94.2**
192	484	94.7	2,070	94.2
Urban outside NCR	**907**	**83.4**	**4,759**	**83.4**
Gumamela	239	74.2	1,315	74.8
Magbangon	154	80.6	855	80.7
Poblacion III	299	86.7	1,555	87.1
Villa Angeles	215	93.9	1,034	93.8
Rural	**1,599**	**85.5**	**8,467**	**85.4**
Ando	93	73.8	568	73.9
El Rio	168	84.9	921	86.6
Maligaya	596	96.1	2,796	95.8
Masikap	117	77.0	619	80.3
Piglawigan	133	55.9	799	58.5
Salvacion	176	95.7	911	95.1
San Miguel	151	86.3	901	85.1
San Vicente	165	93.2	952	93.9
Total	**2,990**	**86.2**	**15,296**	**85.8**

Source: CBMS 2009.

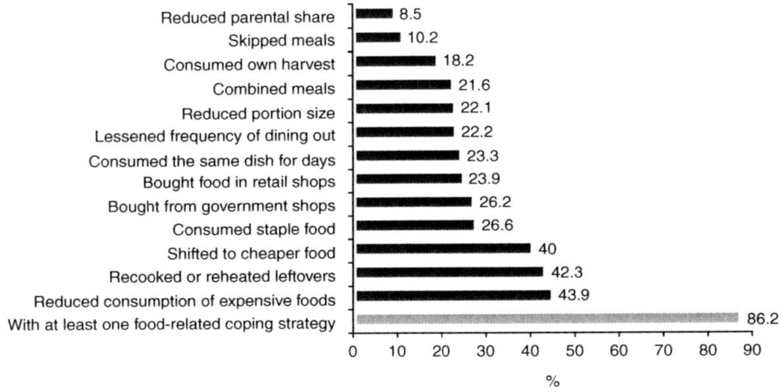

Figure 8.3 Coping strategies adopted by households with children age 0–17 years related to food consumption, 2009

Source: CBMS 2009.

consumption of expensive food; in rural areas it was re-cooking and reheating leftovers.

Some households adopted strategies that could sacrifice their members' health. Results show that about 61.7 per cent of households with children resorted to changing their health-seeking behaviour during the crisis period (Figure 8.4). This translates to about 61.3 per cent of children whose health may be affected as a result of these changes, with urban NCR recording an even higher proportion of about 71.7 per cent (Table 8.10).

Meanwhile, malnutrition still existed among children 0–5 years old. In fact, about 2.4 per cent of children in this age range were classified as malnourished during the reference period. Urban NCR recorded the highest proportion, at 2.0 per cent.

Social protection programmes for children in the Philippines

In recent years, the Philippine government has put in place social protection programmes to protect vulnerable populations and households from different types of risks. However, these programmes could be improved, based on additional insights from CBMS data.

For instance, the Department of Social Welfare and Development (DSWD), the lead government agency in charge of implementing

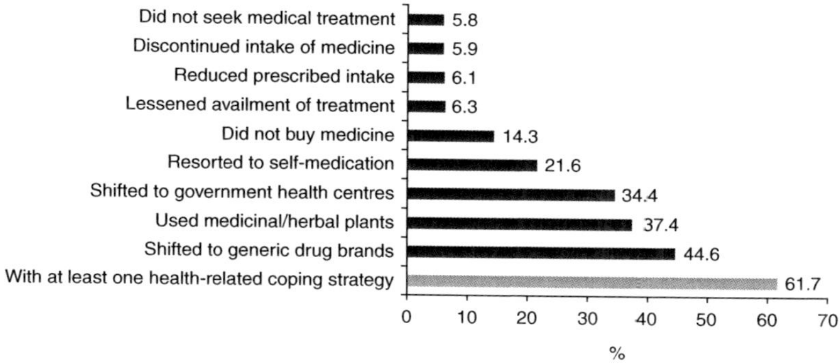

Figure 8.4 Coping strategies adopted by households with children age 0–17 years related to health, 2009

Source: CBMS 2009.

Table 8.10 Households with children age 0–17 that adopted at least one coping strategy related to health, and children who belonged to these households by site, 2009

	Households with children		Children	
	No.	%	No.	%
Urban NCR	**372**	**72.8**	1,576	71.7
192	372	72.8	1,576	71.7
Urban outside NCR	**549**	**50.5**	**2,922**	**51.2**
Gumamela	95	29.5	543	30.9
Magbangon	74	38.7	406	38.3
Poblacion III	220	63.8	1,189	66.6
Villa Angeles	160	69.9	784	71.1
Rural	**1,220**	**65.2**	**6,418**	**64.7**
Ando	74	58.7	436	56.7
El Rio	122	61.6	645	60.7
Maligaya	517	83.4	2,471	84.7
Masikap	66	43.4	320	41.5
Piglawigan	102	42.9	590	43.2
Salvacion	114	62.0	613	64.0
San Miguel	117	66.9	715	67.5
San Vicente	108	61.0	628	61.9
Total	**2,141**	**61.7**	**10,916**	**61.3**

Source: CBMS 2009.

programmes that assist vulnerable groups in society including children, has rolled out specific programmes meant to protect and encourage household investments in child health and nutrition. Its conditional cash transfer (CCT) programme, or the Pantawid Pamilyang Pilipino Program (4Ps), has recently been expanded to cover 2.3 million poor households by the end of 2011. Under this programme, eligible families with a maximum of three children receive a monthly allowance of P1,400, a P500 monthly allowance for nutrition and health expenses and P3,000 for one school year or P300 per month for educational expenses per child. Beneficiaries have to comply with certain conditions to continue receiving the cash grants. These include ensuring that children attend school at least 85 per cent of the time and receive vaccinations and health care. On the supply side, local government units have to provide basic facilities and supplies for health, like vaccines and family planning services, and education.

As with CCT programmes in other developing countries, policymakers face implementation challenges in relation to the 4Ps. Problems include benefit leakages to non-poor households, exclusion of poor households, delays in payments, poor education and health facilities in coverage areas, noncompliance with conditions and corruption. Reyes et al. (2010) found that in two 4Ps implementing sites, although the poorest quintile had the largest proportion of households who were able to access the programme, a significant proportion of households in the upper quintiles were still benefiting. Leakage and exclusion rates among households for the two *barangays* were estimated at 21.2 per cent and 44.4 per cent, respectively. In order to respond systematically to these issues, the 4Ps has established a grievance redressal system, through which stakeholders can voice their concerns, complaints and suggestions regarding the programme.

Based on CBMS findings, some 4Ps beneficiaries should not qualify for the programme. Although the model used in selecting beneficiaries for the 4Ps is not available to the authors at this time, it is important to note that some beneficiaries may not necessarily be considered 'poor' based on some obvious household characteristics. Table 8.11 shows the socioeconomic characteristics of four beneficiary households in El Rio and Piglawigan in Agusan del Sur. One important characteristic is that all four households were classified as non-poor in terms of income, as their annual per capita income did not fall below the income poverty threshold. At the same time, these households are not proxy means test poor.[7] In addition, Household 2 in El Rio owned all types of assets, which may also be an indication that the household was not necessarily

Table 8.11 Socioeconomic characteristics of four beneficiary households of 4Ps

	Piglawigan		El Rio	
Characteristics	**Household 1**	**Household 2**	**Household 1**	**Household 2**
Household size	5	7	5	6
Annual per capita income	P23,349	P77,280	P10,5100.0	P154,200
Educational attainment of head	Grade 6	4th year high school	1st year high school	High school graduate
Educational attainment of spouse	4th year high school	Grade 6	Grade 5	High school graduate
Head is working	Yes	Yes	Yes	Yes
Spouse is working	No	No	Yes	No
Industry where head is working	Transportation and storage	Agriculture	Agriculture	Agriculture
Industry where spouse is working	N/A	N/A	Hotels and restaurants	N/A
With children	Yes	Yes	Yes	No
With malnourished children	No	N/A	No	N/A
With children who are not studying	Yes	No	Yes	N/A
Income-poor	No	No	No	No
Food-poor	No	No	No	No
Proxy means test poor	No	No	No	No
Assets				
Radio	No	No	Yes	Yes
TV	Yes	No	Yes	Yes
DVD/VCD/VHS player	Yes	No	Yes	Yes
Stereo	No	No	N/A	N/A
Karaoke	No	Yes	N/A	N/A
Refrigerator	Yes	Yes	Yes	Yes
Electric fan	No	Yes	N/A	N/A
Iron	Yes	Yes	Yes	Yes
Stove	No	No	Yes	Yes
Washing machine	No	No	No	Yes
Microwave	No	No	No	Yes
Computer	No	No	No	Yes
Cellular phone	Yes	No	Yes	Yes
Telephone	No	No	No	No
Air conditioner	No	No	No	Yes
Sewing machine	Yes	Yes	N/A	N/A
Car	No	No	No	Yes

Source: CBMS 2009.

poor. Note also that the same household had no child members. These results therefore highlight the potential to improve on programme implementation.

In addition, DSWD, the Department of Education (DepEd) and NFA have put in place programmes aimed at mitigating hunger and addressing calorie and nutrition deficiencies among young children. One of these is the Food-for-School Programme implemented by DSWD and DepEd. This covers pupils from day care level to Grade 3, including special education and preschool. In exchange for school attendance, each child receives 1 kg of iron-fortified rice per day for a specified period of time. Assessments conducted by implementing agencies have observed improved school attendance and improved weight of children from targeted schools as a result of the programme.

A similar programme, the Breakfast Feeding Programme, implemented by DepEd, aims to improve not only children's nutrition but also their performance in class through the provision of specially formulated noodles to Grades 1 and 2 pupils in selected schools. However, no information is available regarding the programme's achievements.

Although not directed solely at children, another programme worth mentioning is NFA's Tindahan Natin Project, which provides low-price but high-quality rice and noodles to low-income families through shops. The programme focuses on areas identified by the National Nutrition Council as having high hunger and poverty incidences. This loosely targeted programme is highly subsidised, with critics pointing to substantial benefit leakages to non-poor households. Reyes et al. (2011) found that in three *barangays* surveyed during the height of food and fuel price shocks in 2008, not all poor households were able to access NFA rice, whereas some non-poor households could do so. Leakage and exclusion rates for the programme were estimated at 76.6 per cent and 35.7 per cent, respectively, indicating problems with the targeting of the subsidised rice programme.

Suffice it to say that this additional evidence shows that there is still scope to improve the effectiveness and efficiency of government programmes to protect poor households and children. CBMS could provide useful data and evidence to complement government data, offering credible and timely information that would allow for stronger policy responsiveness to the challenges at hand.

Conclusion

Based on national data, many children in the Philippines are already suffering many deprivations, especially in terms of lack of access to shelter, water and sanitation. Some children are also deprived in terms of health and education. Household-level data collected through the CBMS mechanism further confirms that children are deprived in many dimensions.

CBMS results also show that crises, such as price shocks and the global economic slowdown, could maintain, if not worsen, the poverty situation among children. Estimates for 2006 for the Philippines showed that about 17,000 children in the country were suffering from simultaneous deprivations in terms of shelter, sanitation and water (PIDS, 2009). Meanwhile, the 2008 CBMS in three sites showed that about 5.1 per cent of children were deprived on at least two dimensions of deprivation in terms of shelter, water and sanitation. In addition, the 2009 survey in the 13 global financial crisis sentinel sites revealed multiple deprivations for 2.1 per cent of children. Additional CBMS results showed that some children were also deprived in terms of health, nutrition and education, among others.

Recent increases in the prices of food and fuel may trigger the same impacts again. Given this, there is a critical need for a ready menu of safety nets that can be implemented quickly to avert the negative long-term consequences of shocks and coping strategies adopted. Great challenges also lie in improving the targeting of programmes. A real-time monitoring system such as CBMS that can generate data at the community and household level could be critical to better arming policymakers with the necessary information and evidence to respond quickly and effectively to such crises. Equally important, CBMS could help identify possible inefficiencies and inequities in programme implementation and thus offer scope for improvement in government programmes to protect the poor and vulnerable.

Notes

1. This section draws largely on chapter 2 'Poverty and Children' prepared by Celia Reyes and Aubrey Tabuga as part of the Global Study on Child Poverty and Disparities in the Philippines conducted by the Philippine Institute for Development Studies (PIDS) and the UN Children's Fund (UNICEF).
2. This is part of a multi-country initiative of the Poverty and Economic Policy (PEP) CBMS Network to assess the impact of the food and fuel shocks on poverty. Similar studies have been carried out in Cambodia and Ghana.
3. The complete results of the study can be accessed at www.pep-net.org/programs/cbms/special-initiatives/impact-of-rising-prices-of-food-and-oil.
4. In 2009, the Philippines experienced very strong typhoons, suffering significant damage to lives and property.
5. Wave 1 for Barangay 192, Villa Angeles, Gumamela, San Vicente, Magbangon, El Rio and Piglawigan refers to the year 2005; Wave 1 for Ando, San Miguel and Maligaya refers to 2006. Wave 2 for all sites refers to 2009.
6. Those who were affected through the two key transmission channels for the Philippines: domestic employment and overseas employment and remittance

channels. This includes households that experienced a reduction in the amount and frequency of remittances; with a member who lost a job; that experienced a reduction in wage, working hours and employment benefits; that saw a decline in income and employed workers from an entrepreneurial activity.

7. This refers to the model developed by Reyes used in identifying poor households. The model was estimated using Family Income and Expenditure Survey data and then applied to CBMS data to be able to identify which households were poor based on household characteristics.

References

Development Academy of the Philippines (2009) 'The Review and Strengthening of the National Social Protection and Welfare Program.' Project Terminal Report.

PIDS (2009) 'Global Study on Child Poverty and Disparities: The Case of the Philippines.' Discussion Paper 2009-27. Makati: PIDS.

Reyes, C., Sobreviñas A. and de Jesus, J. (2010). 'The Impact of the Global Financial and Economic Crisis on Poverty in the Philippines.' Eighth PEP Network Policy Conference. Dakar, 15 June.

Reyes, C. Sobreviñas A., Bancolita, J. and de Jesus, J. (2011) 'Analysis of the Impact of Changes in the Prices of Rice and Fuel on Poverty in the Philippines.' In Reyes, C. and Sobreviñas, A. (eds) *Impact of Rising Prices of Food and Fuel on Poverty in Cambodia, Ghana, and the Philippines*. Manila: PEP-CBMS Network Coordinating Team.

9

Turning Crisis into Opportunity for Children Affected by HIV/AIDS: Responding to the Financial, Fuel and Food Crises

Nicola Jones with Caroline Harper

Introduction and conceptual framework

In September of 2010, the Joint UN Programme on HIV/AIDS (UNAIDS) lauded global progress towards curtailing the HIV/AIDS epidemic. Executive Director Michel Sidibé announced, 'For the first time change is happening at the heart of the epidemic. In places where HIV was stealing away dreams, we now have hope' (UN News Centre, 2010). Nearly two dozen countries in Sub-Saharan Africa (SSA) have seen a 25 per cent decline in the number of new infections since the millennium. There has also been a 12-fold increase in the number of patients on antiretroviral (ARV) medication and HIV-related deaths are declining correspondingly. Nearly half of all HIV-positive pregnant women now have access to treatment protocols to prevent vertical transmission to their infants (WHO et al., 2009).

However, evidence indicates that the effects of the 2008–10 food, fuel and financial crisis are poised to wipe out much of this hard-won progress towards Millennium Development Goal (MDG) 6. Although it is difficult to isolate these effects for a given country, Figure 9.1 provides an indication of the differential impacts of the financial crisis on the HIV/AIDS situation internationally. The Democratic Republic of Congo (DRC), Eritrea, Ethiopia, Mozambique, Niger, Rwanda, Tanzania, The Gambia and Zambia are facing the greatest overall vulnerability.

Similarly, UNAIDS and World Bank (2009a; 2009b) highlight that countries most at risk are those that (1) have the highest HIV prevalence,

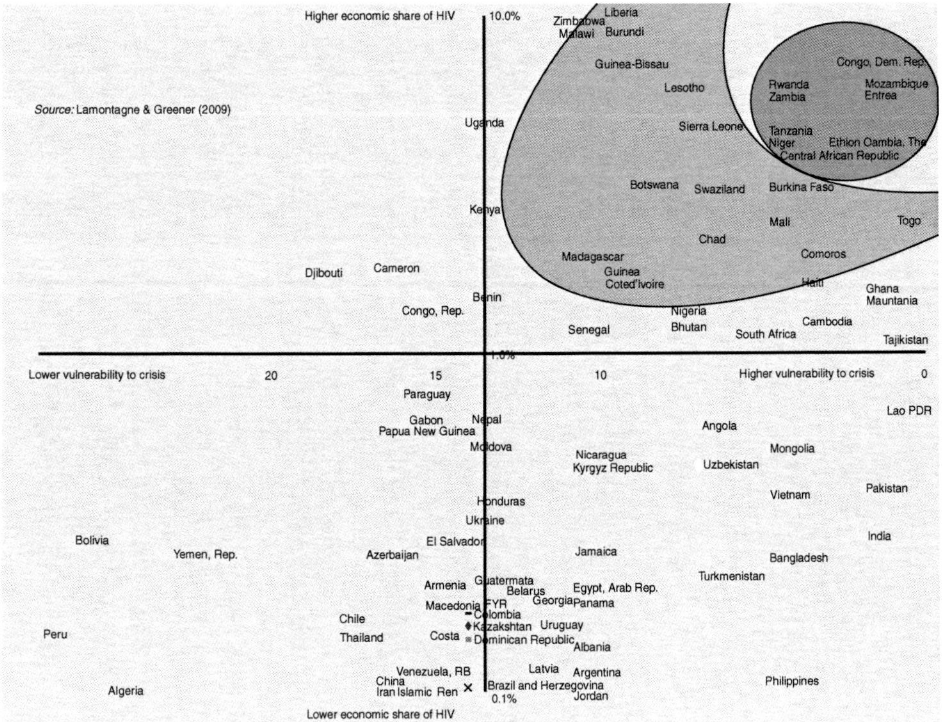

Figure 9.1 Impact of the financial crisis on HIV/AIDS by country, according to economic share[1] of HIV/AIDS and vulnerability to crisis

Source: Based on UNAIDS (2009b).

and thus the largest financial resource requirements; (2) are most exposed to a combination of external shocks, such as declines in foreign investment, volumes and prices of exported commodities, workers' remittances and external aid and (3) rely primarily on domestic resources to finance their national HIV response. Political commitment by national leaders is likely to have a strong influence on countries' ability to address the negative impacts of the financial crisis (ibid.).

While evidence is patchy,[2] it is generally agreed that the financial crisis is exacerbating previous difficulties and vulnerabilities rather than creating new ones. In particular, as we elaborate below, pre-existing challenges related to budgeting and social protection have intensified as a result of the crisis. By late 2009, more than 50 per cent of countries surveyed reported that both treatment and prevention efforts had been compromised, and more than three-quarters indicated that developmental efforts towards universal access had been derailed (UNAIDS, 2009c). The ramifications of this could extend for years. While prevention lacks 'the glamour' of treatment, and it has had to make do with smaller and often more vulnerable budgets, it is the cornerstone of the global strategy to wipe out HIV/AIDS. Backsliding now could reverse years of work. And, of course, treatment is also vital: disrupted protocols leave patients more infectious, further hindering global prevention efforts.

Crisis-related reversals are expected to have the largest impact on children. Despite this, there has been no comprehensive review of HIV/AIDS-related crisis impacts specific to children and their caregivers. This is critical, given that the mortality rate among infected children is disproportionate to that among adults, and that relatively fewer children have access to antiretroviral therapy (ART) which, if used effectively, could virtually eliminate vertical transmission rates, ensuring an HIV-free generation (GFATM, 2010). However, many governments lack policy strategies to address the child-specific dimensions of the epidemic, and thus there is a risk of children living with or highly vulnerable to the disease remaining invisible in the context of the crisis.

In order to understand how the macro-level changes brought by the crisis translate into meso- and micro-level effects on children living with or vulnerable to HIV/AIDS and their caregivers, it is important to understand the impact pathways through which changes in the global macroeconomic environment filter through country-specific policy and institutional frameworks at national and sub-national levels to affect communities, households and individuals. The conceptual framework that underpins this approach draws on Harper et al. in this volume.

We first look at micro-level effects on families, children and communities, and then at meso- and macro-level effects and how these shape economic and social policy choices. In this, we discuss both HIV/AIDS-specific pre- and post-crisis policy and programming, and social protection initiatives that may provide more general support to children and their families affected by or vulnerable to HIV/AIDS. We conclude with a discussion of policy implications and ways this global crisis could be turned into an opportunity for children affected by HIV/AIDS.

Crisis impacts on children: current and new infections

The crisis is likely to affect infants, children and youth differently, through the following key variables. Most of these are a product of the economic risk and intensification of poverty that both HIV/AIDS-affected households and children vulnerable to HIV infection face in times of economic downturn.

Food consumption

Both quantity and quality of food intake have suffered significantly (Hossain, 2009), due to lower household income, local currency depreciations and/or food price hikes. For instance, a focus group of HIV-infected people in Nairobi reported that they could no longer provide adequate food for their HIV-infected children, who in turn could not understand why they were being given so little to eat (ICAAP, 2009). Reductions in food intake and shifts to low-quality food products raise concerns relating to higher levels of malnutrition, including wasting, anaemia and other micronutrient deficiency conditions, as well as impaired mental development, diminished learning ability, reduced work productivity and increased prevalence of chronic disease among poor populations in general, especially women and children (WHO, 2008). These impacts are likely to be particularly severe for HIV-infected individuals, as they tend to suffer from more frequent and severe opportunistic infections, due to a lack of immune response. Adults living with HIV require 10 per cent to 30 per cent more energy than before infection, and children may need up to 100 per cent more (IFPRI, 2008). Meanwhile, even a small decline in the quantity and quality of food may lead to heightened risk of HIV infection for children and young people, as their vulnerability to infection increases simultaneously with malnutrition and the resulting dampening of their immune systems.

Furthermore, food insecurity is likely to have significant impacts for those being treated for HIV/AIDS, for several reasons: food weakens some of the negative side effects of taking ARVs; ARV patients experience increased appetite and, if cash is diverted into food purchases, there may not be sufficient household funds left over for transportation to clinics (ibid.). Evidence also suggests that those who are malnourished when they begin therapy have much lower survival rates, and blood plasma concentrations of some drugs have been found to be lower in malnourished individuals, suggesting a relationship between adequate food intake and ARV absorption efficacy. Moreover, 'Where food insecurity translates into increased rates of maternal under-nutrition, we can expect to see a rise in babies born with low birth weight, who in turn may be at higher risk of vertical (mother to child) HIV transmission' (ibid.: 1).

Moreover, studies in Botswana, Malawi, Swaziland, Tanzania and Zambia have demonstrated associations between acute food security and unprotected transactional sex for poor women, while sudden increases in food insecurity can often result in distress migration and increased risk of HIV exposure (IFPRI, 2008) (see below). Children may be taken out of school to work for cash or food, which not only denies them an education (including on HIV prevention) but also increases their risk of HIV infection. Rising food prices may also mean fewer extended families can provide homes for those orphaned by HIV/AIDS, and programmes providing essential care for orphans and vulnerable children (OVC) are having to reduce the length of time they can offer support (ibid.).

Health-seeking behaviour

Although ART is free in many countries, patients still need to pay other costs, often including bribes for tests and services. Travel costs are repeatedly cited as hindering access to clinics and drugs.[3] The time involved can also stop parents seeking treatment for children.

Even in 'committed' households, unexpected or sudden shocks can interrupt care by making planned-for treatment prohibitively expensive in terms of time or money: the rise in food prices has 'forced people to choose between taking ART on an empty stomach or foregoing treatment to keep food on the table' (World Bank, 2011). This can have considerable detrimental effects in terms of responsiveness to a future cure as a result of developing viral resistance to first-line drugs (UNAIDS, 2009a). Furthermore, discontinuing ART treatment can increase the risk of contracting preventable HIV-connected diseases.

Financial hardships often lead families to seek alternatives to costly allopathic health care, increasing reliance on traditional medical practitioners (including witch doctors) who are often of questionable benefit (and are sometimes harmful) to infected individuals or children. In Zimbabwe, for example, the crisis led to a resurgence of traditional forms of medicine as an alternative to unaffordable orthodox treatment: it is estimated that 80 per cent of the population is currently relying on traditional medicine (IRIN, 2007).

Crisis effects can also result in increased numbers of HIV infections through cutbacks in health care seeking compounded by cutbacks in services. For example, as pregnant women and new mothers delay testing for HIV and thus reduce their uptake of critical prevention of mother-to-child transmission (PMTCT) interventions, there are implications for both unborn and newborn babies, adding to the 400,000 new infant infections each year (GFATM, 2010).

Social exclusion

While migration is in itself not a risk factor for HIV infection, adult and child migrants often face increased vulnerability through exposure to exploitative situations (Richter, 2009). Under conditions of economic stress, such vulnerabilities may rise. Marginalised groups such as sex workers, injecting drug users, prisoners, refugees and internally displaced persons (IDPs) can be indirectly more prone to HIV infection through stigmatisation by health planners (House of Commons, 2008). In Indonesia and China, for example, many migrants working in the manufacturing and construction sectors lost their jobs as a result of the financial crisis. In Hong Kong, Malaysia, Singapore and Taiwan working conditions worsened, leading to increased concerns that female migrants losing jobs would move into sex work to survive, exacerbating the risk of contracting HIV/AIDS (JUNIMA, 2009). Migrants often do not have access to subsidised ARV treatment, even if it exists in their host country. If they lose work and move into the informal economy, their links to existing HIV programmes can weaken further because of fear of detention when accessing these services (Richter, 2009).

Eroding social capital and increased social violence are common outcomes of economic shocks, often with negative spill-over effects for children (Harper et al., 2009). Marginalisation of children with HIV is already widespread, and it is likely to increase as a result of economic shocks. Violations of children's rights to care and protection and access to education; increased incidence of exploitation and abuse; loss of homes and inheritance rights through property grabbing and increased risk of becoming street children or child trafficking victims are all major impacts of HIV/AIDS on the lives of children (CRIN, 2009).

Loss of livelihood and risky coping strategies

Millions of households across the developing world are facing increased poverty as a result of the crisis (World Bank, 2009), which has led to the adoption of risky coping strategies, exposing both women and children to the vulnerabilities associated with HIV infection. In Jamaica, Kenya, Mozambique and Zambia, there is evidence of children engaging in hazardous forms of labour to supplement declining household incomes, including commercial sex work, transactional sex (trading sex for food or gifts), domestic work, drug peddling and internal migration to look for work (Hossain et al., 2009), all of which increase the risk of infection. Among a sample of Cambodian sex workers, 58 per cent were found to have entered the trade since the onset of the crisis, due to declining family remittances, difficult family circumstances and the ability to earn higher wages (UNDP, 2009). This is likely to have impacts on the quantity and quality of caring time available for younger children especially.

Moreover, in times of financial hardship, women may stop demanding condom use for fear of losing clients. During the 1997–8 East Asian crisis, many vulnerable women entered commercial sex work in informal settings due to a loss of alternative means of income generation, but reduced demand also reduced their power to negotiate condom use (Richter, 2009). This is reportedly also the case in the Philippines in the 2008–10 crisis: lack of employment opportunities are reportedly increasing the number of commercial sex workers but also reducing their bargaining position with clients on condom use (JUNIMA, 2009).

Gender dimensions

Globally, there is increasing evidence of the feminisation of the HIV/AIDS epidemic. In SSA, 61 per cent of those infected are girls and women, many age 15–24. In the Caribbean, 43 per cent are women, and numbers are rising gradually in Latin America, Asia and Eastern Europe (GFATM, 2009a). Given what we know about women serving as shock absorbers in crisis contexts (Holmes et al., 2009), the additional strain of their own HIV status may compromise this important but generally unseen buffering effect, exacerbating impacts on children.

There is also good evidence that gender relations shift in times of economic crisis: there tends to be higher levels of gender-based domestic violence, exacerbated by unemployment, financial stress and changing household membership as migrants come and go (Pearson and Sweetman, 2011). Under such conditions, women's power within the household also shifts – sometimes strengthening, especially if they are bringing in financial resources – sometimes weakening. Expenditures, including on nutrition for children, seem generally dependent on the level of decision-making and bargaining power women have at home (ibid.). For instance, cases of households earmarking food and medical resources for men rather than children were reported in Jamaica in the 2008–10 crisis (Hossain et al., 2009). In addition, worsened access to ART services due to budget cuts means use of home-based care options is likely to increase, exacerbating women's time poverty in particular and potentially raising intra-household tensions. Finally, for girls, simply being enrolled in school is protective against HIV (CRIN, 2009), by delaying sexual activity, improving knowledge on health issues and increasing self-efficacy and control in relationships. However, there are reports that the 2008–10 crisis has led to school dropouts as a result of increased poverty (Hossain et al., 2009).

Policy choices: pre-existing and crisis responses

Pre-existing policy approaches

National political commitments to scaling up HIV prevention, treatment and care have intensified in recent years, with an increasing number of countries moving to national programmes supported by domestic scale up plans and population-based targets. As of 2008, 57 per cent of low- and middle-income countries had implemented national plans for scaling up PMTCT, and 44 per cent had plans to scale up treatment and care for children, compared with 28 per cent and 15 per cent, respectively, three years earlier (WHO et al., 2009). That said, a number of international factors are undermining HIV-related spending, many of them exacerbated by the crisis context: a significant funding gap; generally declining levels of donor commitment to specific HIV/AIDS funding; the expiry of committed funds and health sector human resources constraints (including increased demand on health systems, reduced health care training opportunities and brain drains).

Although spending today is much higher than it was before the millennium, thanks in significant part to global financing mechanisms, current funding levels remain insufficient to tackle the epidemic. In 2008, during its eight round for proposals, the Global Fund to Fight AIDS, Tuberculosis and Malaria (GFATM) identified a funding gap of approximately $4 billion for 2008–10; demand during the period has been estimated at approximately $13.5 million, and donor funding based on pledges already received and indicated amounts to only $9.5 billion (GFATM, 2009b). This budget deficit is not a direct outcome of the 2008–10 crisis, but rather originates from the fact that grant proposals have doubled as a result of the huge need for the continuation and scale up of programmes to move towards universal access to treatment.

Meanwhile, 2009 funding levels were reported at a full $10 billion under optimum levels, and 2010 was the first year in which President's Emergency Plan for AIDS Relief (PEPFAR) funding did not increase (UN News Centre, 2010). While this funding freeze was offset partially by President Obama's 2010 pledge to GFATM, the largest ever received, concerns over funding levels remain (GFATM, 2009c). Despite heavy lobbying, the US, which contributes one-third of GFATM's budget, has not given any specific amounts for future pledges (IRIN, 2010). Given that PMTCT programmes are particularly dependent on external aid, it is possible these will be short-changed disproportionately as global funding levels off in the wake of the downturn (UNICEF, 2009).

Meanwhile, a notable 'backlash' against disease-specific initiatives such as HIV/AIDS has developed over the past few years. Donors are increasingly seeking to ensure that their funds are distributed across health systems in order to strengthen infrastructural capacities. Only when these are efficient and running well do they extend support to disease-specific initiatives such as in HIV/AIDS (Nattrass and Gonsalves, 2009).

Furthermore, despite a number of general commitments at the international level, a widespread dispersion of responsibility and lack of coordination are compromising policy approaches to HIV/AIDS-affected children, resulting in fragmented responses among national governments, the international community and civil society. The positioning of AIDS agencies within ministries of health leads to a neglect of policy responses related to social welfare and social protection. Additional complications arise because of often limited agreement on funding priorities among child-sensitive HIV/AIDS interventions in resource-poor governments, and/or because government and development partner spending is too narrowly defined.

Pre-existing treatment and prevention programmes

HIV develops much faster in children than in adults: without treatment, half of all children infected at birth die by their second birthday (Newell et al., 2004). In recent years, paediatric HIV treatment has benefited from the general push for access to adult treatment, UNITAID's negotiations for reduced drug prices and the World Health Organization's (WHO's) user-friendly fixed-dose ART for children. This contributed to a 70 per cent increase in the number of children receiving ART in

2004–06 (UNICEF, 2007b). Yet, children's overall access to treatment, care and support services remains generally poor, with fewer than 4 per cent of the total number of children exposed to HIV during gestation and birth receiving appropriate prophylaxis by two months of age (JLICA, 2009). At the end of 2008, fewer than two out of five HIV-positive children in lower- and middle-income countries were receiving ART (WHO et al., 2009). Globally, children make up 6 per cent of the infected population but 14 per cent of HIV/AIDS-related deaths (House of Commons, 2008).

Child prevention initiatives focus largely on PMTCT and preventative education. Mother-to-child transmission during pregnancy, childbirth and breastfeeding can be linked to 90 per cent of all infections in children. Without treatment, between 20 per cent and 40 per cent of all infants born to HIV-positive mothers will become HIV positive themselves. With optimal treatment, the rate of transmission falls to 2 per cent: even a single, inexpensive dose of medication cuts transmission rates in half (GFATM, 2010). Progress is being made: in low- and middle-income countries the proportion of pregnant women receiving ART increased from 10 per cent to 45 per cent between 2004 and 45 (ibid.). Uptake is generally affected by poor geographical reach; fear and stigma of being tested and weak health systems (UNICEF, 2007b) – in particular human capital capacity constraints; but also poor early infant diagnosis, limited numbers of women giving birth in hospital settings that offer PMTCT services; poor targeting, especially among rural populations and out-of-pocket payments at health facilities, reducing attendance by women.

Post-crisis treatment and prevention programmes

Budget allocations

Evidence from past crises suggests that spending on HIV may suffer disproportionately (Holmes and Jones, 2009), and crisis-related HIV budget cuts have already affected testing and diagnosis, treatment, resistance monitoring and prevention as a result of the 2008–10 crisis (UNAIDS, 2009a; 2009c), although impacts have varied between countries. Some countries have already witnessed a significant fall in HIV spending, with widespread expectations that cuts will be even more visible going forward, as old funding pledges expire and are replaced by new pledges made under conditions of fiscal restraint. For example, in March 2009, four countries in East and Southern Africa (ESA) were already implementing health budget reductions (UNAIDS, 2009a). ART shortages were reported in six African countries (Congo, Guinea, Malawi, South Africa, Uganda and Zimbabwe) (MSF, 2009a).

There is a risk that interventions to treat opportunistic infections will be cut even more due to lack of earmarked funding (UNAIDS, 2009a), and that ART programmes for marginalised groups such as men who have sex with men, sex workers and injecting drug users and their children will be undermined further, as they are often not recognised by their state, do not have strong political support and therefore are either de-prioritised in funding allocations or excluded totally from public services. HIV/AIDS workplace programmes are also impacted, as highlighted recently in SSA (ILO, 2010).

Despite overwhelming evidence that prevention programmes make a difference, they are often among the first cut in times of budgetary crises. Evidence arising from the Thai government's 50 per cent cut in the number of free condoms distributed in brothels and commercial sex establishments during 1996–99 (Richter, 2009) raises concern that such programmes will be among the first to suffer in the global economic downturn. For example, excluding ARVs, Mexico's budget for HIV prevention is estimated to be 30 per cent lower in 2010 than it was in 2009 (UNAIDS, 2009a). Other marginalised groups, such as migrants, may also be excluded from prevention initiatives, as even in good economic times they are often unreachable by such services (ibid.). In addition, flat global funding for HIV prevention research may limit the ability of researchers to move forward promising approaches (HVMRTWG, 2009).

Differential regional impacts

Impacts vary markedly across regions. UNAIDS (2009a) notes that, in ESA, 'where the highest levels of HIV infection and prevalence are occurring and the largest share of the population is in need of treatment, concerns about the impact of the economic crisis are, perhaps paradoxically, less severe than in some other regions'. UNAIDS suggest this could be because external funders prioritise these countries, although middle-income countries in this region, such as Botswana and South Africa, are seeing growing financial pressures as a result of declines in economic growth and reduced government revenues. Relatively less impact is reported in Latin America and in the Asia and Pacific region, which is attributed to 'lower HIV prevalence, early economic recovery in Asia, and strong commitment of some governments to providing treatment' (ibid.: 4).

Concern about specific types of programmes has also been found to vary greatly by region (UNAIDS and World Bank, 2009b). For example, there is limited concern about ARVs, OVC, pre/postnatal care and tuberculosis programmes in the Middle East and North Africa (MENA) region, mainly because of the low proportion of populations affected. Meanwhile, concern about ARV programmes is especially high in Eastern Europe and Central Asia (EECA), where 70 per cent of countries are expected to be affected. Concerns about OVC programmes are highest in ESA and second-highest in West and Central Africa (WCA), following the global pattern of parental deaths from AIDS. Pre- and postnatal primary health care programmes are of most concern in EECA and WCA, and concerns about tuberculosis are highest in Latin America and EECA. Nutrition is a particular concern in ESA and the Caribbean, with patients discontinuing treatment, both temporarily and permanently, because of food shortages. Finally, Prevention of Mother to Child Transmission (PMCTC) is a key concern in MENA and WCA.

Causes of concern also vary (UNAIDS and World Bank, 2009b). For example, reduced household income is an issue most frequently in the Caribbean, Latin America, WCA and ESA, where the private sector is a major supplier of services. Concern about external aid is reported everywhere except Asia and the Pacific, and ECA and Latin America see cuts in external funding for drug users and other high-risk groups as a particular concern due to lack of political support for these groups. In WCA, there is concern that governments will not have sufficient fiscal capacity to respond to reduced external aid, while government funding cuts are seen as the chief cause for concern in ESA, where HIV/AIDS programmes represent a significant proportion of government health expenditures. Finally, concern about the costs of AIDS drugs is especially high in EECA and the Caribbean.

Donor funding

Reports highlight that total funding for HIV/AIDS decreased by 2 per cent in 2008–9, while the total given by US-based philanthropies decreased from $618 million in 2008 to $585 million in 2009, a reduction of 5 per cent and the first decrease on record since disbursements started being tracked in 2005 (UNAIDS, 2010b). Funding from the Bill and Melinda Gates Foundation, which represented 57 per cent of all US-based philanthropic HIV/AIDS-related funding in 2009, decreased to $334 million in 2009, from $378 million in 2008. Furthermore, donor government funding for HIV/AIDS, which represents a much larger share of global resources for HIV/AIDS than the philanthropic sector does, remained essentially flat over the same period, decreasing from $7.7 billion in 2008 to $7.6 billion in 2009. This is in contrast with annual double-digit percentage point increases in donor support for international AIDS assistance since at least 2002 (UNAIDS, 2010c).

Indeed, a reduction in external financing was the most-mentioned factor in terms of negative impacts of the crisis by those surveyed by UNAIDS and the World Bank in 2009 (UNAIDS and World Bank, 2009a; 2009b). There is now a widespread fear that the GFATM funding gap and the severe impacts of the crisis could prevent G8 countries from delivering on their commitments. For example, Swaziland, which has the highest HIV prevalence in the world, has had to lower its 2011 treatment coverage target from 60 per cent to 50 per cent due to reductions in donor funding (ibid.). Non-governmental organisations (NGOs) in Swaziland have faced similar cuts, and such situations have also been reported in Uganda and Tanzania, with the latter having to cut its HIV and AIDS budget by 25 per cent for the 2009–10 financial year (ibid.).

Delivery of ART is perhaps the area of most concern. In Rwanda, where PEPFAR funds half of care and support services and GFATM funds the other half, second-line treatment for children funded by UNITAID is under immediate threat; it may take longer for first-line treatment to be affected.[4] In Uganda, where ART programmes are highly politicised, PEPFAR is currently cutting funding and creating a supply scare.[5]

In addition, exchange rate devaluations make it more costly for governments to obtain imported drugs, supplies and equipment (World Bank, 2009). For example, in Mexico, increased peso prices have affected the costs of condoms, lubricants and didactic supplies (UNAIDS, 2009a). Exchange rate fluctuations have also worked against GFATM, reducing the overall amount available for 2008–10 by 5 per cent, or $0.7 billion. If exchange rates had remained constant, it is estimated that contributions would have been around $10.2 billion higher (GFATM, 2009b).

Social protection programmes

Pre-existing social protection approaches

Social assistance initiatives supporting children affected by HIV/AIDS comprise income transfers, which can be in kind (food transfers), in cash or in the form of exemptions (from school and medical fees for instance). Social assistance can focus specifically on children affected by the pandemic or, more broadly, on households or children, producing positive externalities for HIV/AIDS-affected children. General cash transfer schemes in low-income, high-prevalence countries such as Malawi, South Africa and Zambia reach approximately 80 per cent of HIV/AIDS-affected households experiencing chronic poverty and labour constraints, and 60 per cent of these households' constituents are children (Nolan, 2009). Unconditional cash transfers in Africa increase food consumption and school attendance, and conditional cash transfers (CCTs) in Asia and Latin America both increase health service utilisation and reduce incidence of illness (JLICA, 2009). This suggests that cash transfers can prevent uptake of damaging coping strategies (Nolan, 2009). There is also evidence that untargeted transfers have an impact on the incidence of HIV infection in girls: a CCT scheme in Malawi found that keeping girls in school decreased the rate of infection (Baird et al., 2009).

Furthermore, even in countries highly impacted by HIV/AIDS, the overwhelming majority of children in institutional care are not actually orphaned; most have a surviving parent or other close relative who could care for them if they had the economic ability to do so (UNICEF, 2009). Lastly, there is growing concern over the adequacy of targeting AIDS-affected families or orphaned children rather than the most extreme poor households or other orphans (Slater, 2004), for reasons to do with equity, justice, accuracy and stigma (Adato and Bassett, 2008). There are, therefore, a variety of sound reasons for bolstering social protection schemes in general, rather than developing a parallel system addressing the specific needs of groups impacted by HIV/AIDS. Broad social protection programmes have the potential to address the inequality, stigma and discrimination that impact all vulnerable populations, regardless of disease status (UNICEF and UNAIDS, 2010).

There are, however, some promising programmes that address the specific needs of families living with HIV/AIDS. For example, in Uganda, a pilot study found that providing patients with a small cash transfer designated for transportation increased their adherence to ART protocols (Emenyonu et al., 2010). Since households undertaking ART face significant additional expenses, cash transfers to patients could also address specific health and nutritional needs (UNICEF, 2007a).

Social insurance schemes can also encourage individuals to save and invest in risk reduction, as a valid alternative to user fees. Private health insurance is likely to play a minimal role in protecting the poor, let alone individuals affected by the epidemic, as they generally experience intensified income poverty. National health insurance schemes are generally affected by similar levels of exclusion of the poorest segments of the population, since they are typically available to formal sector employees only – although there are examples of more inclusive expansion in Ghana, Kyrgyzstan, Mongolia and Thailand. Community health insurance is likely to play a significant role in addressing vulnerabilities in the context of the HIV/AIDS epidemic, due to their objective of covering people outside the formal sector and being affordable to the poor. Such schemes have been gaining momentum in WCA especially, but coverage remains limited.

Post-crisis social protection

The fact that a number of countries are continuing to pay significant attention to social protection in the crisis context (WHO, 2009) could be seen as an opportunity to continue with essential treatment, support and prevention for children infected with, or vulnerable to, HIV/AIDS. However, assessing what has been done so far in this respect is a work in progress. Moreover, as social protection coverage rates are weak under normal conditions, given the exclusion of the most vulnerable from the formal employment market, limited coverage, poor targeting mechanisms and sometime counterproductive programme goals, expectations for these same schemes in addressing HIV/AIDS vulnerabilities in times of economic downturn are understandably low.

In settings with scarce national resources and where social sector ministries have weak bargaining power, economic downturns can significantly affect the government's ability to provide public services and prioritise spending on social protection. Social protection nonetheless accounted for a significant portion of the policy response in Southeast Asia during the 1997–8 financial crisis (Holmes and Jones, 2009). For instance, social health insurance targeted poor and vulnerable population groups in Thailand, including HIV/AIDS patients and children, enabling beneficiaries to receive free public health services. Moreover, CCTs seem to have been highly effective in mitigating the health impacts of the crisis in Latin America, in particular in Mexico and Brazil (World Bank, 2009).

More recently, in the context of the global food crisis, the urgent need to implement and scale up social protection and safety nets was one of four policy recommendations on which the UN, the Bretton Woods institutions and international organisations agreed, in the 2008 Comprehensive Framework of Action (CFA) (Holmes et al., 2009). The importance of institutionalising food transfers for the poor and vulnerable in particular, to prevent the negative impacts of HIV/AIDS on children, has been specifically highlighted (Brunelli et al., 2008). Furthermore, given that economic crises can erode the value of income transfers to beneficiaries, the value-added of food over cash transfers that are not linked to the price index has been recognised (Holmes et al., 2008).

Conclusions and policy implications

Our findings highlight that the main impact pathways between the macro-level effects of the 2008–10 crisis and children's micro-level experiences involve current or anticipated budget cutbacks to both treatment and prevention programmes, alongside contraction of specific funds, either planned or because of currency devaluation, and increased drug import costs. Cuts are compounded by increased household difficulties in accessing services because of rising poverty, and related decreases in nutritional status and thus drug efficacy. Moreover, social protection responses, HIV-targeted or general, have so far been limited by both donor and government resource restrictions stemming from the crisis.

Pre-crisis challenges are inevitably exacerbated, especially in child-related policies and services, which already lack strategic direction and priority and which have poor cross-institutional coordination. An over-reliance on civil society hampers large-scale interventions, and policy choices, such as the OVC focus, are not driven by reliable evidence. The lack of focus also extends to daunting pre-existing funding gaps. Weak health systems and prevention services, alongside stigmatisation, social isolation and cultural barriers to changing risky behaviour, compound the long-term nature of the HIV/AIDS crisis. In this context, social protection systems offer important mechanisms to counter vulnerabilities, especially in times of economic crisis, but existing systems are fragmentary. The danger is that ongoing efforts will at best be stalled, but could also face reversals in progress. The opportunity is that economic crisis could stimulate a renewed focus on the most appropriate and cost-effective interventions, including enhancing social protection to address HIV alongside other vulnerabilities.

To prevent reversals and the long-term costly implications of infections, and instead turn crisis into opportunity, the following should be considered:

- Policy debates need to be far better informed, with more timely and systematic age- and gender-disaggregated data collection and crisis monitoring initiatives, paying particular attention to the differential patterning of the epidemic in diverse regional contexts and the specific patterning of child and youth infections. There also needs to be careful monitoring of children and young people, especially girls, at risk of falling into trafficking and/or commercial sex work. Apart from informing policy decisions, these data would highlight the true nature of the dilemma and stimulate action.

- National responses must be strategic and recognise the specificities of children's vulnerabilities to HIV/AIDS. Strategic responses need to work with, but not rely solely on, civil society responses, instead coordinating far more effectively across sectors and actors.
- It is critical to take a countercyclical spending approach and ensure the continued provision of ART during the crisis, given the likelihood of drug resistance developing as a result of interrupting treatment and, furthermore, the significant constraints to providing second-line treatment (which is more costly and often unavailable). Similarly, in the case of prevention services, particular attention needs to be paid to maintaining funding for PMTCT and addressing key pre-crisis challenges, including wastage, general ineffectiveness and high scale up costs.
- Finally, capitalising on the growing international momentum around and support for social protection interventions, a social protection focus on HIV/AIDS-affected children and broader household vulnerability would be opportune. Social assistance measures such as child grants, social health insurance for households in the informal sector, enhanced social welfare services and social equity measures to address discrimination and social exclusion are all vital elements of this package.

Notes

This paper draws on a longer report by Jones et al. (2009). We gratefully acknowledge detailed comments provided by Ken Legins on that report.

1. Economic share of HIV/AIDS refers to the resource needs for HIV/AIDS as a share of gross national income (GNI).
2. For instance, the 2010 UNAIDS Report on the Global Aids Epidemic does not mention the crisis (UNAIDS, 2010a).
3. Interviews with Landry Tsague, UN Children's Fund (UNICEF) Rwanda; Gudren Nadoll, UNICEF Philippines; Policy Advisor, Catholic Relief Services (CRS).
4. Interview with Landry Tsague, UNICEF Rwanda.
5. Interview with African Youth and Adolescent Network on Population and Development, Uganda AIDS Commission.

References

Adato, M. and Bassett, L. (2008) 'What is the Potential of Cash Transfers to Strengthen Families Affected by HIV and AIDS? A Review of the Evidence on Impacts and Key Policy Debates.' Washington, DC: IFPRI.

Baird, S., Chirwa, E., McIntosh, C. and Ozler, B. (2009) 'The Short-term Impacts of a Schooling Conditional Cash Transfer Program on the Sexual Behavior of Young Women.' Policy Research Working Paper 5089. Washington, DC: World Bank.

Brunelli, C., Kenefick, E. and Yamauchi, F. (2008) 'The Impacts of Adult Death on Child Growth and Nutrition. Evidence from Five Southern African Countries. HIV, Livelihoods, Food and Nutrition Security: Findings from RENEWAL Research (2007-2008).' Brief 12. Washington, DC: IFPRI.

CRIN (2009) 'Briefing on Discrimination and HIV and AIDS.' London: CRIN.

Emenyonu, N. et al. (2010) 'Cash Transfers to Cover Clinic Transportation Costs Improve Adherence and Retention in Care in a HIV Treatment Program in Rural Uganda.' Report for Doris Duke Charitable Foundation and Mark and Lisa Schwartz Family Foundation.

GFATM (2009a) 'Scaling up for Impact: Results Report 2008.' Geneva: GFATM.

GFATM (2009b) 'Updated Demands Estimate 2008–10.' Mid-Term Review of the Second Voluntary Replenishment 2008–10. Caceres, 30 March–1 April.

GFATM (2009c) 'President Obama Signs $1.05 Billion Contribution to the Global Fund for 2010.' Geneva: GFATM.

GFATM (2010) 'Born HIV Free – Go Deeper.' Geneva: GFATM.

Harper, C., Jones, N., McKay, A. and Espey, J. (2009) 'Children in Times of Economic Crisis: Past Lessons, Future Policies.' Background Note, London: ODI.

Holmes, R. and Jones, N. (2009) 'Gender Inequality, Risk and Vulnerability in the Rural Economy: Re-focusing the Public Works Agenda to Take Account of Economic and Social Risks.' Draft Background Report for SOFA 2010.

Holmes, R., Jones, N. and Marsden, H. (2009) 'Gender Vulnerabilities, Food Price Shocks and Social Protection Responses.' Background Note. London: ODI.

Holmes, R., Jones, N. and Wiggins, S. (2008) 'Understanding the Impact of Food Prices on Children. How Rising Food Prices Affect Poor Families. What Can Be Done to Protect Children in the Developing World.' London: Plan and ODI.

Hossain, N. (2009) 'Accounts of Crisis: Poor People's Experiences of the Food, Fuel and Financial Crises in Five Countries.' Report on a Pilot Study in Bangladesh, Indonesia, Jamaica, Kenya and Zambia, January–March 2009 (5 April 2009). Available at SSRN: http://ssrn.com/abstract=1879126 or http://dx.doi.org/10.2139/ssrn.1879126.

House of Commons (2008) 'HIV/AIDS: DFID's New Strategy.' 12th Report of 2007–2008 Session. Volume 1. London: IDC.

HVMRTWG (2009) 'Advancing the Science in a Time of Fiscal Constraint: Funding for HIV Prevention Technologies in 2009.' XVIII International AIDS Conference. Vienna, 20 July.

ICAAP (2009) 'Declaration on the Response to HIV and AIDS in Asia and the Pacific.' 9th ICAAP. Bali, 9 August.

IFPRI (2008) 'Food Prices and the AIDS Response: How They Are Linked and What Can Be Done.' Washington, DC: IFPRI.

ILO (2010) 'Income Generation and Sustainable Livelihoods for People Living with and Affected by HIV/AIDS.' Global Jobs Pact Policy Brief. Geneva: ILO.

IRIN (2007) 'Zimbabwe: Clinics Close Down as Economic Crisis Deepens.' 1 May.

IRIN (2010) 'MDGs' Donors Hold Key to HIV-Free Generation.' 23 September.
JLICA (2009) 'Home Truths, Facing the Facts on Children, AIDS and Poverty.' Final Report of JLICA.
Jones, N., Tincatti, C., Harper, C., Mitra, S. and Espey, J. (2009) 'Crisis Impacts on Children Affected by and Vulnerable to HIV/AIDS.' Report for UNICEF. London: ODI.
JUNIMA (2009) *The Threat Posed by the Economic Crisis to Universal Access to HIV Services for Migrants*. Bangkok: JUNIMA.
MSF (2009a) 'Disruptions in HIV Drug Supplies and Funding Endanger Patient Lives.' Press Release, 17 July.
Nattrass N. and Gonsalves, G. (2009) 'Economics and the Backlash against AIDS-specific Funding.' Report for the WHO/World Bank/UNAIDS Economics Reference Group.
Newell, M. et al. (2004) 'Mortality of Infected and Uninfected Infants Born to HIV-Infected Mothers in Africa: A Pooled Analysis.' *The Lancet* 364: 9441.
Nolan, A. (2009) *Social Protection in the Context of HIV and AIDS*. Paris: OECD.
Pearson, R. and Sweetman, C. (2011) *Gender and the Economic Crisis, Working in Gender and Development*. London: Practical Action Publishing and Oxfam GB.
Richter, K. (2009) 'The Threat Posed by the Economic Crisis to Universal Access to HIV Services for Migrants, Preliminary Findings.' Report for JUNIMA.
Slater, R. (2004) 'The Implications of HIV/AIDS for Social Protection.' London: ODI.
UN News Centre (2010) 'UN Agency Reports Significant Progress in Reducing New HIV Infections.' 17 September.
UNAIDS (2009a) *The Global Economic Crisis and HIV Prevention and Treatment Programmes: Vulnerabilities and Impact. Executive Summaries*. Geneva: UNAIDS.
UNAIDS (2009b) 'How the Current Economic Crisis Might Impact HIV in Low and Middle Income Countries?' AIDS Impact Conference. Gaborone, 23 September.
UNAIDS (2009c) 'What Countries Need: Investments Needed for 2010 Targets'. Geneva: UNAIDS.
UNAIDS (2010a) *Report on the Global Aids Epidemic 2010*. Geneva: UNAIDS.
UNAIDS (2010b) 'New Reports Show that, Despite Commitment, Total Philanthropic Funding for AIDS in Slight Decline.' Press Release. Geneva: UNAIDS.
UNAIDS (2010c) 'KFF/UNAIDS Report Finds Donor Nation Support for AIDS Relief Was Flat in 2009 during World Economic Crisis, with US$7.6 Billion Provided during the Year.' Press Release. Geneva: UNAIDS.
UNAIDS and World Bank (2009a) *The Global Economic Crisis and HIV Prevention and Treatment Programmes: Vulnerabilities and Impact*. Geneva: UNAIDS.
UNAIDS and World Bank (2009b) *Update on the Impact of the Economic Crisis: HIV Prevention and Treatment Programmes*. Geneva: UNAIDS.
UNDP (2009) 'The Economic Crisis's Impact on Migrants and AIDS.' New York: UNDP.
UNICEF (2007a) *The Impact of Social Cash Transfers on Children Affected by HIV and AIDS. Evidence from Zambia, Malawi and South Africa*. New York: UNICEF.
UNICEF (2007b) *Children and AIDS: Second Stocktaking Report*. New York: UNICEF.
UNICEF (2009) *Children and AIDS: Fourth Stocktaking Report*. New York: UNICEF.

UNICEF and UNAIDS (2010) 'Enhancing Social Protection for HIV Prevention, Treatment, Care and Support – The State of the Evidence.' Geneva and New York: UNICEF and UNAIDS.
WHO (2008) 'Health Impacts of the Global Food Security Crisis.' Geneva: WHO.
WHO (2009) 'Impact of the Global Financial Crisis on Health.' 27th Meeting of Ministers of Health. Kathmandu, 7–8 September.
WHO, UNAIDS and UNICEF (2009) 'Towards Universal Access. Scaling up Priority HIV/AIDS Interventions in the Health Sector.' Progress Report 2009. Geneva: WHO.
World Bank (2009) *Averting a Human Crisis during the Global Downturn. Policy Options from World Bank's Human Development Network*. Washington, DC: World Bank.
World Bank (2011) 'HIV/AIDS Regional Update-Africa.' Washington, DC: World Bank. Accessed 30 May 2011.

Part III

Policies to Promote Inclusive Recovery

10
Child Poverty Impacts and Public Budgets: Tracking the Global Economic Crisis in Sub-Saharan Africa

Andy Sumner

Introduction

Many of the Millennium Development Goals (MDGs) are unambiguously about children (for example child nutrition, primary enrolment and child mortality). Further, those under 18 years old account for on average 37 per cent of the population in developing countries and 49 per cent in least-developed countries (LDCs); children are also more likely to be poor in the sense that they make up a disproportionate number of the total number of the poor (Gordon et al., 2004). In the long run, impacts of poverty experienced during childhood are well documented in terms of wasting, stunting, delayed school enrolment and reduced grade completion.

This chapter discusses the impact of the 2008–10 global economic crisis in Sub-Saharan Africa (SSA) with particular reference to child poverty and wellbeing, and analyses the outlook with attention to child poverty-related aspects of public budgets. Note that tracking child poverty during a crisis is more complex than tracking adult poverty because monetary-based poverty indicators, which are more quickly and readily available, are at best a rough proxy for child poverty and wellbeing. In addition, there has been considerable variance in estimates of the poverty impacts of the crisis.

The crisis in Africa: an overview

The 2008–10 global economic crisis was different to previous crises in its reach, its size, the speed of its transmission and its compound nature, following as it did the fuel and food shocks in 2007–8. There were large falls in exports, foreign direct investment (FDI) and remittances, although these were quite variable and not all expected impacts materialised. There was a slowdown in growth but few outright recessions. Overall, the impacts were highly country-specific. In SSA, for example, the regional average hides major differences.

Nevertheless, the short- and medium-term impacts of the crisis are beginning to become clearer. There are various concerns regarding the speed of recovery, available fiscal space and impacts on public expenditure in general and social spending in particular, which differ considerably across countries. Fragile states have been especially hurt by slowing growth and fiscal squeezing as a result of the economic downturn. At the same time, aid is under pressure as a result of the crisis.

Meanwhile, the fact that the crisis came on the back of drastic increases in food and fuel prices has had implications for both child nutrition as well as adult nutrition. Food accounts for 50 per cent to 90 per cent of poor families' budgets; when prices rise, poor families adjust the quantity and quality of their food consumption (as well as their expenditure on health and schooling).

It is clear that the assertion that low-income subsistence and/or agricultural economies in Africa are not linked to complex global markets is false. Indeed, the transmission channels of the crisis can be seen at different levels, from global impacts to the national macroeconomy to the household to individual child poverty and wellbeing, including in developing countries (Figure 10.1).

In macroeconomic terms, we can note overall trends in SSA as follows:[1]

- Growth decelerated from 6–7 per cent to around 2 per cent.
- Pre-crisis growth rates are not expected to be attained again before 2015.
- There was a fall in savings as a percentage of GDP.
- There was a significant worsening in the current account position.
- There was an increase in debt service interest of an additional $1–2 billion a year and an apparent trend upward.
- There was a fall in net private capital inflows from $25 billion to $18 billion but then a recovery.
- There were portfolio outflows of $20 billion and a further loss of $20 billion in 2007–9 in other capital.
- ODA increased significantly to compensate during the crisis.
- The volume of exports barely grew in 2008 and contracted by 7 per cent in 2009.

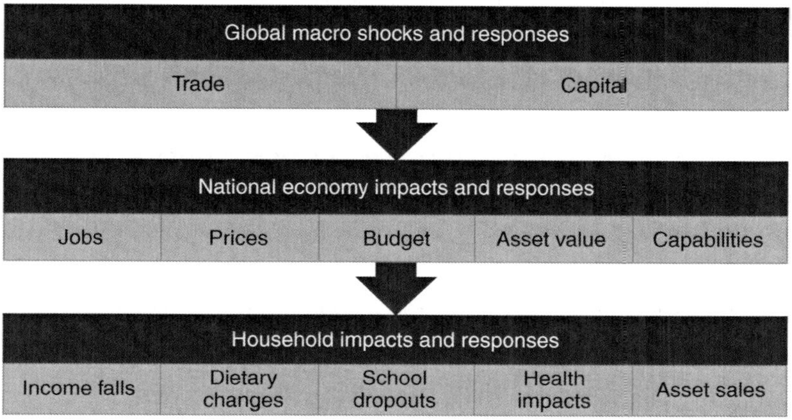

Figure 10.1 Conceptualising the links between the global economic crisis and child poverty
Source: Author's elaboration.

Table 10.1 SSA countries experiencing negative growth in 2009 (GDP per cent change, constant prices)

Country	2004–7 average	2008	2009	2010–15 average
Angola	17.66	13.18	−0.41	6.35
Botswana	4.38	3.12	−6.00	5.60
Chad	10.47	−0.44	−1.58	3.89
Gabon	2.65	2.69	−1.42	3.35
Guinea	2.40	4.94	−0.29	3.68
Madagascar	5.28	7.07	−5.03	3.88
Namibia	6.83	3.32	−0.72	2.59
Niger	4.21	9.29	−0.86	5.56
Seychelles	5.69	−0.88	−7.56	4.84
South Africa	5.23	3.68	−1.79	3.94
Swaziland	2.75	2.40	**0.43**	2.22

Source: www.imf.org/external/pubs/ft/weo/2009/02/weodata/index.asp.

However, the averages hide significant variations. Meanwhile, outright recessions were experienced in 10 of 44 SSA countries. Some countries experienced a double whammy of a large growth deceleration and a slow recovery. Economic recovery has been v-shaped overall.

Given that the macroeconomic impacts and recoveries have been highly variable, we can expect poverty and child poverty estimates to be similarly diverse.

Tracking child poverty in Africa during the crisis

Estimates of crisis impacts on child poverty and MDG indicators have been focused largely on extrapolations based on growth elasticity estimations; research from previous crises (given the time lags in data collection) and new empirical, cross-country research with an emphasis on rapid 'real-time' data collection with largely qualitative and participatory techniques (see Table 10.2). There are also numerous qualitative and/or quantitative country studies that have yet to be synthesised into cross-country findings. Here, the three available cross-country approaches are discussed in terms of tracking and estimating child poverty and wellbeing.

Child poverty estimates based on the growth elasticity of poverty

The starting point for tracking based on the growth elasticity of poverty is the growth–poverty relationship and how changes in growth impact poverty (that is, a deceleration of growth by 1 per cent leads to a 2 per

Table 10.2 Approaches to crisis (child) poverty tracking

	Basic characteristics		
Approach	**Extrapolation to 2008/9 crisis**	**Weaknesses in tracking crisis in general**	**Weaknesses in tracking child poverty and wellbeing in crisis**
Growth elasticity of poverty	Based on historical elasticity and growth estimate	Unstable over time/space; limited account of compound nature of crisis	Child poverty levels are likely weakly linked to average growth due to importance of non-market channels and public goods
Research from previous crises	Based on severity of previous crises in similar context	Based largely on middle-income Asia and Latin America; limited account of compound nature of crisis	Child poverty is defined implicitly; largely material wellbeing indicators (nutrition, health, education)
Rapid qualitative appraisal	New research and sampling method	Sample size and representativeness; delay to results	If designed with child poverty focus useful and relevant

cent increase in poverty). Growth deceleration estimates differ by time of estimate and have differed by agency. These are of little use for child poverty levels, as they are generally weakly linked to average growth due to the importance of non-market channels and public goods.

Furthermore, various issues exist in 'normal' (that is, non-crisis) time periods about making estimates, such as the instability of elasticities over time and space, the wide variation across and within countries and weaker links to non-income or human development measures such as child nutrition. Although it has been asserted strongly that growth is matched by proportionate reductions in overall poverty on average, recent evidence challenges this view, suggesting that the incomes of the poorest may increase less than proportionately with growth (Besley and Cord, 2006; Grimm et al., 2007). Indeed, positive economic growth has been associated with *increases* in poverty in much of SSA, Russia and Eastern Europe (Epaulard, 2003; Mosley, 2004). These issues bring into question both the relevance of the global averages and whether growth responds differently to different kinds of (chronic and transient) income poverty.

In terms of children, MDG indicators such as those on child education, child nutrition and child and maternal health are generally related positively to growth but often less strongly, or over a longer time horizon, than those related to income poverty (Gross et al., 2005). Income levels are therefore far from being the only factor influencing child health; other factors include public health care systems, nutrition and immunisation programmes and maternal education levels, any of which might or might not improve independently of growth. In particular, in relation to child nutrition, economic growth – while crucial – will not take care of malnutrition quickly enough: cross-country studies strongly suggest the two are not as tightly wedded as many imagine (Haddad et al., 2003).

During the 2008–10 crisis, estimates based on growth elasticities became yet more contentious because different estimates were published at different points in time (usually just before G8 and G20 meetings), based on estimates of growth at those points in time from one of three agencies (the International Monetary Fund [IMF], the UN Department of Economic and Social Affairs [UNDESA] and the World Bank); various elasticities and an assumption that GDP deceleration would have a distributionally neutral impact on poverty. One might add that the actual last *real* global poverty estimates, for 2005, have been revised with new purchasing power parity (PPP) data by Ravallion et al. (2009), further complicating matters.

The above points aside, using a growth elasticity approach, estimates made in 2009 of the 'new' poor globally and in Africa (based on a $1.25/day poverty line – a proxy for MDG 1's $1/day) as a result of the crisis and growth decelerations are varied and not child-centred, but are all significant. Given time lags in real data collection, these estimates have received a high profile. In September 2009, there were several:

- UNDESA (2009): 73–100 million 'new' poor people of whom 56–80 million live in East and South Asia, 12–16 million in Africa and 4 million in Latin America and the Caribbean;
- UNGIVAS (2009): 108 million new poor based on UN estimates and World Bank (Global Development Finance) growth data;
- World Bank (Ravallion and Chen, 2009): 89 million new poor, whose estimates were 73 million to 91 million under $1.25/day and $2/day based on country-specific growth projections.

The most recent global estimates (Ravallion and Chen, 2010) revised downwards the World Bank estimates to an extra 50 million people estimated to be living under $1.25/day in 2009 as a result of the crisis (or 57 million under $2/day) and an extra 15 million in 2010 (19 million under $2/day), creating a cumulative impact of 64 million under $1.25 (or 76 million under $2/day). The World Bank's (2010) Global Monitoring Report made estimates for poverty based on different recovery scenarios. If recovery from the current economic recession is rapid, there will be an estimated 918 million poor people in 2015, of whom 40 per cent will be in SSA. If recovery is weak, there will be 1.132 billion poor people in 2015, of whom 421 million will be in SSA (Figure 10.2).

Growth decelerations and elasticities have been used to estimate the impact on infant mortality – one of the health MDGs – both globally and in Africa, with the following assertions and strongly gendered impacts:

- If the crisis persists there will be 30,000 to 50,000 more infant deaths per year in Africa and 200,000 to 400,000 more infant deaths globally and 1.4 million to 2.8 million infant deaths in 2009–15 if the crisis persists (Friedman and Schady, 2009);
- An additional 1.5 infant boy deaths and 7.4 infant girl deaths per 1,000 live births per 1 per cent growth deceleration (Baird et al., 2009).

In terms of child poverty tracking during the crisis that broke out in 2008, one issue has been its compound nature (food, fuel, financial): the

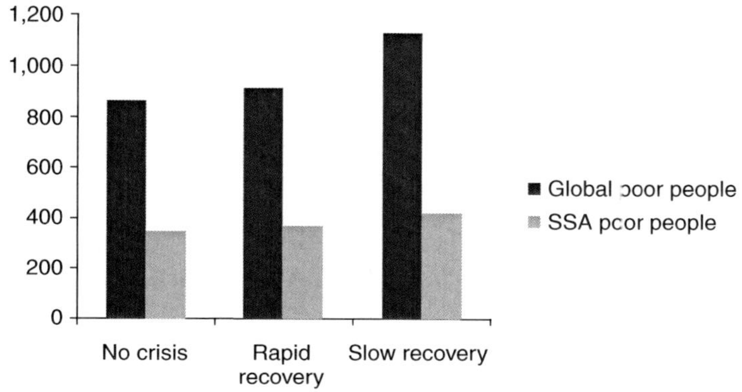

Figure 10.2 Millions of poor people in different recovery scenarios, 2015
Source: World Bank (2011).

Table 10.3 $1.25/day per capita poverty in SSA, alternative scenarios, 1990–2020

Scenario	1990	2005	2015	2020
Post-crisis recovery (millions of people)	296	387	366	352
Without crisis (millions of people)	296	387	346	321
Low growth (millions of people)	296	387	421	428
Post-crisis recovery (% of people)	58	51	38	33
Without crisis (% of people)	58	51	36	30
Low growth (% of people)	58	51	44	40
MDG Target for 2015 (% of people)	58	51	29	

Source: World Bank (2010).

economic shock followed a food and fuel price shock, leading to possible impacts on children's long-term capabilities.

In short, although growth estimates are of limited use for estimating child or adult poverty, not least because of the ambiguous growth–poverty linkages, such estimates do arguably have a use in triggering political action for social policy, released as they are immediately before G8 and G20 meetings. Such estimates do also provide a sense of the magnitude of poverty impacts overall.

Crisis poverty estimates based on research on previous shocks

Research from previous crises has been largely in Asia and Latin America (see Table 10.4). For example, Cline (2002) puts the average poverty impact of a crisis at a 7 per cent increase in the poverty headcount per country. This is consistent with the average of nine crises since 1990, and an average contraction of GDP by 8 per cent increases poverty by 50 per cent. In short, although income poverty is of course a weak proxy for childhood poverty, looking at the poverty impacts of previous crises shows that the total number of poor people is likely to rise dramatically during a crisis (see also Ravallion, 2008).

While noting deficiencies in the data, we find that reported increases in income poverty are significant. More importantly, perhaps, is that the poverty increases do not seem to be tied as closely to the magnitude of the GDP contraction as one might expect (given the approach outlined previously). For example, a 6–7 per cent GDP contraction is associated with an increase in poverty of 200 per cent in Korea but only 115–20 per cent in Malaysia or Mexico.

Meanwhile, we do have better and child-specific indicators in terms of child nutrition, schooling and health. Non-income poverty impacts are particularly child-specific, partly because many households adopt coping mechanisms that include decisions affecting children, such as those related to expenditures on food, education and health (Bhutta et al., 2009; Mendoza, 2009). Indeed, as noted at the outset, there is strong evidence that crises impact the future wellbeing of children. A particular concern is that crisis poverty impacts will have long-term or intergenerational poverty effects.

Through our review of nine crises (see Table 10.4), we can see that child health and child nutrition indicators generally deteriorate during a crisis episode (Table 10.5), but not always. Across those countries with two data points there is a significant rise, from 8.1 per cent to 8.8 per cent.

On the child-related education MDGs, governments can and do intervene successfully to prevent severe crisis impacts. In Indonesia during the 1997–8 crisis, a scholarship scheme was introduced as part of a set of social protection measures to support families experiencing difficulties paying fees. There is also evidence that in some middle-income country crises (but not all) education indicators may be unaffected or actually improve as a result of interventions and the changing opportunity cost of child labour (Table 10.6; Ferreira and Schady, 2008). The average across the countries with two data points is consistent with this.

Gender plays a critical role in any assessment of poverty impacts. Across the nine crises reviewed, gendered impacts are particularly evident via indicators of changes in labour markets (World Bank, 1999). Women are more likely to lose jobs than men, as women dominate

Table 10.4 Impact on national poverty headcount of selected financial crises, 1990–present

Country (date crisis began)	GDP contraction (year of crisis) (per cent)	Change in national poverty headcount (per cent increase)	Poverty headcount (% of population under *national* poverty line)	
			Pre-crisis (year prior to crisis)	Post-crisis (crisis +2 years)
Argentina (December 2001)	–10.9	147.2	35.8 (2001)	53.0 (2002)
Brazil (January 1999)	–4.3	N/A	22.0 (1998)	21.5 (2003)
Indonesia (July 1997)	–13.1	172.6	15.7 (1996)	27.1 (1999)
Korea (October 1997)	–6.9	200.0	9.6 (1996)	19.2 (1998)
Malaysia (September 1997)	–7.4	114.8	6.1 (1997)	7.0 (1998)
Mexico (December 1994)	–6.2	119.4	36.0 (1994)	43.0 (1996)
Russia (August 1998)	–6.4	149.3	21.9 (1996)	32.7 (1998)
Thailand (July 1997)	–10.5	138.8	9.8 (1994)	13.6 (1998)
Turkey (June 2001)	–6.2	N/A	28.3 (1994)	27.0 (2002)
Average	**–8.0**	**148.9**	**20.6**	**27.1**

Source: IMF International Financial Statistics database (www.imfstatistics.org/imf/); World Development Indicators (http://data.worldbank.org/data-catalog/world-development-indicators) December 2008.

export sectors in garments, electronics and agriculture (Buvinic, 2009). Similarly, girls are often affected more than boys: girls are more likely to drop out of school in both low- and middle-income countries (Schady, 2004; Skoufias and Parker, 2006) and the infant mortality rate (IMR) among girls exceeds that among boys during a downturn (Baird et al., 2007). Indeed, Elson (2009) identifies four gender biases during crises: a deflationary bias; a privatisation bias; a male breadwinner bias (protect male jobs if possible) and a reliance on women to provide a safety net bias, through informal work, both paid and unpaid.

During crises, major rural and urban variations are often evident because of different impacts on different production and consumption patterns. The rural poor may have been hit harder during the 2008–10

Table 10.5 Low birth weight babies as a proportion of all births during selected financial crises, 1990–present (%)

Country (date crisis began)	Pre-crisis	Post-crisis
Argentina (December 2001)	7.0 (1999)	8.0 (2003)
Brazil (January 1999)	10.0 (1996)	8.2 (2003)
Indonesia (July 1997)	15.0 (1996)	N/A
Korea (October 1997)	N/A	3.8 (2000)
Malaysia (September 1997)	8.3 (1994)	10.0 (1998)
Mexico (December 1994)	7.9 (1994)	9.0 (1999)
Russia (August 1998)	N/A	6.3 (2001)
Thailand (July 1997)	7.3 (1995)	8.8 (2001)
Turkey (June 2001)	15.1 (1998)	N/A
Average of crises with two data points	**8.1**	**8.8**

Source: World Development Indicators December 2008.

Table 10.6 Primary school completion rate during selected financial crises, 1990–present (% of relevant age group)

Country (date crisis began)	Pre-crisis	Post-crisis
Argentina (December 2001)	98.3 (2001)	100.0 (2003)
Brazil (January 1999)	89.8 (1995)	100.0 (2001)
Indonesia (July 1997)	96.7 (1997)	95.3 (2001)
Korea (October 1997)	98.2 (1996)	91.8 (1999)
Malaysia (September 1997)	92.5 (1995)	94.0 (1999)
Mexico (December 1994)	91.6 (1994)	97.2 (1996)
Russia (August 1998)	91.4 (1995)	94.2 (2000)
Thailand (July 1997)	N/A	96.0 (1999)
Turkey	N/A	N/A
Average of crises with two data points	**94.1**	**95.2**

Source: World Development Indicators December 2008.

global crisis as falling agriculture and export commodity prices have reduced rural employment and incomes (IMF, 2009a). The impact depends on whether or not the household is a net producer or a net consumer of food.

Conceição et al. (2009a; 2009b) note three key conclusions from previous crises for child poverty and wellbeing: (i) the IMR and the under-five mortality rate (U5MR) are significantly worse during economic downturns; (ii) completion rates in primary education, especially for girls, deteriorate rapidly during economic downturns and (iii) female enrolment in primary and secondary education drops during contraction (see also Table 10.7).

Table 10.7 Human development and gender outcomes during crises in SSA (sample averages during growth deceleration v. otherwise)

Indicator	During deceleration	Otherwise	Significance
Life expectancy female (years)	52.26	55.02	**
Life expectancy male (years)	48.87	51.86	**
Life expectancy total (years)	50.52	53.40	**
IMR (per 1,000 live births)	106.62	85.61	**
U5MR (per 1,000 live births)	161.3	139.40	*
Primary completion females	33.83	50.37	**
Primary completion males	48.44	56.55	*
Primary completion total (per cent of cohort)	40.95	53.55	**
Ratio female: male in primary enrolment	77.86	87.27	**
Ratio female: male in secondary enrolment	63.57	79.88	**
Ratio female: male in tertiary enrolment	32.52	62.31	**

Notes: *Difference significant at 5 per cent level; **difference significant at 1 per cent level; U5MR average rises to 172 when three countries in conflict are included.

Sources: Conceição et al. (2009a, 2009b).

What little exists in terms of crisis research on subjective wellbeing is thought provoking, though. For example, there is cross-country evidence of impacts on subjective wellbeing via psychological distress and mental health (e.g., Das, 2008) and via elevated levels of community and intra-household conflict during and post-crisis (e.g., Friedman and Thomas, 2007).

Crisis poverty estimates based on new rapid qualitative appraisal research

New empirical research presents the best prospects for tracking child poverty during an ongoing crisis if designed with child poverty and wellbeing in mind. Three major cross-country pieces of research (all qualitative) have been conducted (Hossain et al., 2009; Oxfam, 2010; World Bank, 2009c). The greatest weakness of the qualitative-led studies is that they are not representative, but they do provide real data and insights into the poverty impacts of the 2008–10 crisis. They thus serve an important function of flagging 'off-radar'-type issues. Unfortunately, none of the three qualitative studies mentioned above used a fully child-specific lens. However, it is possible to use these studies to look across the domains of child wellbeing and differentiate between general impacts reported and child-specific impacts. For example, in terms of child wellbeing and the material wellbeing dimension, there were cross-country reports of school absenteeism and dropout, and some reports of child labour and/or education expenses being reduced. There were also reports across countries of children combining labour with education.

According to the World Bank study, in Ghana families said they would need to take 'drastic measures' to survive. These included sending children away to live with wealthier relatives or getting them involved in income-generating activities to support the family. This would mean less time and worse conditions for study, given that tiredness affects educational performance. Meanwhile, remittances had been delayed or cancelled, which meant children were returning late to school as mobilising funds for school fees was taking longer than usual. Fewer jobs and more competition on the labour market had led households to cut back on expenses, for example on schooling. Small-scale *shea* nut dealers had been particularly affected by the crisis and many had been unable to pay back loans, which may well have an impact on their children's life chances. Responses included making food stretch further – diluting soup, eating fewer times a day (children twice instead of three times) and consuming less expensive food.

In Kenya, the Hossain et al. study found that prices of food, rent, fuel, water and transport had increased, leading to a change in food consumption and a reduction in the number of meals from three in January of 2007 to barely one in February of 2009. Teachers confirmed these trends by reporting that the number of children begging for food in their schools had increased significantly. They also mentioned a drastic decline in enrolment and a rise in absenteeism at school. In some cases, parents were withdrawing their children from school because the fees were unaffordable. Performance of school children had also declined as a result of hunger. There were also reported increases in cases of pupils in schools engaging in crime and prostitution. In Mukuru slum in Nairobi, sex for food had been observed.

In Zambia also, Hossain et al. found that the impacts of the food, fuel and financial crises included prostitution among youths (due to poverty and lack of employment, family problems/lack of income), and reported increases in drunkenness and theft. Money spent on food consumption had declined, and the number and quality of meals eaten a day had reduced. In some cases, parents had failed to pay school fees, and children had been withdrawn from school because of a need for them to get involved in paid activities to support household income. The number of school dropouts had increased in rural areas due to seasonal hunger, which had forced children into casual labour to earn food and cash. In some cases, children were too weak to cover long distances to school because of hunger. Further, health care expenses were said to be competing with households' food needs.

The outlook: public budgets in Africa

Fiscal space and public expenditure has become the new area of impacts of the crisis. In late 2009, the managing director of the IMF was upbeat and noted that, out of 27 low-income countries with available data, 26 had managed to preserve or increase social spending – a significant achievement in the current environment (IMF, 2009b). The claim that there was no immediate need to worry about social spending led to a very public spat with the Centre for Economic Policy Research (CEPR), which argued that, in SSA, although IMF crisis agreements had included expansionary fiscal policy in four countries (Mozambique, Niger, Tanzania, Zambia), there had been contractionary fiscal policy in nine others (Burkina Faso, Burundi, Central African Republic, Congo, Gabon, Ghana, Mali, Senegal, The Gambia) (Weisbrot et al., 2009).

Public expenditure matters in reducing child poverty and attaining the MDGs. The African Economic Outlook for 2010 projected major deteriorations in total revenue and grants while spending was expanding, leaving a fiscal gap of 5 per cent of GDP on average (see Table 10.8), with 13 countries facing a deficit greater than 5 per cent (see Table 10.9).

In terms of child poverty, we need to ask not only what is happening to child-related public expenditures but also whether governments are already meeting their commitments on social expenditures from regional and international agreements. Such agreements (see ACPF, 2008) include 15 per cent of government expenditure to health and 20 per cent to education. Of the 46 countries with health data, only 4 are

Table 10.8 Public finances in Africa, 2007–10 (projected data) (per cent of GDP)

	2007	2008	2009	2010
Total revenue and grants	30.2	31.0	25.7	25.8
Total expenditure and net lending	28.2	28.2	31.1	30.8
Overall balance	**1.9**	**2.8**	**–5.4**	**–5.0**

Source: African Economic Outlook 2010 (www.africaneconomicoutlook.org).

Table 10.9 Overall fiscal balance in Africa, 2007–10 (projected data) (countries above deficit of 5 per cent of GDP in 2009 or 2010)

	2007	2008	2009	2010
Algeria	4.8	6.8	–11.5	–10.9
Angola	11.2	10.8	–8.7	–6.9
Burkina Faso	–5.7	–6.4	–6.9	–7.3
Burundi	–3.0	–8.9	32.4	–9.8
Democratic Republic of Congo (DRC)	–0.3	–5.8	–9.0	–7.9
Egypt*	–5.6	–6.8	–7.1	–6.7
Eritrea	–10.0	–8.3	–8.1	–7.1
Ghana	–8.4	–10.0	–9.2	–9.1
Guinea Bissau	–10.3	1.1	–12.6	–12.5
Mauritania	–2.7	–3.7	–4.7	–5.4
Mozambique	–2.9	–4.4	–5.2	–5.2
Nigeria	0.4	0.9	–11.1	–11.7
Sudan	–5.4	0.5	–10.6	–10.9

Note: *Fiscal year July (n – 1)/June (n); Fiscal year April (n)/March (n + 1).

Source: African Economic Outlook 2010.

reaching the target, and of the 37 countries with education data, only 14 are (CFA, 2010).

If we consider child poverty and wellbeing impacts via education and health budgets in particular, again the picture varies by country. Kyrili and Martin (2010) reviewed data for low-income countries and noted that:

- Two-thirds of countries for which social spending details were available were cutting budget allocations in one or more of the priority social sectors of education, health, agriculture and social protection.
- Education and social protection were particularly badly affected, with average spending levels in 2010 lower even than those in 2008.
- Education spending fell for all groups in 2009. It was estimated to rise in 2010 (sharply in SSA).
- Health spending rose in 2009 and it was estimated to be higher at the end of 2010 than in 2008 for all groups. However, it was forecast to fall for non-SSA countries and to rise less sharply for IMF programme countries than for others.
- Social protection spending fell for all four groups in 2009, it would continue to fall in 2010 and it would be lower in all groups in 2010 than in 2008, but the fall was less steep in countries with IMF programmes.

- Regionally, Africa had done much better than other regions, ending 2010 with higher spending levels in all sectors except social protection. However, its spending levels as a percentage of GDP, while matching those of other regions on education and infrastructure for the first time, and exceeding them on agriculture, were still much lower on health and especially on social protection.
- Among those with IMF programmes, African countries had fared better on education, health and agriculture, and similarly to low-income countries in other regions on infrastructure and social protection.

While it may be true that public expenditures in SSA are not being reduced immediately, as public spending management is typically planned over several future years, the outlook is particularly important for the MDGs and child poverty. More important again is fiscal space.

Table 10.10 Projected sectoral expenditures in Africa, 2008–10 (per cent of GDP)

	Education			Health			Social protection		
	2008	2009	2010	2008	2009	2010	2008	2009	2010
Angola	–	3.9	3.6	–	2.9	2.1	–	4.8	4.1
Benin	3.2	3.2	–	2.6	3.5	–	1.5	2.3	1.9
Cameroon	1.1	1.5	1.5	0.8	1.1	1.1	–	–	–
Central African Republic	1.6	1.5	2.1	1.4	1.2	1.9	0.4	0.2	0.1
Chad	5.6	4.4	4.2	2.0	2.7	3.0	2.6	0.6	0.7
Congo	–	–	3.0	–	–	2.2	–	–	0.5
Côte d'Ivoire	4.7	4.9	5.3	0.9	1.1	1.1	0.1	0.1	0.1
DRC	–	3.7	3.6	–	2.1	2.9	–	–	0.5
Ghana	9.0	6.8	7.4	–	3.5	3.8	–	–	–
Guinea-Bissau	4.2	3.3	5.1	2.7	2.8	3.4	0.7	0.7	0.6
Mali	–	1.3	1.0	–	1.2	1.2	–	0.5	0.6
Mozambique	6.3	7.1	–	–	–	–	–	–	–
Nicaragua	3.7	4.2	3.9	3.7	4.0	3.8	–	–	–
Niger	–	3.8	3.4	–	2.8	2.1	–	–	–
Nigeria	1.1	0.8	0.8	–	0.6	0.5	–	–	–
São Tomé & Príncipe	–	4.9	4.5	–	5.3	4.8	–	–	–
Senegal	4.8	3.4	4.5	1.6	1.5	1.8	–	–	–
Sierra Leone	1.2	1.4	1.8	–	1.8	1.3	–	–	–
Zambia	3.8	4.0	4.4	2.9	2.8	1.8	1.0	0.6	0.6

Source: Kyrili and Martin (2010).

Table 10.11 Fiscal space in SSA (adjusted for 'check' indicators)

	No.	Countries
No space	4	Angola, Burundi, DRC, Liberia
Low space	16	Benin, Congo, Côte d'Ivoire, Djibouti, Ethiopia, The Gambia, Ghana, Guinea, Guinea-Bissau, Kenya, Malawi, Mauritania, São Tomé and Príncipe; Senegal, Tanzania, Togo
Moderate space	10	Cameroon, Central African Republic, Chad, Comoros, Lesotho, Nigeria, Sierra Leone, Sudan, Zambia
High space	6	Madagascar, Mali, Mozambique, Niger, Rwanda, Uganda

Source: Kyrili and Martin (2010).

Kyrili and Martin (2010) have developed a fiscal space index which includes debt, domestic revenues and aid. If a country has no constraint in relation to any source of resources, it is classified as having 'high fiscal space'. If it is constrained on one indicator, it is 'moderate', and if it is constrained on two indicators, it has 'low fiscal space'. 'Zero fiscal space' refers to countries constrained on all three indicators. A second assessment is that of 'check' indicators of fiscal balance and inflation, whereby an account is made of deficits and inflation. Of the African countries in the study, 21 (over half of those in the sample) had no or low fiscal space when adjusted for 'check' indicators.

Conclusions

The macroeconomic impacts of the 2008–10 crisis have been highly variable in SSA, although across the region as a whole they have included a deceleration in growth; a worsening in the current account position; an upward trend in debt service interest; a fall in net private capital inflows (but then a recovery); large portfolio outflows, although ODA increased significantly to compensate and a contraction in the volume of exports. Some countries experienced a double whammy of large growth decelerations and a slow recovery in growth rates.

While we know a great deal about the macroeconomic impacts, we still know only a limited amount about the child poverty impacts of the crisis overall. Child poverty tracking during crises is important because children account for a large proportion of the population in many developing countries, and the long-run impacts of poverty during childhood are well documented. The public budget situation across

Africa is potentially worrisome. Even before the crisis, only 4 out of 46 SSA countries with data were meeting public spending targets on health and 14 out of 37 were meeting those on education. In terms of changes in education, health and social protection spending, again the picture varies depending on the country. The good news is that education spending in SSA is forecast to rise sharply in 2010, although only countries with IMF programmes will have higher spending in 2010 than in 2008. Health spending is also likely to rise overall in SSA. However, social protection spending has fallen and will continue to fall in 2010, and it will be lower in all groups in 2010 than in 2008.

Regionally, Africa has done much better than other regions, ending 2010 with higher spending levels in all sectors except social protection. Nevertheless, its spending levels as a percentage of GDP, while matching those of other regions on education and infrastructure for the first time, are still much lower. Even more concerning is where the money will come from. Of African countries surveyed, half of the sample of countries had no or low fiscal space when adjusted for 'check' indicators. How these budgetary indicators evolve will play a significant role in the final impacts of the crisis on child poverty.

Notes

Special thanks for research assistance go to Chetna Desai, Ben Mann and Apratim Gautam. A longer version of this chapter was published by the African Child Policy Forum (see Sumner, 2010).

1. www.imf.org/external/pubs/ft/weo/2009/02/weodata/index.aspx.

References

ACPF (2008) *African Child Wellbeing Report*. Addis Ababa: ACPF.

Baird, S., Friedman, J. and Schady, N. (2007) 'Aggregate Income Shocks and Infant Mortality in the Developing World.' Working Paper 4346. Washington, DC: World Bank.

Baird, S., Friedman, J. and Schady, N. (2009) 'Aggregate Income Shocks and Infant Mortality in the Developing World.' Washington, DC: World Bank.

Besley, T. and Cord, L. (eds) (2006) *Delivering on the Promise of Pro-poor Growth: Insights and Lessons from Country Experiences*. Basingstoke: Palgrave Macmillan.

Bhutta, Z., Bawany, F.A., Feroze, A., Rizvi, A., Thapa, S.J. and Patel, M. (2009) 'Effects of the Crises on Child Nutrition and Health in East Asia and the Pacific.' *Global Social Policy* 9: 119–43.

Buvinic, M. (2009) *Impact of Financial Crisis on Women and Families*. Washington, DC: World Bank.

CFA (2010) *Still Our Common Future*. London/Addis Ababa: CFA.

Cline, W. (2002) 'Financial Crises and Poverty in Emerging Market Economics.' Working Paper 8. Washington, DC: CGD.
Conceição, P., Kim, N., Mendoza, R.U. and Zhang., Y. (2009a) 'Human Development in Crisis.' Working Paper 534. New York: Levy Economics Institute.
Conceição, P., Kim, N. and Zhang, Y. (2009b) 'Economic Shocks and Human Development: A Review of Empirical Findings.' UNDP/ODS Working Paper. New York, UNDP.
Das, J. (2008) 'Mental Health Patterns and Consequences: Results from Survey Data in Five Developing Countries.' Policy Research Working Paper 4495. Washington, DC: World Bank.
Elson, D. (2009) 'Gender Equality and the Economic Crisis.' IDRC/SID-OG Meeting. Ottawa, 27 November.
Epaulard, A. (2003) 'Macro-economic Performance and Poverty Reduction.' Working Paper 03/72. Washington, DC: IMF.
Ferreira, F. and Schady, N. (2008) 'Aggregate Economic Shocks: Child Schooling and Child Health.' Working Paper 4701. Washington, DC: World Bank.
Friedman, J. and Schady, N. (2009) 'How Many More Infants Are Likely to Die in Africa as a Result of the Global Financial Crisis?' Policy Research Working Paper 5023. Washington, DC: World Bank.
Friedman, J. and Thomas, D. (2007) 'Psychological Health Before, during and after an Economic Crisis: Results from Indonesia 1993–2003.' Policy Research Working Paper 4386. Washington, DC: World Bank.
Gordon, D., Nandy, S., Pantazis, C., Pemberton, S. and Townsend, P. (2004) 'The Distribution of Child Poverty in the Developing World.' Report to UNICEF. Bristol: Centre for International Poverty Research, Bristol University.
Grimm, M., Klasen, S. and McKay, A. (2007) *Determinants of Pro-poor Growth: Analytical Issues and Findings from Country Cases*. Basingstoke: Palgrave Macmillan.
Gross, M., Klasen, S. and Harttgen, K. (2005) 'Measuring Pro-poor Growth with Non-income Indicators.' Discussion Paper 132. Göttingen: IAI, University of Göttingen.
Haddad, L, Alderman, H., Appleton, S., Song, L. and Yohannes, Y. (2003) 'Reducing Child Malnutrition: How Far Does Income Growth Take Us?' *World Bank Economic Review* 17(1): 107–31.
Hossain, N. (2009) 'Accounts of the Crisis: Poor People's Experiences of the Food, Fuel and Financial Crises in Five Countries.' Brighton: IDS.
IMF (2009a) *The Implications of the Global Financial Crisis for Low-income Countries*. Washington, DC: IMF.
IMF (2009b) 'Low-income Countries Need Increased Financing to Cope with Crisis Says IMF Managing Director Strauss-Kahn.' Press Release 09/305, 17 September.
Kyrili, K. and Martin, M. (2010) 'The Impact of the Global Financial Crisis on the Budgets of Low-Income Countries.' Oxford: Oxfam.
Mendoza, M. (2009) 'Aggregate Shocks, Poor Households and Children: Transmission Channels and Policy Responses.' *Global Social Policy* 9: 55–78.
Mosley P. (2004) 'Severe Poverty and Growth: A Macro-micro Analysis.' Working Paper 51. Manchester: CPRC.

Oxfam (2010) 'The Global Economic Crisis and Developing Countries: Impact and Response.' Oxford: Oxfam UK/Australia.
Ravallion, M. (2008) 'Lessons from World Bank Research on Financial Crises.' Policy Research Working Paper 4779. Washington, DC: World Bank.
Ravallion, M. and Chen, S. (2009) 'The Impact of the Global Financial Crisis on the World's Poorest.' www.voxeu.org/index.php?q=node/3520.
Ravallion, M. and Chen, S. (2010) 'Updated Poverty Estimates of the Global Economic Crisis.' Washington, DC: World Bank.
Ravallion, M. Chen, S. and Sangraula, P. (2009) 'Dollar-a-day Revisited.' *World Bank Economic Review* 23(2): 163–84.
Schady, N. (2004) 'Do Macroeconomic Crises Always Slow Human Capital Accumulation?' *World Bank Economic Review* 18(2): 131–54.
Skoufias, E. and Parker, S. (2006) 'Job Loss and Family Adjustments in Work and Schooling during the Mexican Peso Crisis.' *Journal of Population Economics* 19(1): 163–81.
Sumner, A. (2010) *Child Poverty Impacts and Public Budgets: Tracking the Global Economic Crisis in Sub-Saharan Africa.* Addis Ababa: ACPF.
UNDESA (2009) *World Economic Situation and Prospects 2010.* New York: UNDESA.
UNGIVAS (2009) *Voices of the Vulnerable.* New York: UNGIVAS.
Weisbrot, W., Ray, R., Johnston, J., Cordero, J.A. and Montecino, J.A. (2009) 'IMF Supported Macroeconomic Policies and the World Recession: A Look at Forty One Borrowing Countries.' Washington, DC: CEPR.
World Bank (1999) *Gender Dynamics of the East Asian Crisis.* Washington, DC: World Bank.
World Bank (2009a) 'Swimming against the Tide: How Developing Countries Are Coping with the Global Crisis.' Washington, DC: World Bank.
World Bank (2009b) 'Women in 33 Countries Highly Vulnerable to Financial Crisis Effects.' Press Release 245/PREM, 6 March.
World Bank (2009c) 'Rapid, Qualitative Assessments of the Impacts of the Economic Crisis: Overview of Findings from Eight Countries.' Washington, DC: World Bank.
World Bank (2011) *Global Monitoring Report 2011: Improving the Odds of Achieving the MDGs.* Washington, DC: World Bank.

11

Social Protection Responses to Crises and Their Impacts on Children: Learning from Past Lessons in Indonesia and Ethiopia

Maricar Garde and Jenn Yablonski

Introduction

The global economic crisis is estimated to have had a substantial impact on the number of people living in poverty in developing countries. Children tend to be disproportionately affected by aggregate shocks: as households are forced to make difficult choices, tradeoffs often result in a worsening of children's wellbeing. While such coping strategies may be temporary, some have been proven to bring about long-term consequences for children.

There has been increased attention to social protection since the global economic crisis which broke out in 2008.[1] Past experience indicates that social protection programmes can play a significant role in helping households cope during crises, and in mitigating or preventing negative consequences for children. Learning from these experiences may provide important lessons when designing responses, not only to economic crises but also to other types of aggregate shocks.

This chapter discusses the development and evolution of social protection programmes in two countries during previous crises, and the consequent impacts for households and children. The two case studies cover the introduction of the National Safety Net programme in Indonesia during the 1997–8 East Asian financial crisis and the evolution of the Productive Safety Net Programme (PSNP) in Ethiopia as a response to repeated food crises. It examines the characteristics of the programmes, how they were adopted and implemented, their mitigating effects for children and their potential to turn into long-term anti-poverty schemes. The two cases were chosen for their contrasting contexts, but importantly because many countries are currently facing the effects of overlapping shocks and trends: spikes in food and fuel prices, financial crises, economic downturns, fiscal and political pressures on public spending and so on. The chapter closes with lessons from the case studies that warrant reflection for the current context.

Impacts of shocks on children and households

There is a broad literature on how aggregate shocks affect households, which is treated here only briefly. Aggregate shocks in developing countries are likely to result in increased poverty and a deterioration of social indicators such as education, health and nutrition. The effects of shocks differ across households, and factors such as wealth, geographic location, demographics and education determine the severity, depth and nature of the impacts. Within households as well, shocks may affect members unequally, with some members bearing the burden disproportionately dependent on age, gender, birth order and so on. Figure 11.1 illustrates how an aggregate shock might affect households and channels through which government social protection responses can have an effect.

At the macro level, economic shocks can have direct effects on trade, investments, remittances and possibly official development assistance (ODA), which in turn affect household income and consumption. Crises also affect government revenue and spending, as officials may face increased demand for social services in the face of shrinking budgets.

During difficult times, households often resort to networks and coping mechanisms to maintain their living standards. Even where strong networks and private transfers exist, however, shocks can strain these systems beyond their capacity. Additionally, the poorest and most marginalised are less likely to have access to these networks. The mechanisms the poor can use to protect their consumption, including selling off productive assets, getting into debt, withdrawing children from school and sending children to work, often bring long-lasting consequences (Ravallion, 2008).

It is worth looking at some of the evidence on the effects of crises on children, taking the examples of nutrition, education and child work. Starting with nutrition, the East Asian crisis contributed to food insecurity and reduced high-quality food intake in parts of Indonesia. For example, 11 per cent of respondents in a survey in Java in 1998 reported weight loss in the previous year owing to lack of food (Studdert et al.,

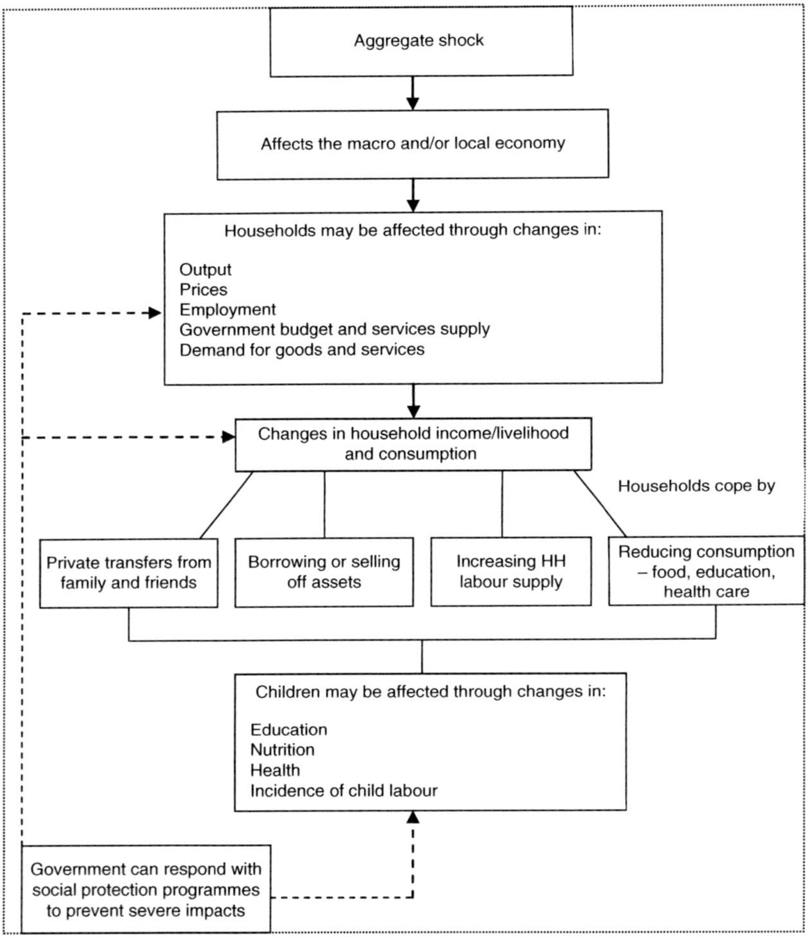

Figure 11.1 How aggregate shocks might affect households and how government can respond

2001). Rapid monitoring initiatives conducted by the UN Children's Fund UNICEF in 2008–9 in a range of countries indicated that households were experiencing increased difficulties in covering expenses, therefore decreasing food consumption and/or switching to cheaper foods (Mendoza, 2010).

Crises can also cause withdrawals of children from school as families can no longer afford the direct costs or need the children to work at home or for pay. The Argentinean recession in the late 1990s reduced the probability of schooling attendance by 12 per cent and 8.6 per cent for males and females, respectively (Rucci, 2003). Unemployment spells in Brazil, captured in monthly surveys from 1982 to 1999, increased the probability of a child entering the labour force, dropping out of school and failing to advance in education (Duryea et al., 2007). Crop shocks in the Kagera region of Tanzania caused transitory income shocks and an increase in the level of child labour (Beegle et al., 2006), but households with assets were able to mitigate the impacts of these shocks.

Children also suffer disproportionately from crises due to irreversible and long-term consequences of negative impacts during childhood. For example, malnutrition in early childhood has permanent effects on physical and cognitive development and educational achievement. These outcomes have been found in turn to impact adult productivity and adult earnings negatively.[2] Similarly, missed years in school alter children's earning potential during adulthood, with school dropouts earning less as adults (Ravallion, 2008).

Social protection responses to crises: Indonesia and Ethiopia

Social protection systems can offer an important mechanism for protecting children and their families from immediate and long-term consequences of crises. India, Malawi, Nicaragua and Zambia provide evidence of the potential for different types of social protection to protect household consumption and wellbeing (Singh, 2008; Yablonski and O'Donnell, 2009). In policy discussions of the response to the current economic crisis, there is considerable discussion of the need to expand or develop new social protection programmes. In this context, it is useful to examine what we can learn from past experiences of designing or expanding social protection in developing countries as a response to crises – in terms of impacts but also policy development and implementation. What factors lead to the adoption of programmes? What makes them more or less effective in protecting children and households from potentially negative impacts?

As mentioned above, the two cases presented here were chosen mainly for their different evolution in response to different types of crises and their relevance to recent crises experienced by developing countries, but also for their different political, regional and economic contexts. The shock in Indonesia stemmed from the financial sector and it was part of a sudden regional financial crisis. Ethiopia suffered from chronic food insecurity brought about by multiple factors, as well as more recent price inflation. These cases bring some parallels with the crises that hit recently. Food prices spiked in the first half of 2008 and the global financial crisis hit later the same year. In many developing countries, households had to cope with very high food prices and economic tightening brought about by the imbalance in the global economy. While economies have started to grow again, unemployment lingers and food commodity prices are starting to go up again after a period of respite. Countries today have to deal with both sudden shocks like the East Asian financial crisis and repeated ones such as food insecurity in Ethiopia. It would be a mistake to make any generalisations based on this short overview of just two cases. However, we do attempt to draw out observations from the Indonesian and Ethiopian cases that may warrant reflection for the current crisis and social protection.

Indonesia

Context

Indonesia, one of the countries that drove the 'East Asian Miracle', experienced fast and sustained economic growth for three decades from the 1970s through the mid-1990s. From 1970 to 1996, Indonesia's per capita income increased at an annual rate of 5.9 per cent in constant US dollars (Ascher, 2008), and the population living below the official poverty line declined sharply by 50 percentage points (Sumarto et al., 2002). By 1996, the poverty rate was 17.4 per cent. Non-income indicators such as infant mortality, life expectancy and student enrolment had also improved.

During this growth period, Indonesia had no large-scale social protection programme in place – just a few small programmes directed at specific disadvantaged groups (for example orphans). The government directed social spending on health and education, with subsidised health care and compulsory social security insurance for those employed in the formal sector (Sumarto et al., 2002). It also provided commodity subsidies, the most significant of which was the fuel subsidy. This was regressive, however, as the richest 40 per cent of the population received almost 70 per cent of the subsidy (Widianto, 2007). The fuel subsidy moved with oil prices, making it burdensome to the government budget during times of oil price hikes.

The East Asian crisis hit unexpectedly and rapidly in July 1997, with regional currencies, including the Indonesian rupiah, losing much of their international value. By 1998, inflation in Indonesia was 78 per cent and export industries had declined by about 40 per cent (ADB, nd). The social cost of the crisis proved to be very deep for Indonesia. Poverty went up from 15 per cent in mid-1997 to 33 per cent by the end of 1998, while the proportion of households facing a high probability of falling below the poverty line almost tripled from 6.8 per cent in 1996 to 18.4 per cent in 1999 (Sumarto et al., 2008). Violent riots occurred as food prices went up and subsidies were dismantled as part of the conditions of the International Monetary Fund's (IMF's) bailout package. The Suharto regime, which many had credited for the country's economic progress, collapsed after decades in power. Most importantly, evidence reflects that the crisis brought about long-term poverty impacts. Ravallion and Lokshin (2007) estimate that about half the country's poverty count in 2002 could be attributed to the crisis, even if the economy had started to recover a few years previously.

Programme design

In the wake of the crisis and social unrest, the Indonesian government introduced several social protection programmes, to respond to social pressure, prevent the poor from falling into deeper poverty and reduce the risks facing vulnerable households. The schemes covered food security, employment, education, health and community empowerment, and they were generally directed at offsetting rising food prices, providing employment and preventing the deterioration of health and education (see Table 11.1).

The social protection response in Indonesia during the East Asian crisis is widely documented, and this paragraph and the next draw on several studies (Sumarto et al., 2002, 2008; World Bank, 2004) that have looked at this issue. Programmes – financed by the national government, the World Bank and the Asian Development Bank (ADB) – were implemented by a patchwork of national government agencies and regional and local authorities. For example, sales of subsidised rice were implemented by the National Logistics Agency (BULOG), an existing agency responsible for the supply and pricing of food, together with village authorities at the local level. In the case of the employment generation scheme – which was composed of 16 programmes – various national ministries (for example public works, forestry) and their local branches were involved in implementation.

The government relied on existing household data, self-selection and local officials' assistance to target beneficiaries. For instance, the BKKBN ranking of households was used to select who could participate in the sales of subsidised rice programme. Initially, only households which fell into the lowest official category of poverty were eligible to buy subsidised rice, but this was later expanded to those who were in the second-lowest category. Education scholarships were awarded by a school committee composed of the principal, a teacher representative, a student representative, the head of the parents' association and

Table 11.1 Programmes implemented in Indonesia in response to the East Asian crisis

Safety net area	Programme	FY 98–9 budget (billion rupiah)	Planned coverage	Targeting FY 1998–9
Food security	Sale of subsidised rice: eligible households allowed to purchase 10 kg of rice monthly at a subsidised price of price of Rp1,000 compared with average market price of Rp3,000	5,450	12.8 million of the bottom and second to the bottom categories of households designated by the BKKBN prosperity ranking	Geographic: none Household: BKKBN list
Employment	Employment creation programmes through labour-intensive public works projects	2,066	12.7 million person days	Geographic: none, various ministries Household: weak self-selection (arbitrary wage rate)
Education	Scholarships of Rp10,000, Rp20,000 and Rp30,000 for primary, lower secondary and upper secondary students; block grants to poor schools	1,138	Scholarships: 6 per cent of primary school students, 17 per cent of lower secondary school students and 10 per cent of upper secondary school students nationwide Block grants: 60 per cent of poorest schools in each district	Geographic: data on enrolment in 1997 Household: school committees based on the following criterion – students must be from poor households as classified by BKKBN and not in receipt of any other scholarship

Health	Health care subsidies: free medical and family planning services Nutrition programme to improve nutritional status of certain individuals especially children of preschool age	1,043	7.4 million of the lowest categories of households designated by BKKBN	Geographic: BKKBN poorest households rates Household: BKKBN list
Community empowerment	Community fund programme: block grants extended directly to villages for public works or a revolving credit fund	1,701		Geographic: pre-crisis poverty data by district Household: local decision-making

Note: BKKBN = National Family Planning Agency.

Source: Sumarto et al. (2002, 2008).

the village head following administrative criteria. While employment programmes targeted certain areas, the government relied on self-selection – those who had lost their jobs and were willing to work – to populate the scheme.

Coverage, targeting and impacts

The following analysis synthesises information from various studies that evaluated the implementation and impacts of the Indonesian social protection programmes. The safety nets were introduced in early 1998 but they were implemented only in the second half of that year, by which point the crisis had already affected millions. Some households relied on private transfers to protect themselves from the impacts of the downturn. Sumarto et al. (2005) provide evidence that households can partially protect their consumption from income shocks. However, the magnitude of the crisis pushed many into poverty and heightened vulnerability, and the tendency was for informal social protection to be stretched to capacity. The social effects of the crisis within its first year might have been dampened if programmes were implemented immediately, but the political unrest at that time limited the government's response capacity.

Coverage varied across the programme, as Figure 11.2 shows. The rice subsidy scheme had the highest coverage, at 40 per cent of all households, followed by the nutrition scheme, which reached 16 per cent of all households. The rice subsidy scheme covered over half of poor households; the rest covered a comparatively lower proportion.

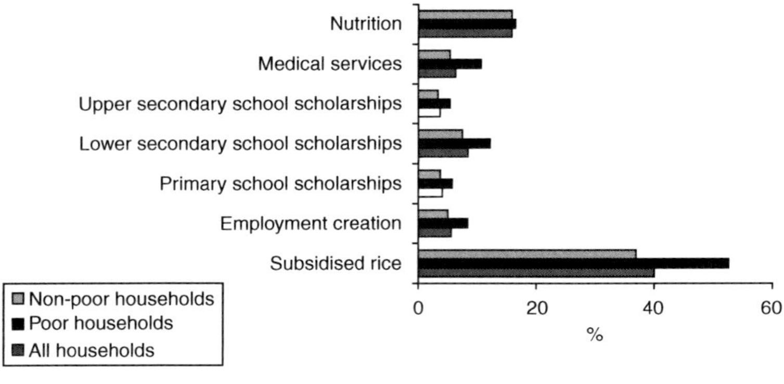

Figure 11.2 Household coverage of social protection programmes
Source: Sumarto et al. (2002).

Targeting across all programmes suffered from weaknesses. Notable was significant uptake by non-poor households of the employment creation programme. About 5.6 per cent of households – 8.3 per cent of poor households and 4.9 per cent of non-poor households – participated in the scheme. Sumarto et al. (2002) attribute this to the level of wages the programme offered (Rp6,073), close to the average daily wage in the food crop sector (Rp6,350). In some regions, the scheme's wage rate was higher than the prevailing local rate, which encouraged the employed and non-poor to switch to the programme (ODI, 2006), making self-selection ineffective.

Scholarship programmes, which had the lowest coverage of all the schemes, also faced targeting problems. Some scholarships were extended to families from higher levels (Cameron, 2000), even though only students from households in the two lowest BKKBN rankings were supposed to benefit from them.

Programmes which selected beneficiaries on the basis of BKKBN household rankings failed to reach those who were experiencing transitory shocks. For instance, the rice subsidy programme was targeted at the permanently poor and not necessarily those experiencing a shock due to the crisis (Sumarto et al., 2002). However, in some cases, village chiefs did not limit distribution of the subsidised rice to the list of eligible households, and extended it to families they perceived as being in need of the subsidy. Olken et al. (2001) show that the more near poor there were in the village, the more difficult it was to distinguish between poor and non-poor households, although wider rice distribution may have been welfare-enhancing for some families. Pritchett and Sumarto (2002) present some arguments on the merits of allowing communities to target beneficiaries – for example local officials may have better information on households' needs – but caution that too much discretion can lead to abuses.

Empirical studies show that some of the programmes brought benefits to participating households. Of all the schemes, however, only the rice subsidy programme was found to reduce the risk of falling into poverty significantly. According to Sumarto et al. (2005), a household that benefited from the subsidy had a 4 per cent lower chance of falling below the poverty line compared with one with similar characteristics but which did not receive the benefit.

The programmes saw mixed results for children and women. The education and nutrition programmes aimed to protect children's wellbeing. While the former had the lowest coverage, Cameron (2009) finds that the scholarship programme reduced dropout by 3 percentage points at lower secondary level but did not affect dropouts at primary level. As historically most dropouts have occurred at the lower secondary level, the scholarships helped students who were the most susceptible to leaving school early.

Children who participated in the nutrition (supplementary food) programme achieved better nutritional status than those who did not (Satriawan, 2006). Although the subsidised rice programme was not targeted directly at children, it helped households maintain their staple food consumption, which presumably freed up resources for other needs, including children's. There is evidence, however, that the shock brought about long-term nutritional impacts, which the programme was not able to avert. Block et al. (2004) indicate that, while child weight-for-age did not fall during the crisis, children's micronutrient levels deteriorated. In addition, mothers protected their children's caloric intake, leading to higher maternal wasting. While the programmes may have prevented more immediate nutrition indicators from slipping, impacts on vulnerable groups such as children and women may have consequences for a longer period.

Overall, the safety nets achieved mixed results and suffered from some weaknesses. The analysis above suggests that Indonesia needed swifter and larger-scale social protection, with better targeting strategies. Evidence synthesised from the various studies also indicates that social protection responses to shocks need to be more sensitive to long-term impacts that may disproportionately affect women and children. Indonesia has scaled up social protection in past years, and some of the schemes introduced in 1998 have continued in some form. This makes it important for the government to take note of existing evidence and use it to improve current programmes.

Ethiopia

Context

With a reach of over 8 million people, Ethiopia's PSNP is the largest social protection programme in Africa outside of South Africa. This is particularly impressive, and challenging, given overall poverty levels and levels of development. Ethiopia ranked 171 (out of 182) on the 2009 Human Development Index (HDI). A total of 39 per cent of people live below the $1.25 per day international poverty line and 48 per cent of children under five years are stunted.[3] The country's population also faces serious threats to food security, having experienced three major famines in recent history, in 1973–4, 1984–5 and 2002–3 (Pankhurst, 2009). Between 1998 and 2003, an estimated average 5 million people each year were identified as 'at risk', with the number of people receiving food aid ranging up to 14 million (Devereux et al., 2006).

As a response to chronic food insecurity and periodic crises owing to droughts and conflict, Ethiopia has a history of relief interventions, usually in the form of food aid or food relief (Adams and Kebede, 2005). Although this response was based on an emergency relief model, a large population was in fact chronically food-insecure even in good years, and it was rendered increasingly vulnerable over time as recurrent shocks forced them to deplete their assets (Devereux et al., 2006; Save the Children UK, 2009).

Evidence on these shocks in Ethiopia indicates immediate and longer-term impacts beyond the immediate crisis. Various studies find negative effects of income shocks (measured by droughts, crop damage and so on) on child health status (Dercon and Hoddinott, 2003; Woldehanna, 2009). Woldehanna (2009) also finds negative impacts of aggregate shocks on children's height for age, and that these effects are stronger when they occur before a child was born – indicating enduring consequences on households and children, as well as likely impacts of shocks on women's health and wellbeing. The gendered nature of risks and vulnerabilities in Ethiopia results in women bearing the consequences of crises heavily, with likely impact for children also (Jones et al., 2010). There is also some evidence that the impact of droughts on households and children is mitigated by factors such as asset holdings, family size and adult education (Yamauchi et al., 2009).

During the 1990s and early 2000s, a series of programmes attempted to tackle development and food security issues. Following the famine of 2002–3, there was increased recognition among donors and the government that emergency relief was not addressing the underlying vulnerability of a large proportion of the population, and that there was a need to shift towards a more regular and systematic safety net approach which would protect households from shocks (Pankhurst, 2009). In 2004, the government and donors designed the PSNP, which was viewed as a shift from repeated annual appeals to a predictable, multiyear response which would deliver support in a timely manner and reduce household vulnerability over time (Devereux et al., 2006; Food Security Coordination Bureau, 2008).

Programme design

The objective of the PSNP is 'to provide transfers to food insecure population in chronically food insecure *woredas* [districts] in a way that prevents asset depletion at the household level and creates assets at the community level' (Government of Ethiopia, 2004). From an original scale of 5.2 million beneficiaries in 2005, it currently reaches approximately 8.2 million people in four regions: Oromia, Tigray, Amhara and the Southern Nations, Nationalities and Peoples Region (SNNPR) (Gibson and Nyhus, 2009).

The PSNP is one of three elements of the government's Food Security Programme (FSP), alongside the Other Food Security Programme (OFSP) and the Resettlement Programme (Food Security Coordination Bureau, 2008). In combination, these programmes are intended to address food insecurity and help move people out of chronic poverty. Responsibility for implementation of the PSNP lies with the Ministry of Agriculture and Rural Development. While actual implementation is carried out by the government in some areas, in others it is implemented through non-governmental organisations (NGOs).[4] The OFSP has substantial financing from the national government, but the PSNP is financed entirely through multiyear funding from eight international donors (ibid.; Gibson and Nyhus, 2009).

The PSNP has two components. The first is a public works component, which takes up the bulk of the resources. In this, households are required to work 5 days per month for each member of the household up to a maximum of 20 days per able-bodied member. The second component is direct support for households unable to supply adult labour[5] for participation in public works; approximately 20 per cent of PSNP beneficiaries receive this support. Beneficiaries are expected to stay in the programme three years.

Transfers occur in the six-month period between January and June, to coincide with the lean season. The package received by households varies substantially by area and, in some cases, over time. There are numerous combinations of food and cash, with some households receiving food, some cash and some a combination of both. There has also been some variation in the food basket received.[6]

Coverage, targeting and impacts

Discussing in detail the impacts of the PSNP in terms of mitigating the effects of crises on children and their families is beyond the scope of this chapter. Indeed, the outcomes have been challenging to measure, in part because they are complex and vary across regions, populations and time, due to a number of factors. In this section, we attempt to highlight some of the major impacts that have been measured, with an emphasis on those mitigating the effects of crises on children.

Initial problems in the implementation of the PSNP related to effectiveness of targeting; understanding and transparency of the targeting process among communities; timeliness of transfers; and amount of employment per household. These have seen significant improvements over time, thanks to investment in training, capacity-building and planning and systems (Slater et al., 2006). Nonetheless, these improvements are not consistent across regions and are stronger in some aspects than others (Gilligan et al., 2009).

These early implementation problems had serious implications for the impacts of the programme during the initial period. A survey conducted in 2006 found that 22 per cent of households that had not participated in public works that season had participated in the previous season. Among households that were participating, half had not received assistance in the previous year. This variability of participation in the programme, combined with late payments and actual employment days being less than expected, meant that impacts among participants were on average less than expected. In 2006, research indicated that food security had not improved among households that had received at least some payment from the PSNP relative to similar households that had not participated. Although PSNP participant households reported increased ability to avoid depleting assets and savings during lean periods, they were still more likely than non-beneficiaries to adopt strategies such as reducing food consumption or selling assets. However, when measuring impact among households that had received at least half of intended payments over the year (Birr 90), some measures of food security and livelihoods activities improved (Devereux et al., 2006; Gilligan et al., 2008).

Despite initial challenges, evidence suggests there have been some modest improvements in household consumption and food security over time as a result of the PSNP. Based on household surveys conducted in 2006 and repeated in 2008, Gilligan et al. (2009) find that consumption by public works beneficiaries during this period rises more than for non-beneficiaries. During a period marked by a reported modest rise in climatic shocks and a marked increase in input shocks, non-beneficiary households report a fall in food security, while those in the public works programme report no change. Outcomes are similar for livestock holdings, with beneficiaries' holdings increasing between 2002 and 2007 and then levelling off in 2008, as compared with a slight fall among non-beneficiaries. Beneficiaries themselves report improved capacity to cope with the lean season and with drought (Jones et al., 2010). These findings suggest the PSNP is protecting beneficiaries from shocks to some extent.

In terms of child- and gender-specific outcomes, there are a number of positive indications. In 2006, many households receiving cash were spending part of it on education (15 per cent of households) and health (29 per cent). Households reported increased use of health care facilities and increased enrolment and longer attendance of children in school, and attributed these changes to the PSNP (Devereux et al., 2006; Slater et al., 2006). Interestingly, Yamauchi et al. (2009) find that the public works programme decreased school progression in the absence of a drought, but increased progression otherwise, and that this effect is more important than prior household assets. The direct support component also is viewed as having important benefits for women in addressing some of the gender-specific vulnerabilities they face – as female-headed households or during pregnancy. Women and teenage girls in some areas suggest they are less vulnerable to 'labour abuse' in terms of wages and abuse by employers due to the alternative offered by the PSNP (Jones et al., 2010).

There are some concerns when we examine the programme using a gender or child lens, however. In particular, the labour requirements of the PSNP may affect who is selected for the programme and who is able to participate, resulting in unintended impacts for some women and children. Who benefits from the PSNP, and from the OFSP, appears to be affected by household demographics. Households with older or heads who are female or higher dependency ratios are less likely to participate in public works, and households headed by females are less likely to get access to OFSP services[7] (Gilligan et al., 2009). While this may in part reflect that more of these households are receiving direct support, it is unclear whether this is in fact the case. These finding are particularly concerning given that households headed by females and olderadults are on average worse off in terms of assets and food security (Devereux et al., 2006). A number of design and implementation issues mitigate the potential positive impacts for women: inconsistent implementation of the maternity leave provisions and equal wages for men and women; payments made to the household head and limited consideration given to women's additional time burden (Jones et al., 2010). There is also some evidence that the work requirements of the PSNP cause children's work at home to increase, as they replace adult labour which is being used for PSNP work (Slater et al., 2006; Woldehanna, 2009). Among those selected for the PSNP but who do not participate, conflicts with child care and needing to spend time on the family farm are cited as reasons (Gilligan et al., 2009). These findings suggest that a different approach may be needed for a subset of households, particularly to achieve the programme's aim of a more sustainable movement of households out of poverty (Pankhurst, 2009).

Another important lesson from the PSNP relates to high rates of inflation experienced in 2007–8. While in theory the transfers received, whether in cash or in kind, are supposed to be equivalent in value, in practice this is often not the case. Particularly during the 2007–8 period, the purchasing power of the PSNP payment decreased drastically for households receiving cash (Gilligan et al., 2009). For instance, households in Amhara lost 56 per cent in purchasing power over seven months. This led to increasing demands from beneficiaries to receive food instead of cash. In addition, differences in prices between and within regions meant that the real value of cash payments varied substantially across beneficiary households. Combined with the fact that households were already receiving different combinations of food and cash, this meant PSNP beneficiaries were receiving very different levels of transfers (Hobson, 2009; Save the Children UK, 2009).

Concluding observations

Forming generalisations from the analysis is not the intention here, but some useful insights can be gleaned from the discussion in this chapter. First, the nature of the shock affects both the social protection response of the government and possibly the longer-term prospects of a programme. Programmes developed in response to crises may require explicit changes in policy objectives in order to address longer-term vulnerability. Ethiopia's experience of periodic shocks combined with underlying food insecurity eventually led to the development of a more predictable and multiyear safety net programme, designed to reduce household vulnerability over time. Nonetheless, the PSNP's origins as an evolution of humanitarian response combined with dependence on donor funding make its future unclear. Pressure for the graduation of beneficiaries stands in contrast with growing numbers of beneficiaries and the fact that, while important improvements are being achieved, the time horizon for sustainable reductions of food insecurity are not short.

Indonesia faced a sudden and large crisis after a period of growth and improvements in human development. The government responded with hastily designed and implemented social protection programmes to address economic and social turmoil. The programmes were patchy and suffered from targeting weaknesses. The government has scaled up social protection since that crisis and introduced other schemes such as cash transfers, but some of those from 1998 have continued.

Second, poor coverage and targeting are often a problem but can be improved as the programme progresses. That the Indonesian government relied on dated national household data for coverage meant the programmes failed to capture those experiencing transitory shocks, but in some cases this was rectified by local-level distribution. Indonesia's experience also highlights the importance of developing countries' capacity to collect real-time data as part of strategies to build resilience to future crises. In the Ethiopian case, achievement of desired coverage (in terms of consistency of payment, numbers of beneficiaries and so on) required time and investment in systems and human capacity. Ethiopia was able to enhance the PSNP's targeting over time, but improvements were unequal across regions. In both cases, this points to the importance of systems being in place before a crisis occurs, especially where overall administrative capacities are low.

The Indonesian case also suggests that the poor and the non-poor can end up competing for limited benefits during times of shocks. There is a tension for safety nets between cushioning the impacts of a crisis on the poor and preventing households from falling into transitory poverty. A role for local actors in identifying beneficiaries and distributing benefits might help, but this obviously carries the risk of mal-distribution.

Third, programme design needs to ensure that programmes are not having negative differential impacts for different households or household members. The PSNP is likely creating conflicts in the use of time and labour among household members and *de facto* limitations to participation, particularly for those who are labour-constrained. Gendered and child-specific outcomes of programmes must be anticipated and monitored. This includes careful consideration of labour requirements and child care provision. Programmes otherwise risk failing to address the long-term impacts on children and women in favour of more visible and immediate needs.

Finally, social protection programmes in Ethiopia and Indonesia have produced some positive results for women and children despite implementation challenges – even when not directly targeted at children. The most obvious impact is on protecting consumption during times of insecurity. Participating households in both countries increased consumption compared with households that did not participate in the programmes. Evidence also shows that the PSNP protected participating households from future shocks. As such, well-implemented social protection programmes can prevent aggregate shocks from having long-term impacts on children, but this potential requires attention to a range of design and implementation issues.

Notes

1. For example, the Communiqué of the London G20 Summit in 2009 and the launch of the Social Protection Floor Initiative by the UN Chief Executives Board in the same year.
2. Grantham-McGregor et al. (2007); Strauss and Thomas (1998); Victora et al. (2008).
3. www.unicef.org/infobycountry/ethiopia_statistics.html.
4. The implementing agency is linked to the funding source, with US Agency for International Development (USAID) funding for the PSNP implemented through NGOs.
5. Including pregnant and lactating women.
6. Food Security Coordination Bureau (2008); Gibson and Nyhus (2009); Gilligan et al. (2008); Save the Children UK (2009).
7. Access to the OFSP is important, as preliminary evidence suggests that households that are able to access both the PSNP and the OFSP are better able to protect and accumulate assets over time (Slater et al., 2006).

References

Adams, L. and Kebede, E. (2005) 'Breaking the Poverty Cycle: A Case Study of Cash Interventions in Ethiopia.' HPG Background Paper. London: ODI.

ADB (nd) 'The Asian Financial Crisis and Indonesia's Labor Intensive Work Program.' Project Brief. Manila: ADB.

Ascher, W. (2008) 'Mineral Wealth, Development, and Social Policy in Indonesia.' Working Document. Project on Social Policy in Mineral-rich Countries. Geneva: UNRISD.

Beegle, K., Dehejia, R. and Gatti, R. (2006) 'Child Labor and Agricultural Shocks.' *Journal of Development Economics* 81(1): 80–96.

Block, S., Kiess, L., Webb, P. and Kosen, S. (2004) 'Macro Shocks and Micro Outcomes: Child Nutrition during Indonesia's Crisis.' *Economics and Human Biology* 2(1): 21–44.

Cameron, L. (2000) 'An Analysis of the Role of Social Safety Net Scholarships in Reducing School Drop-out during the Indonesian Economic Crisis.' Working Paper 82. Florence: UNICEF Innocenti Research Centre.

Cameron, L. (2009) 'Can a Public Scholarship Program Successfully Reduce School Drop-outs in a Time of Economic Crisis? Evidence from Indonesia.' *Economics of Education Review* 28(3): 308–17.

Dercon, S. and Hoddinott, J. (2003) 'Health, Shocks and Poverty Persistence.' Working Paper 2003/08. Helsinki: UNU-WIDER.

Devereux, S., Sabates-Wheeler, R., Tefera, M. and Taye, H. (2006) 'Ethiopia's PSNP: Trends in Transfers within Targeted Households.' Brighton and Addis Ababa: IDS and Indak.

Duryea, S., Lam, D. and Levison, D. (2007) 'Effects of Economic Shocks on Children's Employment and Schooling in Brazil.' *Journal of Development Economics* 84(1): 188–214.

Food Security Coordination Bureau (2008) *Food Security Focus – Quarterly Newsletter of the Federal Food Security Programme* 1(1).

Gibson, J. and Nyhus, C. (2009) 'Research Programme on the Impacts of Cash Transfers on Children in Eastern and Southern Africa: Ethiopia Country Report.' Save the Children UK/UNICEF. Mimeo.

Gilligan, D., Hoddinott, J. and Taffesse, A. (2008) 'The Impact of Ethiopia's Productive Safety Net Programme and Its Linkages.' Discussion Paper 00839. Washington, DC: IFPRI.

Gilligan, D., Hoddinott, J., Kumar, N., Taffesse, A., Dejene, S., Gezahegn, F. and Yohannes, Y. (2009) 'Ethiopia Food Security Program: Report on 2008 Survey.' Washington, DC: IFPRI.

Government of Ethiopia (2004) 'Productive Safety Net Programme: Programme Implementation Manual.' Addis Ababa: MoARD.

Grantham-McGregor, S.M., Cheung, Y.B., Cueto, S., Glewwe, P., Richter, L., Strupp, B. and the International Child Development Steering Group (2007) 'Developmental Potential in the First 5 Years for Children in Developing Countries.' *The Lancet* 369(9555): 60–70.

Hobson, M. (2009) 'The Food Price Crisis and Its Impact on the Ethiopian Productive Safety Net Programme in 2008.' *Humanitarian Exchange Magazine* 42.

Jones, N., Tafere, W. and Woldehanna, T. (2010) 'Gendered Risks, Poverty and Vulnerability in Ethiopia: To What Extent is the Productive Safety Net Programme Making a Difference?' Draft. London: ODI.

Mendoza, R. (2010) 'Inclusive Crises, Exclusive Recoveries, and Policies to Prevent a Double Whammy for the Poor.' Social and Economic Policy Working Paper. New York: UNICEF.

ODI (2006) 'Social Safety Nets: Indonesia.' Inter-regional Inequality Facility Policy Brief 5. London: ODI.

Olken, B., Nabiu, M., Toyamah, N. and Perwira, D (2001) 'Sharing the Wealth: How Villages Decide to Distribute OPK Rice?' Working Paper. Jakarta: SMERU Research Institute.

Pankhurst, A. (2009) 'Rethinking Safety Nets and Household Vulnerability in Ethiopia: Implications of Household Cycles, Types, and Shocks.' World Conference of Humanitarian Studies. Groningen, 4–7 February.

Pritchett, L. and Sumarto, S. (2002) 'Targeted Programmes in an Economic Crisis: Empirical Findings from the Experience of Indonesia.' Working Paper. Jakarta: SMERU Research Institute.

Ravallion, M. (2008) 'Bailing out the World's Poorest.' Policy Research Working Paper 4763. Washington, DC: World Bank.

Ravallion, M. and Lokshin, M. (2007) 'Lasting Impacts of Indonesia's Financial Crisis.' *Economic Development and Cultural Change* 56(1): 27–56.

Rucci, G. (2003) 'Macro Shocks and Schooling Decisions.' Los Angeles, CA: UCLA.

Satriawan, E. (2006) 'Does Supplementary Food Program Help Children during the Crisis? Evidence from Indonesian Panel Data.' American Agricultural Economics Association Annual Meeting. Long Beach, CA, 23–26 July.

Save the Children UK (2009) 'Cash, Food, Payment and Risk: A Review of the Productive Safety Net Programme.' Addis Ababa: Save the Children UK.

Singh, A. (2008) 'Do School Meals Work? Treatment Evaluation of the Midday Meal Scheme in India.' Student Paper. Oxford: Young Lives.

Slater, R., Ashley, S., Tefera, M., Buta, M. and Esubalew, D. (2006) 'PSNP Policy, Programme and Institutional Linkages.' Final Report. London and Addis Ababa: ODI and Indak.

Strauss, J. and Thomas, D. (1998) 'Health, Nutrition, and Economic Development.' *Journal of Economic Literature* 36(2): 766–817.

Studdert, L., Frongillo, E. Jr. and Valois, P. (2001) 'Household Food Insecurity Was Prevalent in Java during Indonesia's Economic Crisis.' *Journal of Nutrition* 131(10): 2685–91.

Sumarto, S., Suryahadi, A. and Bazzi, S. (2008) 'Indonesia's Social Protection during the Crisis.' In Barrientos, A. and Hulme, D. (eds) *Social Protection for the Poor and the Poorest: Concepts, Policies and Politics*. Houndsmills: Palgrave Macmillan.

Sumarto, S., Suryahadi, S. and Widyanti, W. (2002) 'Designs and Implementation of Indonesian Social Safety Net Programme.' *The Developing Economies* 40(1): 3–31.

Sumarto, S, Suryahadi, S. and Widyanti, W. (2005) 'Assessing the Impact of Indonesian Social Safety Net Programmes on Household Welfare and Poverty Dynamics.' *The European Journal of Development Research* 17(1): 155–77.

Victora, C., Adair, L., Fall, C., Hallal, P.C., Martorell, R., Richter, L. and Sachdev, H.S. (2008) 'Maternal and Child Undernutrition: Consequences for Adult Health and Human Capital.' *The Lancet* 371(9609): 340–57.

Widianto, B. (2007) 'Are Budget Support and Cash Transfers Effective Means of Social Protection?' Forum on Inclusive Growth and Poverty Reduction in the New Asia and the Pacific. Manila, 8–9 October.

Woldehanna, T. (2009) 'Productive Safety Net Programme and Children's Time Use between Work and Schooling in Ethiopia.' Working Paper 40. Oxford: Young Lives.

World Bank (2004) 'The Case of a Post-Crisis Country: Indonesia.' Conference on Protecting the Vulnerable: The Design and Implementation of Effective Safety Nets. Washington, DC, 29 November–10 December.

Yamauchi, F., Yohannes, Y. and Quisumbing, A. (2009) 'Risks, Ex-Ante Actions, and Public Assistance: Impacts of Natural Disasters on Child Schooling in Bangladesh, Ethiopia and Malawi.' Discussion Paper 00990. Washington, DC: IFPRI.

Yablonski, J and O'Donnell, M. (2009) 'Lasting Benefits: The Role of Cash Transfers in Tackling Child Mortality.' London: Save the Children.

12
Social Protection in Fiscal Stimulus Packages

Yanchun Zhang, Nina Thelen and Aparna Rao

Introduction

Many countries have responded to the financial and economic crisis by implementing expansionary monetary and/or fiscal policies. The extent of the monetary easing varies from country to country, as does the size and composition of the fiscal stimuli. Some countries have included certain measures in their fiscal stimulus plans to protect the most vulnerable members of society, including children. This chapter presents information on the extent of these social protection measures in order to better understand how policy responses to the crisis addressed concerns about poverty, vulnerability and deterioration in human development outcomes.

There is a growing literature on the size of national stimulus packages. Some studies show compilations of stimulus measures for specific 'groups of countries', such as Organisation for Economic Co-operation and Development (OECD) countries (OECD, 2009a), G20 countries (IMF, 2009a; Prasad and Sorkin, 2009), European Union (EU) countries (Saha and von Weizsäcker, 2009), Latin American and Caribbean countries (ECLAC, 2009) and Asia-Pacific countries (ESCAP, 2009). Other studies give a general overview of worldwide stimulus packages (ILO, 2009a; 2009b; Ortiz, 2009). For the most part, these studies focus on aggregate macroeconomic issues, including expected/projected effect on economic growth and implications for fiscal balances as well as for longer-term debt burdens.

There are some attempts to disentangle the various components of fiscal stimulus packages. The International Labour Organization (ILO, 2009a), for instance, provides an overview of fiscal initiatives directed at supporting the labour market. A number of studies analyse the so-called 'greening' or 'climate-friendly' component of stimulus packages (for instance Hoehne et al., 2009; Klepper, 2009). The UN Development Fund for Women (UNIFEM, 2009) assesses the gender implications of the economic crisis in Asia and how stimulus packages can help mitigate these.

This chapter contributes to the literature by first presenting a collection of data on 48 fiscal stimulus packages worldwide announced by individual countries and areas;[1] and second taking a closer look at measures of the stimulus packages that may be categorised as social protection components.[2] The size of social protection measures is relevant because they could directly help prevent people from losing their income, shedding their assets or reverting to coping strategies that may be harmful to their and their children's current and future wellbeing (for example by cutting spending on health or education). Indirectly, social protection measures can help to build a more sustainable and resilient economy by providing the poor with the capacity to climb out of poverty.

Definitions and methodologies

We collected fiscal stimulus data mainly from official sources (mostly government and central bank websites but also International Monetary Fund (IMF) Article IV consultations).[3] Financial support measures (including financial bailouts; measures taken by the central bank; granting of public loans and government guarantees; and acquisition of securities and loans issued by the private sector) are excluded from our calculations. Due to the often limited information, we focus on fiscal stimulus plans announced, not necessarily on what the legislature has passed or what has been implemented, although we do provide anecdotal evidence on implementation.

Only discretionary measures in the announced fiscal stimulus packages are included.[4] Non-discretionary measures (automatic fiscal stabilisers) are excluded from our computation. Non-discretionary dimensions of fiscal policies include, for example, degree of progressiveness of the tax system and unemployment insurances. Non-discretionary fiscal measures are important mechanisms that can help smooth households' income fluctuations and stabilise the economy without any deliberate fiscal policy changes. In contrast, discretionary fiscal measures arise from deliberate actions by policymakers.[5] As this chapter focuses on deliberate fiscal policy changes adopted by governments to stimulate economies, only discretionary fiscal measures are counted.

There is no unanimous definition of social protection or clear categorisation of social protection measures in the literature or in policy practice.[6] When measuring the social protection components of each fiscal stimulus package, we define social protection measures as policy interventions that are intended to reduce poverty and vulnerability (including transitory poverty and vulnerability due to economic or other shocks) and to improve human welfare. Many social protection measures support poor and vulnerable groups of people, which includes the (non-working) young, unemployed, working poor, non-working elderly and special groups (children, sick, disabled, elderly and minorities) to cope with economic hardships.[7]

Examples of interventions in our computation include measures taken in the areas of public education, health, housing, labour market policy, social services and both contributory social insurance programmes and non-contributory safety net (social assistance) programmes.[8] For the purpose of clarification, the latter two categories are explained in more detail below.

Social insurance programmes, in general, include publicly provided or mandated insurance against unemployment, ageing, disability, sickness or death. During economic crisis, governments can help by reducing individual contributions to social insurance programmes and offsetting them with public funding. We count such government assistance in terms of individual social insurance contributions as social protection measures.

Safety nets, often referred to as social assistance or social welfare programmes, are non-contributory transfer programmes targeted at the poor and those vulnerable to poverty and shocks.[9] There is no universal consensus on the types of interventions covered by the safety net label. When we compute social protection measures, we include cash transfers (needs-based transfers, food stamps, non-contributory pensions); food and nutrition (quantity rations, in-kind transfers, supplemental feeding and nutrition, school feeding, emergency food distribution); general commodity price subsidies (price support for food, subsidised sales of food, subsidies for energy prices); public works (the poor working for food or cash); conditional cash transfers (CCTs) (transfers to poor households conditional on specific behaviour); fee waivers (health fees, school fees, scholarships) and so on. Although some measures may not be aimed directly at children, many of them (for instance school fee waivers, cash transfers and so on) do have an impact on societies' youngest members.

Size of fiscal stimulus packages[10]

Annex 3 lists the sources of the fiscal stimulus packages considered in the chapter.

Overview of the scale of fiscal stimulus

Table 12.1 shows individual countries' fiscal stimulus plans in total size and as a percentage of gross domestic product (GDP). According to our calculations for 48 countries and areas, the total fiscal stimulus size amounts to $2.4 trillion (about 3.9 per cent of global GDP in 2008).[11]

With $787 billion, the US government has announced the largest fiscal stimulus in terms of absolute amount. China's package, equivalent to $585 billion, is the second largest; Japan, with a package equivalent to $298 billion, and Germany, with $81 billion, follow in third and fourth places. Russia and Korea have been hit hard, as the global crisis crashed demand for their exports; both countries responded by stimulating the domestic economy with a fiscal package of about $50 billion each. Thailand and India also announced much bigger fiscal stimulus packages than many much richer economies. The smallest fiscal packages were announced by Honduras ($1.03 billion), Lithuania ($0.92 billion), Kenya ($0.28 billion) and Sri Lanka ($0.08 billion).

On average, the 48 countries are spending about 4.3 per cent of their 2008 GDP on fiscal stimulus. We find that four countries have announced a fiscal stimulus accounting for more than 10 per cent of their 2008 GDP.[12] Despite having the largest fiscal stimulus in terms of total size, the US stimulus package accounts for 6 per cent of its 2008 GDP. China plans to spend 13 per cent of 2008 GDP on its fiscal stimulus.

Although data are scarce, some attempt has been made to track actual implementation of some of the announced measures. IMF (2010a) shows that implementation of fiscal stimulus packages in 2009 in G20 countries was broadly in line with expectations. India, Russia, Turkey and the UK, for instance, implemented their fiscal stimulus packages in 2009 as expected. Indonesia implemented about 85 per cent of its announced 2009 stimulus measures (ibid., 2010b).

The picture for 2010 is a divergent one. IMF (2010c) reports that fiscal exit has been set in motion in countries where economic activity is gaining speed (for example Korea) or which have been exposed to market pressure (for example Portugal). On the other hand, some countries, like Russia, are reported to have added fiscal stimulus measures in 2010.

Table 12.1 Summary of individual countries' fiscal stimulus plans

	Converted ($ billions)	**% of 2008 GDP**
Argentina	3.85	1.27
Australia	47.04	5.75
Austria	16.25	4.14
Bangladesh	1.15	1.38
Belgium	4.93	1.03
Canada	42.15	3.22
Chile	4.00	2.84
China, PR	585.26	13.30
China, PR: Hong Kong	11.30	5.22
Czech Republic	3.91	2.04
Egypt	2.72	1.67
Finland	10.89	4.20
France	36.18	1.34
Georgia	2.28	19.92
Germany	80.50	2.32
Honduras	1.03	7.24
India	38.39	3.53
Indonesia	6.33	1.40
Israel	2.80	1.47
Japan	297.52	5.32
Kazakhstan	18.21	13.83
Kenya	0.28	1.04
Korea	53.35	6.56
Lithuania	0.92	2.02
Malaysia	12.12	5.67
Mexico	13.32	1.49
Netherlands	8.35	1.02
Nigeria	1.55	0.82
Norway	2.86	0.79
Peru	3.20	2.69
Philippines	6.95	4.40
Poland	10.64	2.49
Portugal	3.03	1.31
Russia	53.64	3.78
Singapore	10.21	5.71
Slovenia	1.20	2.32
South Africa	9.90	4.03
Spain	15.55	1.02
Sri Lanka	0.08	0.22
Sweden	13.44	3.33
Switzerland	1.97	0.39
Taiwan	15.26	4.04
Tanzania	1.33	6.85
Thailand	44.92	17.22
Turkey	37.95	6.09
UK	29.16	1.39
US	787.00	5.52
Vietnam	8.42	9.68

Source: Authors' calculations based on official government documents (see Annex 3); IMF (2009b).

IMF (2010b) shows that, for 2010–11, it expects China to continue and complete the stimulus programme that was announced at the end of 2008.

Recent data show a consolidation of the recovery, and fiscal exit strategies are expected to start in 2011 for most countries, although at different speeds (IMF, 2010c). This means some of the fiscal stimulus measures announced for the longer term of several years may ultimately not be implemented.

Social protection components of fiscal stimulus packages[13]

Table 12.2 summarises the total amount of social protection components of the 35 fiscal stimulus packages that provided information on social protection measures. These total amounts may understate the actual size of social protection components of the fiscal stimulus in some countries because information broken down by component on some countries' plans is incomplete. Moreover, additional social protection measures may have been put in place that were not included in the stimulus plans. Thus, the size of social protection stimulus in Table 12.2 reflects only those spending or tax cut items announced in official sources that are included in stimulus plans and that fall in the social protection category as defined above.

We find that the 35 countries on average spend about 25 per cent of their stimuli on social protection measures. In total, this amounts to about $653 billion, almost 1 per cent of 2008 global GDP.

Out of 35 countries, 29 will spend more than 10 per cent of their fiscal stimulus on social protection. South Africa (56 per cent), Singapore (52 per cent), Taiwan (47 per cent) and Finland (43 per cent) are the biggest spenders on social protection calculated as a percentage of their stimulus packages. Peru (7 per cent), Mexico (6 per cent), Israel (4 per cent), Chile (3 per cent) and Turkey (1 per cent) will spend the least of their stimulus on social protection.

Among the 19 countries whose social protection components of the fiscal stimulus plan exceed $1 billion, the top two social protection spenders are the US and China. The US plans to spend $310 billion and China $135 billion on social protection. The smallest social protection spender is Bangladesh in terms of absolute size.

We see developing countries tend to spend less of their fiscal stimulus on social protection measures. Out of six countries that spend less than 10 per cent of their total stimulus on social protection, five are developing countries (Chile, Indonesia, Mexico, Peru and Turkey). Financing

Table 12.2 Summary of social protection components of fiscal stimulus packages

	Social protection components ($ billions)	% of stimulus package
Australia	10.46	22.24
Austria	4.08	25.10
Bangladesh	0.05	12.79
Belgium	0.51	10.44
Canada	11.02	26.16
Chile	0.11	2.70
China	134.61	23.00
Czech Republic	0.95	24.34
Finland	4.67	42.89
France	5.85	16.15
Georgia	0.96	42.11
Germany	20.03	24.89
Honduras	0.38	37.30
Indonesia	0.55	8.77
Israel	0.11	3.76
Japan	82.64	27.78
Kenya	0.11	38.70
Korea	6.11	11.46
Malaysia	4.16	34.29
Mexico	0.74	5.55
Netherlands	2.58	30.92
Norway	0.91	32.00
Peru	0.24	7.48
Philippines	1.05	15.15
Portugal	0.81	26.61
Russia	17.87	33.32
Singapore	5.35	52.38
Slovenia	0.35	29.15
South Africa	5.52	55.72
Switzerland	0.31	15.63
Taiwan	7.15	46.82
Thailand	10.53	23.45
Turkey	0.56	1.48
United States	310.44	39.45
Vietnam	1.41	16.79

Source: Authors' calculations based on official government documents (see Annex 3); IMF (2009b).

and institutional constraints for broader fiscal stimulus measures could be one explanation for a weakened ability to protect the most vulnerable groups in times of crisis in many developing countries. Creating a composite index of 'lack of space for fiscal stimulus', Calderón and

Fajnzylber (2009) find that, to a certain degree, Mexico and Peru are restrained in scaling up fiscal spending. Political aspects may also play a role in explaining the composition of fiscal stimulus packages. Öniş and Güven (2010) report that the fiscal response in Turkey was mainly a reaction to business protests, hence it lacks a focus on the poor and vulnerable. Some studies focusing on general social protection measures (not necessarily only discretionary fiscal stimulus measures) adopted in light of the global economic crisis argue that social protection provision in reaction to the crisis has not been large enough (for instance McCord; 2010; McCord and Vandemoortele; 2009).

It is also useful to examine which social protection items each country has been focusing on. Many stimulus packages include labour market measures to cushion the negative effects of the economic downturn on workers. Social safety net measures are also commonly adopted to protect low-income households.

Spending on public and social housing construction and maintenance is adopted by 10 of the 35 countries we have data on (Australia, China, France, Honduras, Malaysia, Russia, South Africa, Switzerland, the US, Vietnam). For example, China announced it would spend ¥400 billion, 10 per cent of its total stimulus, on public housing. Vietnam will spend VND24 trillion, 17 per cent of its total stimulus, on houses for workers and low-income families. Advanced economies like Australia (A$6 billion on social housing construction, A$0.4 billion on public housing repair and maintenance) and France (building 100,000 social housing units at €1.9 billion) will also dedicate more than 40 per cent of social protection spending to public housing.

A total of 12 countries also explicitly announced direct or indirect stimulus funding to health, such as increasing spending on public health (China, Honduras, Indonesia, Japan, Kenya, Peru, South Africa, Thailand, the US), compensating for contributions to statutory health insurance (Germany), providing health insurance assistance (Switzerland, the US) or lowering the value-added tax (VAT) rate for medication (Austria).

Meanwhile, 13 countries have new measures on education (Austria, China, Finland, Honduras, Malaysia, Netherlands, Peru, Russia, South Africa, Switzerland, Taiwan, Thailand, the US). Developing countries tend to focus on primary education, including China's ¥150 billion on pro-poor and pro-rurual health care and education and Malaysia's RM0.2 billion for preschool education. Developed countries choose to support professional schools for the unemployed or non-working young (the Netherlands, Switzerland).

Out of 35 countries, 21 announced specific and direct labour market measures to support employment (Austria, Belgium, Canada, Finland, France, Germany, Israel, Japan, Kenya, Korea, Malaysia, Mexico, the Netherlands, Portugal, Russia, Singapore, Slovenia, South Africa, Switzerland, Thailand, the US). Other countries, like China, announced big spending on infrastructure projects which will help in creating many new jobs.

Overall, eight countries have announced direct measures to assist and enhance social security (Australia, Bangladesh, the Czech Republic, Finland, Philippines, Russia, Turkey, Vietnam).

Some social protection measures are aimed directly at children and clearly have age-sensitive effects. For example, Korea plans to repair and improve old social welfare facilities for children, and South Africa will expand its school nutrition programme to feed more children more often. Germany, Japan and the US also announced additional measures to support families with young children.

Evidence on actual impact of fiscal stimulus measures, and especially on the impact of social protection components of fiscal stimulus measures, is scarce and usually takes time to emerge. But history does reveal the importance of financial cushions provided by fiscal stimulus to protect the most vulnerable groups during crises.

Harper et al. (2009) identify fiscal stimulus as one important option for policy response in order to protect the most vulnerable members of society in times of economic crisis, stressing the importance of approaching fiscal stimulus decisions for tackling poverty and vulnerability using a gender- and child-sensitive lens. Based on evidence from past crises, the authors argue that fiscal stimulus packages need to include increased investment in education, health, nutrition, water and sanitation as well as programmes to protect parents' economic security and child safety.

As for the impact of fiscal stimulus rolled out after the latest economic crisis, most available analysis has focused on the labour market. Ever since the onset of the global economic crisis, the International Labour Organization (ILO) has been closely monitoring developments in labour markets. The organisation provides estimates of the impact of fiscal stimulus measures on the labour market in G20 countries. According to ILO (2010), discretionary fiscal stimulus measures in G20 countries may have created or protected 8 million jobs in 2009 and 6.7 million in 2010. In light of the nascent withdrawal of fiscal stimulus measures and in order to sustain the recovery, ILO (2011) calls for a continued focus on job creation.

While the impact of fiscal stimulus on children is not easy to review at the current time, information on actual household coverage of increased investment in anti-hunger programmes during the economic downturn allows for some conclusion as to whether fiscal stimulus measures are inclusive of children. Anti-hunger programmes can help a parent who becomes unemployed or whose job pays a low wage to feed her/his children until the situation improves. The Center on Budget and Policy Priorities (CBPP) provides information on the impact of the boost for food stamps that is part of the US fiscal recovery package. According to this, the US American Recovery and Reinvestment Act temporarily boosted benefits under the Food Stamp Program by 13.6 per cent, starting in April 2009. All food stamp-recipient households (close to 20 million households with around 43 million people) are reported to benefit from the increase. The increase to food stamp benefits is considered one of the most effective and fast-acting provisions of the US fiscal stimulus package (CBPP, 2010).

More analysis on the impact of social protection components of discretionary fiscal stimulus measures is needed and it could inform more efficient policy responses to future crises.

Conclusion

This chapter collected evidence on fiscal stimulus packages announced by 48 governments in reponse to the current financial and economic crisis. Drawing on the official sources, we identified a total fiscal stimulus size for 48 countries and areas of $2.4 trillion (about 3.9 per cent of global GDP in 2008). Four countries announced a fiscal stimulus accounting for more than 10 per cent of their 2008 GDP. Our data also show that a few developing countries (for example India and Thailand) announced much bigger fiscal stimulus packages relative to their national GDP than many much richer economies.

This chapter contributes to an understanding of how policy responses to the crisis address concerns about poverty, vulnerability and deterioration in human development outcomes. Analysing the social protection component of the announced stimulus measures for 35 individual governments, we found that, on average, they spend about 25 per cent of their packages on social protection measures. This amounts to about $653 billion, almost 1 per cent of 2008 global GDP. Out of these 35 countries, 29 will spend more than 10 per cent of their fiscal stimulus on social protection.

The chapter also provides evidence on the impact of fiscal stimulus measures. Discretionary fiscal stimulus measures in G20 countries may have created or protected 8 million jobs in 2009 and 6.7 million in 2010 (ILO, 2010). The US American Recovery and Reinvestment Act is reported to have temporarily boosted benefits under the Food Stamp Program by 13.6 per cent, starting in April 2009 (CBPP, 2010), helping parents feed their children in difficult times.

More analysis – including using a child-sensitive lens – on the impact of social protection components of discretionary fiscal stimulus measures is needed and it could inform more efficient policy responses to future crises.

Annex 1 Definitions of social protection

ADB (ADB, 2009): '...policies and programs designed to reduce poverty and vulnerability by promoting efficient labor markets, diminishing people's exposure to risks, enhancing their capacity to protect themselves against hazards and interruption/loss of income.' ADB names five main areas in social protection: labour markets, social insurance, social assistance, micro- and area-based schemes and child protection.

DFID (DFID, 2005: 6): '...a subset of public actions – carried out by the state or privately – that address risk, vulnerability and chronic poverty.' For operational reasons, DFID (2005) subdivides social protection into three key components: social insurance, social assistance and setting and enforcing minimum standards.

ILO (García and Gruat, 2003: 13–14): '...the set of public measures that a society provides for its members to protect them against economic and social distress that would be caused by the absence or a substantial reduction of income from work as a result of various contingencies (sickness, maternity, employment injury, unemployment, invalidity, old age, and death of the breadwinner); the provision of health care; and, the provision of benefits for families with children. This concept of social protection is also reflected in the various ILO standards.'

IMF (IMF, 2001: 106–7): '...government outlays on social protection include expenditures on services and transfers provided to individual person and households and expenditures on services provided on a collective basis....Collective social protection services are concerned with matters such as formulation and administration of government policy; formulation and enforcement of legislation and standards for providing social protection; and applied research and experimental development into social protection affairs and services.' Health care is not included in the IMF definition of social protection expenses as it is classified as a separate expense.

OECD (OECD, 2009c): '...social protection and empowerment provide security and unlock human potential and thereby encourage poor people to take advantage of opportunities, which in turn promotes more sustainable pro-poor growth strategies. Social protection cuts across all sectors, and is considered important for breaking the intergenerational cycle of poverty, and for achieving a social contract on nation-building and accelerating progress towards the MDGs.' OECD also states that social protection measures are '... investments in people of all ages [that] ... have a clear gender dimension.'

UN (ECOSOC, 2000: 4): '... a set of public and private policies and programmes undertaken by societies in response to various contingencies to offset the absence or substantial reduction of income from work; to provide assistance for families with children as well as provide people with health care and housing. This definition is not exhaustive; it basically serves as a starting point of the analysis ... as well as a means to facilitate this analysis.'

Annex 2 Definitions of safety nets and social assistance

ADB (social assistance): programs designed to assist the most vulnerable individuals, households, and communities meet a subsistence floor and improve living standards.

DFID (social assistance): non-contributory transfers to those deemed eligible by society on the basis of their vulnerability or poverty. Examples include social transfers and initiatives such as fee waivers for education and health and school meals.

ILO (social assistance): tax-financed benefits to those with low incomes.

IMF (safety nets): instruments aimed at mitigating possible adverse effects of reform measures on the poor.

OECD (social assistance): support targeted to households that are clustered within the lower segment of the income distribution and provided to prevent extreme hardship among those with no other resources, reduce social exclusion, minimise disincentives to paid employment, and promote self-sufficiency.

FAO (social safety nets): cash or in-kind transfer programs that seek to reduce poverty by redistributing wealth and/or protect households against income shocks. Social safety nets seek to ensure a minimum level of wellbeing, a minimum level of nutrition, or help households manage risk.

Source: Adapted from Grosh et al. (2008: 5).

Annex 3 Announcement dates and source links of stimulus plans

	Announced date of stimulus	Covering years
Argentina	December 2008	N/A
www.casarosada.gov.ar/index.php?option=com_content&task=view&id=5307		
www.casarosada.gov.ar/index.php?option=com_content&task=view&id=5306&Itemid=66#		
Australia	October 2008, February 2009	2008–10
www.economicstimulusplan.gov.au/pages/default.aspx		
www.pm.gov.au/node/5331		
Austria	October 2008, December 2008	2009–10
www.oenb.at/en/img/mop_2009_q1_in_focus05_tcm16-111592.pdf		
Bangladesh[14]	April 2009	2009–10
www.mof.gov.bd/en/budget/09_10/mtbf/en/Chapter_I.pdf		
www.mof.gov.bd/en/budget/09_10/speech/bs_09_10_en.pdf		
www.cpd.org.bd/downloads/Implementation%20Challenges%20of%20the%20Budget%20FY2009-10.pdf (unofficial)		
Belgium	May 2009	2009–13
www.stabilityprogramme.be/en/Stability_program_2009_2013_Belgium_Cabinet_Finances_20090424_EN.pdf		
Canada	January 2009	2009–10
www.fin.gc.ca/pub/report-rapport/2009-1/cepexs-eng.asp		
Chile	January 2009	2009–10
Source: www.gobiernodechile.cl/viewNoticia.aspx?idArticulo=26271		
China	March 2009	2008 Q4–2010 Q4
www.ndrc.gov.cn/xwzx/xwtt/t20090306_264928.htm		
China, PR: Hong Kong	May 2009 (part of measures announced before this date)	2008–10
www3.news.gov.hk/isd/ebulletin/en/category/businessandfinance/090526/html/090526en03003.htm		

Czech Republic	End 2008, January 2009, February 2009	2009–11
www.mfcr.cz/cps/rde/xbcr/mfcr/Fiscal_Policy_Response_to_the_Deteriorating_Economic_Outlook.doc		
Egypt	November 2008	N/A
http://www.bloomberg.com/apps/news?pid=newsarchive&sid=aJ06xio48d3I (unofficial)		
Finland	January 2009	2009–10
http://eesc.europa.eu/events/2009-Financial-Markets/2009-03-17/docs/contributions/contribution-FI-EN.doc		
France	December 2008	2009–10
www.relance.gouv.fr/spip.php?page=chiffre-relance www.relance.gouv.fr/IMG/pdf/Allocution_du_Ministre_Senat_7_juillet_030709.pdf		
Georgia	February 2009	N/A
www.president.gov.ge/?l=E&m=0&sm=6&id=2855 www.georgia.gov.ge/pdf/2009_05_15_17_27_09_1.pdf		
Germany	November 2008, January 2009	2009–10
www.vwl.uni-freiburg.de/fakultaet/fiwiI/publikationen/231.pdf (unofficial source) www.bmwi.de/BMWi/Navigation/Wirtschaft/Konjunktur/Konjunkturpaket-2/umweltpraemie,did=287664.html		
Honduras	March 2009	2009–12 (short-term measures of HNL 14.1 billion are budgeted for 2009, some other measures are budgeted up to 2012)
www.sdp.gob.hn/NEWSDP/visorArch.aspx?ID=PCEFI0309.pdf		
India	N/A	2008–9
Source: http://indiabudget.nic.in/ub2009-10/bs/speecha.htm		
Indonesia	March 2009	2009
www.bi.go.id/web/en/Publikasi/Investor+Relation+Unit/Government+Press+Release/The+2009+Revised+Budget+Fiscal+Stimulus+Programme.htm www.bi.go.id/NR/rdonlyres/AE350D5E-BCB8-4AA4-BE29-9FB44C66B04B/15743/APBNPenyesuaian_2009_ENGLISH1.pdf		
Israel	December 2008	N/A
www.bankisrael.gov.il/develeng/develeng123/develeng.pdf		

Continued

	Announced date of stimulus	Covering years
Japan	October 2008, December 2008, April 2009	2008–10
www.kantei.go.jp/foreign/asospeech/2009/05/21speech_e.html www5.cao.go.jp/keizai1/2009/0420economic_effects.pdf www5.cao.go.jp/keizai1/2009/0420summary-english.pdf www.kantei.go.jp/foreign/asospeech/2009/04/090410siryou.pdf		
Kazakhstan	November 2008	2009–10
http://en.government.kz/site/news/112008/05		
Kenya	June 2009	N/A
www.treasury.go.ke/index.php?option=com_docman&task=cat_view&Itemid=54&gid=87&orderby=dmdate_published www.nation.co.ke/News/-/1056/609752/-/ujtf4s/-/index.html		
Korea	N/A	2008–12
www.mosf.go.kr/recover_eng/general_3.html and private communication with Ministry of Strategy and Finance		
Lithuania	N/A	N/A
www.skatinimoplanas.lt/lt/pages/apie-esp		
Malaysia	November 2008, March 2009	2008–9, 2009–10
www.epu.gov.my/html/themes/epu/images/common/pdf/kp/The_Global_Economic_Crisis-ChallengesFacedbytheMalaysianEconomy.pdf		
Mexico	February 2008, April 2008, October 2008, January 2009	2008–09
www.apartados.hacienda.gob.mx/sala_de_prensa/vocero/documentos/2009/vocero_02_2009.pdf www.eclac.org/publicaciones/xml/1/36241/2009-321-ThereactionoftheGovernmentsoftheAmericas-31may-WEB.pdf www.shcp.gob.mx/SALAPRENSA/sala_prensa_presentaciones/1_presentacion_acc_imef_22112008.pdf www.shcp.gob.mx/comunicados_principal/comunicado_023_2009.pdf www.presidencia.gob.mx/prensa/?contenido=34116#b7 ftp://ftp2.sat.gob.mx/asistencia_servicio_ftp/publicaciones/boletines/SHCPcomunicado_021_2008.pdf www.cefp.gob.mx/foro/alimentos/foroalimentos2.pdf www.presidencia.gob.mx/prensa/comunicados/?contenido=40351		

Netherlands	March 2009	2009–11
www.minaz.nl/dsc?c=getobject&s=obj&objectid=118821 www.minaz.nl/english/News/Press_releases_and_news_items/2009/Maart/Balkenende_presents_measures_to_tackle_crisis www.government.nl/Government/Supplementary_policy_agreement		
Nigeria	N/A	N/A
www.fmf.gov.ng/FMF_News.aspx?id=127		
Norway	January 2009	2008–09
www.regjeringen.no/en/dep/smk/Press-Center/Press-releases/2009/norways-government-presents-measures-to-.html?id=543719		
Peru	December 2008	2009
www.mef.gob.pe/PRENSA/discursos/Resumen_Medidas.pdf		
Philippines	January 2009	2009
Source: www.neda.gov.ph/erp/abouterpfunded.asp		
Poland	December 2008	2009
www.mf.gov.pl/_files_/aktualnoci/2009/stability_and_development_plan.pdf?PortalMF=22051b5016643889463b664b613a5025		
Portugal	December 2008	2009
www.portugal.gov.pt/pt/GC17/Governo/Ministerios/MTSS/Documentos/Pages/20081213_MTSS_Doc_IIE_Empregoaspx www.portugal.gov.pt/pt/Documentos/Governo/PCM/Apres_IIE.pdf		
Russia	November 2008	2009
www.premier.gov.ru/eng/anticrisis/		
Singapore	January 2009	2009
www.mof.gov.sg/budget_2009/speech_toc/downloads/FY2009_Budget_Statement.pdf www.singaporebudget.gov.sg/resilience.html		
Slovenia	December 2008, April 2009	2008–10
www.vlada.si/en/projects/measures_taken_in_response_to_global_financial_and_economic_turmoil/the_first_budgetary_stimulus_measures/ www.vlada.si/en/projects/measures_taken_in_response_to_global_financial_and_economic_turmoil/the_second_stimulus_package/		

Continued

	Announced date of stimulus	Covering years
South Africa	February 2009	2009–11
www.treasury.gov.za/documents/national%20budget/2009/guides/Treasury%20budget%20highlights.pdf		
www.info.gov.za/speeches/budget/speech2009.pdf		
Spain	November 2008, May 2009	2008–09
www.imf.org/external/pubs/ft/scr/2009/cr09128.pdf		
www.la-moncloa.es/ActualidadHome/2008/281108-Consejo.htm		
www.la-moncloa.es/ActualidadHome/2009/120509DebateEstado.htm		
Sri Lanka	January 2009, February 2009, May 2009	N/A
www.news.lk/index.php?option=com_content&task=view&id=8255&Itemid=51		
www.news.lk/index.php?option=com_content&task=view&id=8610&Itemid=44		
www.news.lk/index.php?option=com_content&task=view&id=9876&Itemid=51		
Sweden	April 2009 (part of measures announced before this date)	2009–10
www.sweden.gov.se/sb/d/11760/a/124400		
Switzerland	November 2008, February 2009, June 009	2009–10
www.seco.admin.ch/themen/02860/02942/index.html?lang=fr#sprungmarke1_28		
www.seco.admin.ch/aktuell/00277/01164/01980/index.html?lang=de&msg-id=27480		
Taiwan	April 2009	2009–12
www.ey.gov.tw/ct.asp?xItem=51379&ctNode=2313&mp=1		
www.ey.gov.tw/public/Attachment/93915474571.pdf		
Tanzania	June 2009	2009–10
http://allafrica.com/stories/200906150875.html (unofficial)		

Thailand	January 2009, May 2009	1st Package: 2009 2nd Package: 2009–12
http://thailand.prd.go.th/view_inside.php?id=4038 http://thailand.prd.go.th/view_inside.php?id=4210 www.thailandoutlook.com/NR/rdonlyres/B3CA1781-AAED-4363-AAD0-9EB27C1E23B9/0/EconPackageSlideShowENGFinal19jan09200dpi.pdf		
Turkey	2008, June 2009	2008–10
Source: www.treasury.gov.tr/iro_files/Announcements/PEP2008_eng.pdf		
UK[15]	November 2008	2008–09
www.hm-treasury.gov.uk/d/pbr08_completereport_1721.pdf		
US	February 2009	2009–19
www.cbo.gov/ftpdocs/99xx/doc9989/hr1conference.pdf www.usbudgetwatch.org/stimulus www.cbo.gov/ftpdocs/99xx/doc9989/hr1conference.pdf		
Vietnam	December 2008, April 2009	N/A
www.chinhphu.vn/portal/page?_pageid=439,1090459&_dad=portal&_schema=PORTAL&item_id=26437742&p_details=1 http://vietnamnews.vnagency.com.vn/showarticle.php?num=01COM230409		

Notes

The authors thank Pedro Conceição, Gaspar Fajth, Pingfan Hong, Stefan Moog, Isabel Ortíz, Gabriel Vergara and Keping Yao for helpful comments and discussions and Nergis Gulasan and Ye-Won Cho for excellent help in collecting data on Turkey and Korea. The authors would like to express their gratitude for data assistance received from the Indian Mission to the UN, the Italian Ministry of Economy and Finance and the UK's Mission to the UN.

1. These 48 announced stimulus packages are those we were able to find reliable data on. We do not claim this list is exhaustive.
2. Other studies that look into what falls under the broader category of social protection components of stimulus plans include ECLAC (2009) and OECD (2009b).
3. It should be noted that some of these official sources are available only in the native language, which we translated into English to the best of our knowledge but without claim of completeness.
4. Again, it should be pointed out that there is the caveat of data and information availability.
5. IMF (2008: 160) states that 'discretionary fiscal policy...involves active changes in policies that affect government expenditures, taxes, and transfers and are often undertaken for reasons other than stabilization.' See this source for an analysis on the effectiveness of discretionary fiscal policy measures in times of economic downturn.
6. Annex 1 lists different definitions of social protection adopted by several international organisations.
7. Our definition is similar to that in Holzmann and Jorgensen (2001: 536): 'public interventions (i) to assist individuals, households, and communities better manage risk, and (ii) to provide support to the critically poor.' As the authors point out, 'this definition combines the traditional SP [social protection] tools, including labor market interventions, social insurance programs and social safety nets, under a unifying theme.' We are aware that our definition may not be precise and can be broadly looked at as social policy measures, but decided to use it for the purposes of this chapter.
8. Some narrower definitions of social protection used in other studies exclude interventions measures on public health, education, housing or labour market policy (see Annex 1). For the purposes of this chapter, we include in our computation parts of interventions taken in the abovementioned areas that target the poor and the vulnerable, especially in response to the current economic and financial crisis.
9. Annex 2 lists different definitions of safety nets adopted by several international organisations.
10. Cut-off date for data and information collected was 30 June 2009.
11. Several studies have measured the total size of worldwide fiscal stimulus packages announced. The UN Department of Economics and Social Affairs (UNDESA, 2009) estimates the total as of mid-2009 at about $2.6 trillion (about 4 per cent of global GDP) to be spent between 2009 and 2011. Ortiz (2009) estimates the world's total fiscal stimulus amount announced as of March 2009 at $2.18 trillion (3.5 per cent of global GDP).
12. It should be noted that we are computing the size of the fiscal stimulus plans in percentage of 2008 GDP, for reasons of comparability. Many of

these plans' measures enter in effect only in 2009, and most cover various years to come (for more information, see Annex 3).

13. Details of social protection measures we identified are not included here, given space constraints. Please refer to Zhang et al. (2010) for this list.
14. Regarding the social protection component of Bangladesh's stimulus package, we calculate the size and share based on the first fiscal stimulus package only, since details of the second stimulus package are not available. According to our data sources, the first fiscal stimulus package amounted to an estimated Tk29.24 billion, of which Tk3.74 billion was allocated to social protection. A second fiscal stimulus package of Tk50 billion was later announced in the budget speech, indicating that the programmes under the first fiscal stimulus package would be continued.
15. We include only a £20 billion stimulus announced in the Pre-Budget Report 2008. No precise total amount available for further targeted action was announced in the Budget 2009 (Morgan Stanley reported a £5 billion stimulus in 2009/10 from the Budget 2009).

References

ADB (2009) 'Social Protection: Reducing Risks, Increasing Opportunities.' Manila: ADB.

Calderón, C. and Fajnzylber, P. (2009) 'How Much Room Does Latin America and the Caribbean Have for Implementing Counter-cyclical Fiscal Policies?' LCR Crisis Brief. Washington, DC: World Bank.

CBPP (2010) 'Policy Basics: Introduction to the Food Stamp Program.' Washington, DC: CBBP.

DFID (2005) 'Social Transfers and Chronic Poverty: Emerging Evidence and the Challenge Ahead.' Practice Paper. London: DFID.

ECLAC (2009) 'The Reactions of the Governments of the Americas to the International Crisis: An Overview of Policy Measures up to 31 May 2009.' Santiago de Chile: ECLAC.

ECOSOC (2000) 'Enhancing Social Protection and Reducing Vulnerability in a Globalizing World: Report of the Secretary-General.' New York: ECOSOC.

ESCAP (2009) 'Fiscal Stimulus Packages in Selected Asia-Pacific Countries.' Bangkok: ESCAP.

García, A.B. and Gruat, J.V. (2003) 'Social Protection: A Life Cycle Continuum Investment for Social Justice, Poverty Reduction and Sustainable Development.' Geneva: ILO.

Grosh, M., del Ninno, C., Teslius, E. and Ouerghi, A. (2008) 'For Protection and Promotion: The Design and Implementation of Effective Safety Nets.' Washington, DC: World Bank.

Harper, C., Jones, N., McKay, A. and Espey, J. (2009) 'Children in Times of Economic Crisis: Past Lessons, Future Policies.' Background Note. London: ODI.

Hoehne, N., Burck, J., Eisbrenner, K., van der Straeten, L. and Phylipsen, D. (2009) 'Economic/Climate Recovery Scorecards: How Climate Friendly Are the Economic Recovery Packages?' E3G/WWF.

Holzmann, R. and Jorgensen, S. (2001) 'Social Risk Management: A New Conceptual Framework for Social Protection, and Beyond.' *International Tax and Public Finance* 8(4): 529–56.

ILO (2009a) 'The Financial and Economic Crisis: A Decent Work Response.' Geneva: ILO.
ILO (2009b) 'National Stimulus and Recovery Packages.' Geneva: ILO.
ILO (2010) 'Accelerating a Job-rich Recovery in G20 Countries: Building on Experience.' Meeting of the G20 Labour and Employment Ministers. Washington, DC: 20–1 April.
ILO (2011) 'Global Employment Trends 2011: The Challenge of a Jobs Recovery.' Geneva: ILO.
IMF (2001) 'Government Financial Statistics Manual.' Washington, DC: IMF.
IMF (2008) 'Fiscal Policy as a Countercyclical Tool.' In *World Economic Outlook, Financial Stress, Downturns and Recoveries*. Washington, DC: IMF.
IMF (2009a) 'Update on Fiscal Stimulus and Financial Sector Measures.' Washington, DC: IMF.
IMF (2009b) 'World Economic Outlook: Crisis and Recovery.' Washington, DC: IMF.
IMF (2010a) 'Fiscal Monitor May 2010: Navigating the Fiscal Challenges Ahead.' Washington, DC: IMF.
IMF (2010b) 'World Economic Outlook: Recovery, Risk and Rebalancing.' Washington, DC: IMF.
IMF (2010c) 'Fiscal Monitor November 2010: Fiscal Exit: From Strategy to Implementation.' Washington, DC: IMF.
Klepper, G. (2009) 'Greening Global Growth? Climate and Growth Impacts of the Worldwide Stimulus Packages.' IfW Press Release, 8 April.
McCord, A. (2010) 'The Impact of the Global Financial Crisis on Social Protection in Developing Countries.' *International Social Security Review* 63(2): 31–45.
McCord, A. and Vandemoortele, M. (2009) 'The Global Financial Crisis: Poverty and Social Protection.' Briefing Paper 51. London: ODI.
OECD (2009a) 'Fiscal Packages across OECD Countries: Overview and Country Details.' Paris: OECD.
OECD (2009b) 'Strategies for Aligning Stimulus Measures with Long Term Growth.' Paris: OECD.
OECD (2009c) 'Social Protection.' Paris: OECD.
Öniş, Z. and Güven, A.B. (2010) 'Global Crisis, National Responses: The Political Economy of Turkish Exceptionalism.' Economic Research Forum Working Paper 1013. Istanbul: Tüsiad-Koç University.
Ortiz, I. (2009) 'Fiscal Stimulus Plans: The Need for a Global New Deal.' IDEAs.
Prasad, E. and Sorkin, I. (2009) 'Assessing the G-20 Economic Stimulus Plans: A Deeper Look.' Washington, DC: The Brookings Institution.
Saha, D. and von Weizsäcker, J. (2009) 'Estimating the Size of the European Stimulus Packages for 2009: An Update.' Bruegel Policy Contribution.
UNDESA (2009) 'World Economic Situation and Prospects 2009: Update as of Mid-2009.' New York: UNDESA.
UNIFEM (2009) 'Making Economic Stimulus Packages Work for Women and Gender Equality.' High-Level Conference on the Global Economic and Financial Crisis. New York, 24 May–6 June.
Zhang, T., Thelen, N. and Rao, A. (2010) 'Social Protection in Fiscal Stimulus Packages: Some Evidence.' Working Paper. New York: ODS, UNDP.

13
Conclusion: Revisiting the Main Lessons and Rethinking Crisis Response

Ronald U. Mendoza, Erika Strand and David Stewart

Prior to the recent crises, the world was already a highly unequal place. The top 20 per cent of the population accounted for more than 70 per cent of total income, whereas the bottom quintile received a mere 2 per cent.[1] As the chapters of this book have illustrated, in such an already unequal world economic crisis can have unequal impacts, often hitting children, women and the poor with greater force than less vulnerable members of society. From rising infant mortality to swelling youth unemployment, these consequences can further entrench existing inequalities, leaving wide gaps with long-term consequences for children and, in turn, for a country's future.

In making this case, we have underscored the importance of acknowledging the persistent limitations of data in relation to identifying impacts and vulnerable groups and the value of learning from historical crisis episodes, establishing a baseline *ex ante* and/or detecting initial coping strategies that policies should then target. The range of circumstances surrounding each crisis presented in this volume notwithstanding, common themes of impact and recommended response emerge. This concluding chapter summarises observed impacts on the achievement of child rights and child wellbeing, and challenges what has previously been assumed about sound policy responses to crises in light of the evidence and comparative analysis presented.

As noted in the introduction, the contributors to this volume have endeavoured to shed light on the implications of the global financial crisis of the late 2000s for children, women and poor families. Because these crises have been unprecedented in their scope and depth – producing social, economic and political disruption and ripple effects that are likely to extend well beyond this period – the task of assessing their impact on the social sectors has been of paramount concern to policymakers, civil society groups, academia, development organisations and other stakeholders. The underlying motivation is not just a concern for basic rights to survival and wellbeing: the focus on the social sectors stems also from the potential for permanent scars on individuals and families as well as countries' weakened long-run growth prospects.

The analyses in this volume have covered both historical and much more recent empirical evidence on crisis impact, as well as the scope and effectiveness of different crisis response policies. A variety of analytical tools have been deployed to evaluate the implications of the recent crises, including macro–micro modelling, rapid surveys and empirical analyses of historical and recent data on crises. The contributors hope these tools will soon be used more frequently by policymakers and programme implementers, enabling them to better understand and thus respond more effectively to crises and other emerging challenges. The multiregional perspective reflected across the chapter contributions also provides what could be among the first coherent global snapshots of what has happened during this tumultuous period as far as the social sectors are concerned.

What have we learned overall? The emerging policy messages could be summarised as follows. First, crises, if unabated, could turn into 'inequality machines', leading to vastly disparate social and economic outcomes across and within countries that exacerbate persistent inequalities that predate the current crisis. Addressing this rising threat of inequality is surely a critical policy challenge in an era of crises, whether manmade or otherwise. Second, and in response to the first aspect, policymakers need to recalibrate their policy arsenals, focusing on the most effective interventions as validated by evidence, while also encouraging innovation to address old as well as new challenges. Part of what needs to be done, therefore, is to rethink orthodox policy approaches, as we outline in more depth below.

Curbing the threat of crises as inequality machines

Even though the data are still largely preliminary, with more evaluation forthcoming, existing evidence points to the grave risk facing children, women and poor families, not just during these crises years but also during the ensuing difficult recovery if policies are not targeted effectively. A central theme across the country and regional case studies in this book is that crises and inequality tend to be tightly linked.[2]

Crises tend to be anti-poor: aggregate shocks harm vulnerable groups much more easily

First, there is evidence that crises and their market and policy ramifications are 'anti-poor'. That is, in countries which are heavily affected, crises often disproportionately affect poor and low-income segments of the population. Even as the rich and middle classes are typically those with relatively greater access to formal markets – including some of the sophisticated financial products in real estate and commodity trade that may have been linked to crisis propagation – the relative impact of the crisis on human development outcomes is typically much more severe for poor and low-income families, just by the nature of their pre-existing deprivations and vulnerability. Indeed, emerging evidence from a variety of rapid surveys on the recent crises suggests that poor and low-income populations are often pushed to the brink of subsistence very easily, given the limited buffers and protection mechanisms to which they have access.

In many cases, the poorest and most vulnerable – notably children and women – are the least able to adjust and are among the most severely affected, often forced to cope in ways that imply lasting harm. As evidenced by the chapters in this book, increases in infant and under-five mortality follow periods of economic crisis or recession, with thousands of additional deaths in countries such as India and Mexico in recent years. For example, the case of Mexico illustrates the acute vulnerability of children, showing that the under-fives saw the largest increases in mortality following the 1994 economic shock. Comparing cross-country data yields similar results, with declines in gross domestic product (GDP) consistently linked to increases in child mortality. Evidence from Sub-Saharan Africa (SSA) often shows these increases to be concentrated disproportionately among girls as compared with boys, further demonstrating the unequal, and inequality-exacerbating, effect of crises.

Recoveries are not automatically inclusive – but rather tend to marginalise those least able to cope

There have recently been signs of recovery[3] in the banking and financial sectors – where the global financial crisis began in 2008 – but the recovery process may also tend to further marginalise the poor, who are likely at their weakest and most vulnerable point, having undertaken a variety of often adverse coping strategies that are difficult to reverse quickly. Based on the analyses in this volume, these may include, for example, drawing down on assets and possibly selling productive ones; taking on more debt; eating less (and, for certain family members, including children and mothers, increasing risk of malnutrition) and pulling children out of school or spending less on health care. Poor and low-income populations have also faced significant declines in their purchasing power, with little time to recover during the protracted period of difficulty. Moreover, at the time of writing, another round of price shocks is confirming the widespread view that international food and fuel price volatility will remain a threat in the medium term. Under these conditions, any recovery in economic growth is less likely to translate immediately into building the resilience of millions of poor and low-income families.

Too often, policy responses are not protective but can deepen and entrench inequalities

If crises harm the poor and the ensuing recovery process excludes them, then frequent crises and persistent international economic volatility could exacerbate already acute inequity in social and economic development across and within countries. Despite significant progress in promoting human development and reducing poverty, inequality across the world has increased dramatically in the past few decades. This has prompted some analysts to argue that inequality lies at the heart of the recent crises (Mendoza, forthcoming; Ortiz and Cummins, 2011; Rajan, 2010). The sobering reality is that, just as boom periods do not necessarily benefit the poor, so crises often disproportionately harm them and recoveries tend to leave them behind. Here lies the crux of the argument for collective action and intervention. Without sufficient government and donor action, notably in the area of social protection, economic booms and busts as well as crises of various types will lead to a world of vastly disparate human development outcomes.

Shelving orthodox approaches for innovation and evidence

The evidence and examples provided in this volume should help us rethink some of the conventional wisdom that has often underpinned policy responses to economic crises, so we can more effectively target and nuance policy design in order to stem inequality and minimise human capital deterioration. Particularly in the case of children, an acute or chronic period of reduced investment is difficult to compensate for later. Here we present challenges emerging from the book's multiregional analysis to five specific orthodoxies often assumed to guide policy responses based on existing evidence about the impact of crises on children and their caregivers.

A first orthodoxy to debunk is the often-held view that a financial or economic crisis will probably not affect the poorest and low-income segments of the population because they are not well integrated into the economy and financial system.[4] On the contrary, the emerging evidence suggests that the transmission channels of the crisis to poor and low-income households could actually be strong. Essentially, progress in making markets and economic growth much more inclusive also acts to make crises equally inclusive for the poor.[5] Consequently, a vast number of low-income people remain at risk of slipping back into poverty. In addition, even those marginalised in the market economy could still be impacted by crises in various ways, such as through the aftershocks of the crisis on the budget and related services, aid, remittances and persistently high and volatile food, fuel and commodity prices. These transmission channels are elaborated and borne out by evidence presented in this volume, and result in deleterious consequences for the poor. For example, two-thirds of people in the bottom income quintile in transition economies reduced food consumption in the wake of the economic crisis they faced. In Argentina, health insurance declined markedly among the poor, with a 60 per cent drop among the lowest income groups. And in the Philippines, the poorest segments of the population are shown through community-based monitoring to have fared the worst – turning to adverse coping behaviour with potentially severe long-run impacts on children.

Other impacts that children experience disproportionately in times of economic crisis include sexual exploitation, child labour, abandonment or living on the street. In several historical cases of crises, there are accounts of decreased quality of child care practices, resulting from caregivers' stress, family breakdown and weakened mental health. When prices rise, in particular food prices, caregivers are often forced to leave children unaccompanied in order to be able to work sufficient hours to purchase food or other household necessities, presenting dire risks even for families that are not integrated into the economy – and perhaps more so because of their inability to access loans that would allow them to smooth consumption during a time of difficulty.

A second orthodoxy has to do with the view that blanket macro-stabilisation policies are enough to promote rapid and inclusive recovery. Inclusive recoveries are not automatic, and rather require nuanced policy responses that address the vulnerabilities of those who are most disadvantaged, notably children, and in particular children and their families from various marginalised social groups (for example because of caste, ethnicity, gender, HIV/AIDS status, disability and so on). Indeed, several studies in this volume find that many countries have not been able to implement robust countercyclical responses – and fewer still have been able to implement such policies that are sufficiently nuanced and targeted at the social sectors in ways that respond to specific vulnerabilities, notably of children and women. Conversely, the example of South Africa shows that a previously established social protection scheme targeted at children, such as the country's Child Support Grant, has been able to protect children from the worst impacts of the recent crisis.

A third and related orthodoxy is the widespread assumption that policies that target households will automatically solve the poverty and vulnerability of children and women. Accumulated empirical evidence and policy experience suggests that ignoring intra-household power dynamics and unequal distribution of resources, assets and decision-making may leave women and girls severely vulnerable and facing the brunt of the deprivations attached to poverty. Evidence reviewed by several studies in this volume suggests that women and girls sometimes end up shouldering disproportionate burdens of harsh coping strategies, including dangerous work and school dropout, as well as of distress-related effects, such as domestic violence and the repercussions of the compromised mental health of family members. To be clear, boys and men are also likely to be affected by crises; however, the point here is that gender-sensitive analyses and policies will be needed to address the specific challenges of the vulnerable, even within households.

A fourth possible orthodoxy is that countries will necessarily revert back to their long-run growth rates after certain aggregate shocks. Indeed, the orthodox view of financial and economic crises is that these shocks are able to purge inefficiencies and bring about much-needed reforms and corrections in business strategy and government policy. On the contrary, there is empirical evidence that countries affected by financial and other crises, as well as economic volatility, suffer permanently lower long-run growth trajectories (see Cerra and Saxena, 2007). This volume presents the example of Kyrgyzstan, where up to one-third of children were still chronically poor a decade after transition and only 23 per cent were deemed 'never poor', underscoring the potentially permanent harm to children – the country's human development and human capital – that unabated crisis impact brings about.

What we now know is that recoveries may be exclusive in the sense that the impact on children could be permanent (and the detrimental impact on human capital and household assets could be long-lived). It is also likely that pre-existing vulnerabilities and inequity will be exacerbated by policy responses that are not nuanced – for example job creation that ends up mostly for men and programmes that do not consider the burden on women, who become more time-poor. Who benefits from a policy intervention or reform is directly linked to: (1) what this intervention or reform is; and (2) how its benefit incidence is distributed. Groups that are hardest to reach typically do not receive benefits through existing/usual channels, thus relying on the latter may harden existing marginalisation. This underscores the importance of building social protection systems in anticipation of crises – incorporating platforms for designing, implementing and accurate monitoring of innovative policy interventions whose effectiveness is supported by evidence.

All of the above leads to a fifth orthodoxy that needs to be challenged – that human capital investments can be scaled back during a crisis, due to more pressing stabilisation and other related challenges. There is now growing recognition of the importance of preserving social spending and investments, as well as the role of targeted policies that help ensure that the social sectors are supported adequately.[6] As presented in this volume, protecting spending on children affected by HIV/AIDS, which includes maintaining their anti-retroviral treatment, for example, is critical to prevent worsening inequality for this group. In addition, various contributors to this volume present evidence to support the case for countercyclical social spending and investments, and yet show that lower-income countries are those least able to increase spending in critical social sectors such as health and education. Indeed, countercyclical spending could bolster social protection systems, such as those existing in Mexico and South Africa before the crisis, that are based not just on rights but also on the overall macroeconomic objective of bringing about rapid and robust recovery as well as reversion to long-run growth.

In conclusion, the quality of the recovery, the preservation and strengthening of developing countries' human capital (and thus the minimisation of social and economic costs) and their resulting resilience (or continued vulnerability) to future shocks will hinge on more effective crisis response strategies that respond to higher-quality, real-time crisis impact data. The motivation for action is clearly not one of charity. If left unchecked, crises could turn into inequality machines, perhaps leading to a social crisis that makes all others pale in comparison.

Notes

1. See Ortiz and Cummins (2011). For further elaboration on inequality measures and historical trends, see Jomo and Baudot (2007); Milanovic (2009) and Ortiz and Cummins (2011).
2. Parts of the analysis here build on Mendoza (forthcoming).
3. At the time of writing (May 2011), signs of economic recovery have been observed and recognised by most of major international development institutions. However, it should be noted that a new round of commodity price shocks, lingering public debt problems in a number of industrial countries and political instability in the Middle East paint a picture of uncertainty and near-term volatility.
4. A similar initial orthodoxy may have been in place when developing country policymakers initially considered the crisis to be a 'Northern crisis', with few if any ramifications on developing countries and their populations.
5. Indeed, there has been significant progress in most countries in terms of growing more inclusive markets through innovations that empower microfinance institutions, micro borrowers and small and medium-sized enterprises. These innovations help to link millions of individuals, microenterprises and other informal sector actors to value chains which may also link up to international ones. For further discussion, see United Nations Development Programme's (UNDP's) work on growing inclusive markets (www.growinginclusivemarkets.org/).
6. See Andersen (2009), IMF (2011) and Mendoza (forthcoming). Indeed, this rethinking of macroeconomic policy and crisis management strategies is reflected in an increased openness to considering a much broader array of policy options, such as capital controls and countercyclical fiscal policies (for example Ostry et al., 2010; Stiglitz, 2011).

References

Andersen, C. (2009) 'New Rules of Engagement for IMF Loans.' IMF Survey Online.

Cerra, V. and Saxena, S.C. (2007) 'Growth Dynamics: The Myth of Economic Recovery.' Working Paper 226. Paris: BIS.

IMF (2011) 'The IMF's Role in Helping Protect the Most Vulnerable from the Crisis.' Factsheet. Washington, DC: IMF.

Jomo, K.S. and Baudot, J. (eds) (2007) *Flat World, Big Gaps: Economic Liberalization, Globalization, Poverty and Inequality*. London: Zed Books.

Mendoza, R.U. (forthcoming) 'Lessons from the Global Crises of 2008-2010.' *Global Policy*.

Milanovic, B. (2009) 'Global Inequality and the Global Inequality Extraction Ratio: The Story of the Past Two Centuries.' Policy Research Working Paper 5044. Washington, DC: World Bank.

Ortiz, I. and Cummins, M. (2011) 'Global Inequality beyond the Bottom Billion: A Rapid Review of Income Distribution in 141 Countries.' Social and Economic Policy Working Paper. New York: UNICEF.

Ostry, J., Ghosh, A., Habermeier, K., Chamon, M., Qureshi, M. and Reinhardt, D. (2010) 'Capital Inflows: The Role of Controls.' Staff Position Note. Washington, DC: IMF.
Rajan, R. (2010) 'How Inequality Fueled the Crisis.' Project Syndicate, 9 July.
Stiglitz, J. (2011) 'Rethinking Macroeconomics: What Went Wrong and How to Fix It.' *Global Policy* 2(2): 165–75.

Index